28

Breakfast Served Any Time All Day

Breakfast Served Any Time All Day

&

essays on poetry new and selected

Donald Hall

The University of Michigan Press

Ann Arbor

2006   2005   2004   4   3   2

A CIP catalog record for this book is available from the British Library.

Library of Congress Cataloging-in-Publication Data

Hall, Donald, 1928–
    Breakfast served any time all day : essays on poetry : new and
selected / Donald Hall.
      p. cm.
    ISBN 0-472-09852-7 (cloth : alk. paper)
    1. Poetry.   2. American poetry—History and criticism.   3. English
poetry—History and criticism.   I. Title.
PS3515.A3152 B74   2003
811.009—dc21   2003008358

for Kendel Currier

Whatever we think we write, with good fortune
we write something else: The Muse is the Angel
of Accident.

— William Trout, *Early Notebooks*

The sound of the words spoken aloud is itself the
meaning, just as the sound of the notes on the proper
instruments is the meaning of any piece of music.

— Basil Bunting, "A Note on *Briggflatts*"

All writing is information storage. If all writing
is information storage, then all writing is of
equal value.

— Albertine Gaur, *History of Writing*

Contents

Preface

Over the decades, my thinking about poetry has moved from a consideration of process—how does a poem begin and how does it embody inwardness?—to concentrate on the physical and psychic effects of poems, their sounds and intimacies of verbal connection. These essays concentrate on the sensuality of poems, lavish bodies of language created by the senses for the spirit by way of the senses. Poems are an inwardness talking to an inwardness, through the physical medium of sound. I speak little of what poems say, but praise the art for poetry's ability to occupy contrary positions at the same time, to move both north and south—as the human psyche always moves simultaneously in opposing directions. Poetry's illogic is human truth.

Breakfast Served Any Time All Day begins with an essay addressed to the general reader, an attempt to introduce poetry to people not initially comfortable with the art, maybe shy or unsure, but willing to dare an approach. Other essays, like "Polonius's Advice to Young Poets" and "Hall's Index," with its cautionary diatribe against dead metaphor, are addressed to young poets. In *Their Ancient Glittering Eyes* (expanded from *Remembering Poets*) I wrote essays on T. S. Eliot and Marianne Moore, Dylan Thomas, Robert Frost, and Ezra Pound. Here, I mostly avoid writing about poets in order to write about poetry. The poets I quote are largely the poets I have loved my whole life.

—D. H.

⅋

The Unsayable Said

Poems are pleasure first: bodily pleasure, a deliciousness of the senses. Mostly, poems end by saying something (even the unsayable) but they start as the body's joy, like making love. Sometimes a poem provides nothing for paraphrase, but gives pleasure:

> Baa, baa, black sheep,
> Have you any wool?
> Yes, sir. Yes, sir.
> Three bags full.

Maybe these words once referred to taxation, but we hear them now without being tempted to explanation or translation. Instead, we *chew* on them, *taste* them, and *dance* to them. This banquet or ballet starts in the crib, before arithmetic or thought. Everyone was once an infant who took mouth-pleasure in gurgle and shriek, accompanied by muscle-joy as small limbs clenched and unclenched. Poetry starts from the crib. A thousand years later, John Donne makes lovers into compasses, T. S. Eliot contemplates the still point of the turning world, and Elizabeth Bishop remembers sitting as a child in the dentist's waiting room; but if these poets did not retain the mouth-pleasure of a baby's autistic utterance—pleasure in vowels on the tongue, pleasure in changes of volume and pause: *Baa, baa, black sheep*— we would not receive their meditations and urgencies.

The body is poetry's door; the sounds of words—thrust of legs and arms, riches in the mouth—let us into the house.

Styles of architecture: In his spiritual grammar, Walt Whitman often wrote long complex sentences: The first sentence of "Out

---

From *Principal Products of Portugal* (Boston: Beacon Press, 1995).

of the Cradle" is two hundred and eight words, arranged into twenty-two lines so that its subject, verb, and object wait until the last three lines. But the same poet could make a poem both brief and simple: This is "A Farm Picture"—all of it:

> Through the ample open door of the peaceful
> country barn,
> A sunlit pasture field with cattle and horses feeding,
> And haze and vista, and the far horizon fading away.

It's merely a picture, an incomplete sentence—yet if we read it with an appropriate slow sensuous attentiveness, these lines fill us with a luminous beauty. The reader's mouth dwells in luxury on the three long *ay*s of the last line. But pleasure does not reside only in the mouth: Feel the balance of heavy words in the first two lines—three and three, three and three—then the slight variation in the last line, with "haze and vista" and "far horizon fading away." The mouth lolls among diphthongs like a sunbather.

Readers who enjoy this small poem don't think about its balances and variations; we *feel* them, the way we feel a musical theme that returns slightly altered: expectation fulfilled and denied. With this poem as with the black sheep, we don't paraphrase; we take "A Farm Picture" for what it calls itself. But if we notice that the poem first appeared as the Civil War was ending in 1865, we may find the word *peaceful* emphatic. We speculate; speculation does no harm when it acknowledges itself. What the reader must not do (and what the classroom often encourages): We must never assume that the poem, appearing simple, hides an intellectual statement that only professionals are equipped to explicate.

It's true: When we read poems we often feel more emotion than we can reasonably account for. If Whitman's little poem pleases us much, it pleases us more than paraphrase can explain. (To paraphrase this poem we are driven to synonyms—"Through the wide unclosed portal"—which serve only to show that synonyms do not exist.) Feeling bodily pleasure and fulfillment, feeling rightness beyond reason, feeling contentment or even bliss—we cannot account for the extremity of our satisfaction. By its art of saying the unsayable, poetry produces a response in excess of the discernible stimulus.

Pursuing the architectural analogy, I want to call this response the secret room. Friends of mine bought an old house in the country, a warren of small rooms, and after they furnished it and settled down, they became aware that their floor plan made no sense. Peeling off some wallpaper they found a door that pried open to reveal a tiny room, sealed off and hidden, goodness knows why: It was not a station on the underground railway. They found no corpses nor stolen goods. The unsayable builds a secret room, in the best poems, which shows in the excess of feeling over paraphrase. This room is not a Hidden Meaning, to be paraphrased by the intellect; it conceals itself from reasonable explanation. The secret room is something to acknowledge, accept, and honor in a silence of assent; the secret room is where the unsayable gathers, and it is poetry's uniqueness.

Poets are literal-minded, and poetry depends, even when it names marvelous and impossible things, on a literal mind. On the other hand, the conventional intellect wants to translate particulars into abstractions, as if images were allegorical; such translation is the grave error of the philosophers. The unsayable speaks only through the untranslated image and its noises. When we read Blake's "O Rose, thou art sick!" it is useless to ask, "What does 'Rose' mean? What does 'sick' mean?" Good readers imagine a rose and entertain notions of illness, possibly beginning with a plant canker and continuing to a blossom on a breathing tube, or—more historically—petals bled by leeches. When Emily Dickinson writes that "Death . . . kindly stopped for me," we listen to a story in which a horse and carriage— the figure of mortality holding the reins—pause to pick up a walker. We must see the figure. Thomas Hardy, wandering as an old man in a graveyard, speculates on the vegetation growing from graves: Parts of a yew tree must be somebody his grandfather knew, because the yew grows from the burial place. Wandering further he sees a bush by the grave of a girl he knew when he was a young man:

And the fair girl long ago
Whom I vainly tried to know
May be entering this rose.

Here we have two kinds of literalness: Hardy speculates on molecular survival, particles of the girl's body turned into botanical nutrients; but take the lines into the imagination, and we watch her molecules *enter* the rose as a living woman walks through the portals of a church, or as a penis enters a vagina. The poetry, saying the unsayable, resides in the two ways of seeing or understanding brought (impossibly) together.

Anything that can be thoroughly said in prose might as well be said in prose. The everyday intellect remains satisfied with abstraction and explanation in prose; the poetic mentality wants more. In narrative poems, the poetry adds the secret (unsayable) room of feeling and tone to the sayable story. Philosophy in its more logical incarnations strives to eliminate powers of association because they are subjective and uncontrollable. Poetry, on the other hand, wants to address *the whole matter of the human*— including fact and logic, but also the body with its senses, and above all the harsh and soft complexities of emotion. Our senses, excited by sound and picture, assimilate records of feeling that are also passages to feeling. Poems tell stories; poems recount ideas; but poems *embody* feeling. Because emotion is illogical—in logic opposites cannot both be true; in the life of feeling, we love and hate together—the poem exists to say the unsayable. Contradictory reality, embodied in language, depends on distinctions and associations. If Hardy told us that the fair girl "Might be marching into this cactus," his associations would have failed him—and we would not read his poem. Marianne Moore finds poetry in definition: "Nor was he insincere in saying, 'Make my house your inn.' / Inns are not residences." Sometimes definitions, plain in talk, combine logical impossibility with ironic witness, as in Geoffrey Hill:

this is a raging solitude of desire,
this is the chorus of obscene consent,
this is a single voice of perfect praise.

Poems embody the coexistence of opposites that together form an identity; the Roman poet Catullus wrote, "odi et amo": I hate and I love.

We come to poetry for the pleasure of its body, but also for the accuracy and confirmation of its feeling. When we grieve we go to poems that grieve; but mostly we read poetry for the love of it, not in search of consolation. In the act of reading, we exercise or practice emotion, griefs and joys, erotic transport and the anguish of loss—as if poems were academies of feeling, as if in reading poems we practiced emotion and understandings of emotion. Poetry by its bodily, mental, and emotional complex educates the sensibility, thinking and feeling appropriately melded together.

Words are to poems as stone to the stone-carving sculptor. When we say that we are parking the car we use the material of poetry; we are not speaking poetry, any more than the contractor, using granite for a pediment, makes sculpture. Poetry is the only art that uses as its material something that everyone uses—and this commonness is both a strength of poetry and an impediment to reading it. *Poetry is not talk.* It sounds like talk. At least from Wordsworth on, or even from Dante, it has been a commonplace that speech is our material—but poetry is talk altered into art, speech slowed down and attended to, words arranged for the reader who contracts to read them for their own whole heft of noises and associations. If we try reading poetry with our eyes, as we learn to read newspapers, we miss its bodiliness as well as the history bodied into its words. Reading with care, so that a wholeness of language engages a wholeness of reading body and reading mind, we absorb poetry not with our eyes only, nor with our ears. We read with our mouths that cherish vowel and consonant; we read with our limbed muscles that enact the dance of the poem's rhythm; we read alert to the history and context of words. Robert Creeley's poem ends:

> Be for me, like rain,
> the getting out

of the tiredness, the fatuousness, the semi-
lust of intentional indifference.
Be wet
with a decent happiness.

When we read these lines with the slow attention we give to
Whitman or to Hill, this rain sinks in.

All of us can ask directions or remark that it looks like snow.
When we wish to embody in language a complex of feelings or
sensations or ideas, we fall into inarticulateness; attempting to
speak, in the heat of love or argument, we say nothing or we say
what we do not intend. Poets encounter inarticulateness as
much as anybody, or maybe more: They are aware of the word's
inadequacy because they spend their lives struggling to say the
unsayable. From time to time, in decades of devotion to their
art, poets succeed in defeating the enemies of ignorance, deceit,
and ugliness. The poets we honor most are those who—by stu-
dious imagination, by continuous connection to the sensuous
body, and by spirit steeped in the practice and learning of lan-
guage—say the unsayable.

⨲

Death to the Death of Poetry

Some days, when we read the newspaper, it seems clear that the United States is a country devoted to poetry. We can delude ourselves reading the sports pages. After finding two references to "poetry in motion," apropos figure skating and the Kentucky Derby, we read that a shortstop is the poet of his position and that sailboats raced under blue skies that were sheer poetry. On the funny pages, Zippy praises Zerbina's outfit: "You're a poem in polyester." A funeral director, in an advertisement, muses on the necessity for poetry in our daily lives. It's hard to figure out just what he's talking about, but it becomes clear that this *poetry* has nothing to do with *poems*. It sounds more like taking naps.

Poetry, then, appears to be:

1. a vacuous synonym for excellence or unconsciousness.

What else is common to the public perception of poetry?

2. It is universally agreed that no one reads it.
3. It is universally agreed that the nonreading of poetry is
   (a) contemporary and
   (b) progressive.

From (a) it follows that sometime back (a wandering date, like "olden times" for a six-year-old) our ancestors read poems, and poets were rich and famous. From (b) it follows that every year fewer people read poems (or buy books or go to poetry readings) than the year before.

4. Only poets read poetry.
5. Poets themselves are to blame because "poetry has lost its audience."

From *Death to the Death of Poetry: Essays, Reviews, Notes, Interviews* (Ann Arbor: The University of Michigan Press, 1995).

6. Everybody today knows that poetry is "useless and completely out of date"—as Flaubert put it in *Bouvard and Pécuchet* in 1881.

For expansion on and repetition of these well-known facts, look in volumes of *Time* magazine, in Edmund Wilson's "Is Verse a Dying Technique?," in current newspapers everywhere, in interviews with publishers, in book reviews by poets, and in the August 1988 issue of *Commentary*, where the essayist Joseph Epstein assembled every cliché about poetry, common for two centuries, under the title "Who Killed Poetry?"

Time, which reported *The Waste Land* as a hoax in 1922, canonized T. S. Eliot in a 1950 cover story. Certainly *Time*'s writers and editors altered over thirty years, but they also stayed the same: Always the giants grow old and die, leaving the pygmies behind. After the age of Eliot, Frost, Stevens, Moore, and Williams, the wee survivors were Lowell, Berryman, Jarrell, and Bishop. When the survivors died, younger elegiac journalists revealed that the dead pygmies had been giants all along—and *now* the young poets were dwarfs. Doubtless obituaries lauding Allen Ginsberg are already written.* Does anyone remember *Life* on the new Beat Generation?

In "Is Verse a Dying Technique?" in 1928, Edmund Wilson answered yes to his own question. It is not one of the maestro's better essays. Wilson's long view makes the point that doctors and physicists no longer use poetry when they write about medicine and the universe. Yes, Lucretius is dead. And yes, Coleridge had a notion of poetry rather different from Horace's. But Wilson also announced in 1928 that poetry had collapsed because "since the Sandburg-Pound generation, a new development in verse has taken place. The sharpness and the energy disappear; the beat gives way to a demoralized weariness." (He speaks, of course, in the heyday of Moore, Williams, Frost, H. D., Stevens, and Eliot; reprinting the essay in 1948, he added a paragraph nervously acknowledging Auden, whom he had put down twenty years before.) He goes on to explain the problem's source: "The trouble is that no verse technique is more obsolete

---

* They were. (2003)

today than blank verse. The old iambic pentameters have no longer any relation whatever to the tempo and language of our lives. Yeats was the last who could write them."

Yeats wrote little blank verse of interest, bar "The Second Coming." As it happens, two Americans of Wilson's time wrote superb blank verse. (Really I should say three, because E. A. Robinson flourished in 1928. But his annual blank verse narratives were not so brilliant as his earlier work; and of course he antedated "the Sandburg-Pound generation.") Robert Frost, starting from Wordsworth, made an idiomatic American blank verse, especially in his dramatic monologues, which is the best modern example of that metric; and Wallace Stevens, starting from Tennyson, made blank verse as gorgeous as "Tithonus." Read Frost's "Home Burial" and Stevens's "Sunday Morning" and tell me that blank verse was obsolete in 1928.

Poetry was never Wilson's strong suit. It is worthwhile to remember that he found Edna St. Vincent Millay the great poet of her age. In a late self-interview by Wilson in the *New Yorker,* he revealed that among contemporary poets only Robert Lowell was worth reading. It saves a lot of time, not needing to check out Geoffrey Hill, Elizabeth Bishop, John Ashbery, Galway Kinnell, Adrienne Rich, Philip Larkin, Sylvia Plath, Robert Bly, John Berryman . . .

Sixty years after Edmund Wilson told us that verse was dying, Joseph Epstein in *Commentary* revealed that it was murdered. Naturally, Epstein's golden age—Stevens, Frost, Williams—is Wilson's era of "demoralized weariness." Everything changes and everything stays the same. Poetry was always in good shape twenty or thirty years ago; *now* it has always gone to hell. I have heard this lamentation for many decades, not only from distinguished critics and essayists but from professors and journalists who enjoy viewing our culture with alarm. Repetition of a formula, under changed circumstances and with different particulars, does not make formulaic complaint invalid; but it suggests that the formula represents something besides what it repeatedly affirms.

In asking "Who Killed Poetry?" Joseph Epstein begins by insisting that he does *not* dislike it. "I was taught that poetry was itself an exalted thing." He admits his "quasi-religious language" and asserts that "it was during the 1950s that poetry last had this religious aura." Did Epstein go to school "during the 1950s"? If he now attended poetry readings, with unblinkered eyes, he would watch twenty-year-olds undergoing quasi-religious emotions. One of the undergraduates, almost certainly, will write an essay in the 2020s telling the world that poetry is moldering in its grave.

Worship is not love. People who at the age of fifty deplore the death of poetry are the same people who in their twenties were "taught to exalt it." The middle-aged poetry detractor is the student who hyperventilated at poetry readings thirty years earlier. After college many English majors stop reading contemporary poetry. Why not? They become involved in journalism or scholarship, essay writing or editing, alcoholism or adultery, brokerage or social work. They backslide from the undergraduate Church of Poetry. Years later, glancing belatedly at the poetic scene, they tell us that poetry is dead. They left poetry; therefore they blame poetry for leaving them. Really, they lament their own aging. Don't we all? But some of us do not blame current poets.

Epstein localizes his attack on two poets, unnamed but ethnically specified: "One of the two was a Hawaiian of Japanese ancestry, the other was middle-class Jewish." (They were Garrett Hongo and Edward Hirsch, who testified on behalf of American poetry to the National Council of the Arts, where Joseph Epstein as a Councilor regularly assured his colleagues that contemporary American writing was dreck.) Epstein speaks disparagingly of these "Japanese" and "Jewish" poets, in his ironic mosquito whine, and calls their poems "heavily preening, and not distinguished enough in language or subtlety of thought to be memorable." Epstein does not quote a line by either poet he dismisses. His disparagement is pure blurbtalk. As with the aging Edmund Wilson, Epstein saves time by ignoring particulars of the art he disparages.

Dubious elegies on the death of poetry shouldn't need answers. A frequently reported lie, however, can turn into fact. In his essay, Joseph Epstein tells us that "last year the *Los Angeles Times* announced it would no longer review books of poems." In the *Washington Post,* Jonathan Yardley referred to the same event, which never happened, and applauded what never happened. The editor of the *Los Angeles Times Book Review* had announced that his paper would review *fewer* books of poems; instead, the *Review* would print a whole poem in a box every week, with a note on the poet. In the years after instituting this policy, the *LATBR* continued to review poetry—more than the *New York Times Book Review* did—and in addition printed an ongoing anthology of contemporary American verse.

Yet when the *LATBR* announced its changed policy, poets picketed the paper. Poets love to parade as victims; we love the romance of alienation and insult.

More than a thousand poetry books appear in this country each year. More people write poetry in this country—publish it, hear it, and presumably read it—than ever before. Let us quickly and loudly proclaim that no poet sells like Stephen King, that poetry is not so popular as professional wrestling, and that fewer people attend poetry readings in the United States than in Slavic countries. Snore, snore. More people read poetry now in the United States than ever did before.

When I was in school in the 1940s, there were few poetry readings; only Frost did many. If we consult biographies of Stevens and Williams, we understand that for them a poetry reading was an unusual event. In those decades, the magazine *Poetry* printed on its back cover Walt Whitman's claim that "to have great poets there must be great audiences too" but it seemed an idle notion. Readings picked up in the late 1950s, avalanched in the 1960s, and continue to increase in number every decade.

Readings sell books. When trade publishers in 1950 issued a third book by a prominent poet, they printed only hardbound copies, possibly a thousand. If the edition sold out in three or four years, everybody was happy. The same trade publisher fifty years later would likely print the same poet in an edition of five or ten thousand cloth, and more later in paper. (Often the cloth edition would be reprinted.) Recently, a dozen or more American poets have sold by the tens of thousands: Adrienne Rich,

Robert Bly, Allen Ginsberg, John Ashbery, Galway Kinnell, Robert Creeley, Gary Snyder, Denise Levertov, Carolyn Forché; doubtless others.

A few years back, a journal of the publishing industry printed a list of all-time trade paperback best-sellers, beginning with *The Joy of Sex,* which sold millions, down to books that had sold two hundred and fifty thousand. It happened that I read the chart shortly after learning that Lawrence Ferlinghetti's *Coney Island of the Mind,* a trade paperback, had sold more than a million copies. Because the book was poetry, the magazine understood that its sales did not count.

When I make these points, I encounter fierce resistance. No one wants to believe me. If ever I convince people that these numbers are correct, they come up with excuses: Bly sells because he's a showman; Ginsberg is notorious; Rich sells because of feminist politics. People come up with excuses for these numbers because the notion of poetry's disfavor is important— to poetry's detractors and to its supporters. Why does almost everyone connected with poetry claim that poetry's audience has diminished? Of all people, they should know that it has increased. Doubtless the response is partly pursuit of failure and humiliation. Another source is lovable if unobservant: Some of us love poetry so dearly that its absence from *everybody's* life seems an outrage. Our neighbors don't read Geoffrey Hill! Therefore, exaggerating out of foiled passion, we claim that "nobody reads poetry."

When I contradict such notions, at first I insist merely on numbers. If everybody artistic loathes statistics, everybody still tells us that "nobody reads poetry," which is a numerical notion. Of course, the numbers I recite have nothing whatsoever to do with the quality or spirit of the poetry sold or read aloud. I include no Rod McKuen in my figures; I don't speak of performance poetry, open mike, or hip-hop. I include only poetry that intends artistic excellence, to be read on the page as well as from the platform. My numbers counter only numbers—and not assertions of value or its lack.

Separately I need to insist: I believe in the quality of the best contemporary poetry; I believe that the best American poetry of our day makes a considerable literature. *American Poetry after*

Lowell—an anthology of four hundred pages limited, say, to women and men born from the late 1920s through the 1940s— would collect a large body of diverse, intelligent, beautiful, moving work that should endure. Mind you, it would limit itself to one-hundredth of one percent of the poems published. If ever you write about Poetry Now, you must always acknowledge that *most* poetry is terrible—that *most* poetry of *any* moment is terrible. When, at any historical moment, you write an article claiming that poetry is now in terrible shape, you are always right. Therefore, you are always fatuous.

Our trouble is not with poetry but with the public perception of poetry. Although we have more poetry today, we have less poetry reviewing in national journals. Both *Harper's* and the *Atlantic* have abandoned quarterly surveys of poetry. The *New York Times Book Review* never showed much interest, but as poetry has increased in popularity, the *Times* has diminished attention. The *New York Review of Books,* always more political than poetical, gives poetry less space every year. The greatest falling-off is at the *New Yorker.* The *New Yorker* once regularly published Louise Bogan's essays on "Verse." In the past, men and women like Conrad Aiken, Malcolm Cowley, and Louise Bogan practiced literary journalism to make a living. Their successors now meet classes MWF. People with tenure don't need to write book reviews.

Their absence is poetry's loss, and the poetry reader's—for we need a cadre of reviewers to sift through the great volume of material. The weight of numbers discourages readers from trying to keep up. More poetry than ever: How do we discriminate? How do we find or identify beautiful new work? When there are sufficient reviewers, who occupy continual soapboxes and promote developing standards, they provide sensors to report from the confusing plentitude of the field.

Besides the weight of numbers, another perennial source of confusion is partisanship. When I was in my twenties and writing iambic stanzas, Allen Ginsberg's *Howl* was a living reproach. For a while I denigrated Allen: "If he's right, I must be wrong." Such an either/or is silly and commonplace: Restrictions are impoverishments. In the 1920s one was not allowed to admire both T. S. Eliot and Thomas Hardy; it was difficult for intellectuals who admired Wallace Stevens and his bric-a-brac to find house-room for Robert Frost and his subjects. Looking back at the long heyday of modern poetry, removed by time from partisanship, we can admire the era's virtuosity, the *various* excellences of these disparate characters born in the 1870s and 1880s, who knew each other and wrote as if they didn't. What foursome could be more dissimilar than Moore, Williams, Stevens, and Frost? Maybe the answer is: some foursome right now.

There are a thousand ways to love a poem. The best poets make up new ways, and the new ways mostly take getting used to. The poetry reading helps toward understanding (which explains how poetry thrives without book reviewing) because the poet's voice and gesture provide entrance to the poetry: a way in, a hand at the elbow. The poetry reading helps—but, as a substitute for reviewing, it is inefficient.

⅊

Metallic Flowers

Some years ago I noticed that Wordworth's poem "I wandered lonely as a cloud" was about economics. The surface, or plot, of the poem says that the poet takes a walk, sees a field of daffodils, and that his pleasure endures. Here are the first three stanzas of the poem:

> I wandered lonely as a cloud
> That floats on high o'er vales and hills,
> When all at once I saw a crowd,
> A host, of golden daffodils;
> Beside the lake, beneath the trees
> Fluttering and dancing in the breeze.
>
> Continuous as the stars that shine
> And twinkle on the milky way,
> They stretched in never-ending line
> Along the margin of a bay:
> Ten thousand saw I at a glance,
> Tossing their heads in sprightly dance.
>
> The waves beside them danced; but they
> Out-did the sparkling waves in glee:
> A poet could not but be gay,
> In such a jocund company:
> I gazed—and gazed—but little thought
> What wealth the show to me had brought:

The poem is, of course, about daffodils, and shows a genuine joy in flowers. Yet there is another side to the poem, which

From *To Keep Moving: Essays, 1959–1969* (Geneva: Hobart and William Smith Colleges Press, 1980).

exists in the words and can be derived from the words by close attention, and which belongs to a world entirely different from the world of nature and daffodils.

For many years I read the poem with pleasure, but with a dim sense that something was happening in it which I did not understand. I took a closer look at it. Really, Wordsworth is rather odd about these daffodils. Indeed he emphasizes the pleasure they gave him, but in describing the flowers themselves, he does two unusual things. First, he does not talk about a single daffodil, which one might want to isolate and contemplate; rather, he emphasizes the *quantity* of the daffodils. Even before we have the name of the flower, we have "a crowd, / A host." Then the imagery multiplies them—"Continuous as the stars . . . on the milky way" and "never-ending line"—and finally he names a falsely specific large number (false specificity is a common tradition of lively speech and of poetry)—"Ten thousand."

Second, Wordsworth talks in a peculiar way about the *color* of the flowers. Daffodils are yellow, indeed, and in his first reference to the daffodils Wordsworth uses the alternative word, "golden." It is a perfectly fine word, but there is no such thing as a synonym, and there are various ways in which "yellow" and "golden" differ. Some of the differences are trivial, perhaps, but some are certainly not. The difference that Wordsworth's poem exploits is the metallic overtone in "golden"—an overtone which supplies an intimation of riches. Words like "shine" and "twinkle" would not seem normally appropriate to daffodils. Those numerous stars have intervened; but what applies to stars must apply to daffodils as well. "Shine" and "twinkle" work in this poem because of the metallic connotation of "golden." "Sparkling" continues the image, and then Wordsworth ends the third stanza by bringing together in one metaphor his two themes of quantity and gold. What happens if you have a lot of this metal? You're rich, that's what happens. "I gazed—and gazed—but little thought / What wealth the show to me had brought." Wordsworth makes inescapable his comparison: Looking at the daffodils was like inheriting a great deal of money. It takes skill to combine two different lines of imagery, two remote metaphorical areas (one of color, and one of quantity) and to bring them together in a single word, so that they remain inescapably together. The word "wealth" performs just this act of skill. Doubtless Wordsworth was unaware of his economic metaphor. He provides an example of poetic genius which is surely unconscious.

Wordsworth carries the comparison further. He asks himself, "What does a sensible person do when he acquires a great deal of money?" and he answers, "He invests it, and lives on the income." Look at the fourth and final stanza of the poem:

> For oft, when on my couch I lie
> In vacant or in pensive mood,
> They flash upon that inward eye
> Which is the bliss of solitude;
> And then my heart with pleasure fills,
> And dances with the daffodils.

Let me set an arithmetic problem: Ten thousand daffodils at six percent is how many daydreams a year?

Ever since I noticed this covert meaning to the poem—that it is about money as well as about flowers—I have delighted in telling people about it. Some people think I am joking, possibly satirizing a sort of criticism, and many others are outraged at what they consider a sacrilege. I *do* think that the disparity between the two levels of the poem is comical, but I am not making a joke. (I could assert that "the margin of a bay" is a reference to buying on the margin.) I believe that this meaning exists in the poem as a result of the unconscious intention of the poet. Far from ruining the poem, this further level increases its fascination. The first few times we read the poem with the covert meaning in mind, the comic disparity may split our vision a trifle, but eventually we can hold both meanings in mind at once, and appreciate the poem as the complicated act of a human psyche.

Unconscious intentions are common to good poetry. T. S. Eliot said somewhere that the meaning of a poem is always only ostensible. If the poem lives, there is a content that was hidden from the poet at the time he wrote. If I write a poem about X, and someone later points out to me that it is also about Y, I am pleased: Only an unacknowledged power can make the engine go; only the mysterious *works*.

Unconscious content is unconscious for strong reasons, because we do not wish to acknowledge it. Here Wordsworth writes a poem in praise of money and investment. Wordsworth's England was Marx's England, the England of child labor and the slums of Manchester. Wordsworth turned his back on the slums, the child labor, and the factories. They were ugly and nasty, and he could not bear to see them. He could look at London only before the day's work had started. But there is a strange justice in the psyche: If you live in the country, to forget that your prosperity derives from industry and exploitation, you will look at flowers and praise them in terms of money. I remember the anecdote that gave John O'Hara the title of a novel: The old Sultan, noticing the figure of Death lurking in his courtyard, hurriedly departs for Samarra to hide from him. Another person seeing Death stops for a chat, but Death says he has no time to talk; he has an appointment in Samarra.

Anyone who feels that his appreciation of the poem is harmed by this reading never appreciated it in the first place; he is thinking only of some picture postcard of the English countryside which a teacher substituted for the poem. Postcards are easier to handle than poems, which are as complicated as people. If we read the poem openly, it seems to me, the daffodils are still there, and the imagination that walks among them dreams of them later. But the imagination is specifically capitalist, not feudal or socialist, and as the daffodils move in the breeze and touch each other, they make a clinking sound.

When I published some of these paragraphs in the *New York Times Book Review,* I received a welter of letters from outraged Wordsworthians. One told me that the only clinking sound was in my head. Another letter made me realize that unconscious intentions exist in critical essays too and not just in poems. When I was about sixteen I had an English teacher who ridiculed me before my classmates, under circumstances that were traumatic. A few days after my article had been published, I received a letter from him enclosing a postcard of daffodils in the lake country. He said that doubtless my fingerprints were still on the card. I did not remember, and still do not, that he handed the postcard around. But I have a strong suspicion that he did, and that some part of me remembered it, and that my phrase, "some picture postcard . . . which a teacher substituted for the poem"—which I thought I made up—was a piece of unconscious revenge.

The Expression without the Song

Recently a friend showed me a passage from Wittgenstein. In the fourth of his *Lectures on Aesthetics,* Wittgenstein says, "A man may sing with expression and without expression. Then why not leave out the song—could you hear the expression then?" I love the notion. The question is intended to expose nonsense, but I want to brush aside the logic and take the phrase for my own purposes. Some poetry gives us the expression without the song.

The song is the old baggage of ostensible content. "The leaves fall in the autumn and come back in the spring," etc. "I am historically determined to lack Christian faith, alas," etc. Who needs this junk? If poetry were judged by what usually passes for *content,* the best of it would be eighth-rate philosophy, on the intellectual level of textbooks and the *Reader's Digest.* If you love old poems, you have always loved the expression and not the song, though your brain may have concentrated on the song. You have loved the shapeliness of the words in your mouth, and you have loved the inward speech of the second language of poetry—the private voice underneath the public speech, that the poet may not be aware of.

There is another poetry, a poetry of the intelligence and without mystery. In his later poetry, Auden is an example. These poems resemble the conversation of an intelligent man. Occasionally the second language comes through, but mostly we have the *pages de journal* of a literate intellectual, and not the poetry of expressiveness. For me, it is a lesser kind of poetry. When I read essays, I would just as soon they came in paragraphs. Poetry is written in lines because lines are a way of controlling what happens in the mouth. Poetry happens in the mouth, and the mouth opens up the imagination, the way into the dream coun-

From *To Keep Moving: Essays, 1959–1969* (Geneva: Hobart and William Smith Colleges Press, 1980).

try of wishes and fears. Ideas happen in the eye, and from the eye to the top of the mind—the place of reason, civilization, charm, wit, governments, profit and loss.

But song and expression need not be enemies; they can exist together. Most great poetry has used the hook of a song (reflections and stories and arguments) to hang its expression on, just as old painting used verisimilitude (to landscape and figure) as a vehicle for its expressions of feeling in color, shape and texture. When you liberate the poem from the obligation to have an ostensible meaning, strange things happen. Images set free from realistic narrative or from logic grow out of each other by association, and poems move by an inward track of feeling. Perhaps the song in some sense is still there, but you are not left humming the tune.

Much great poetry has a song and expression, too. Here is Thomas Hardy's "During Wind and Rain":

> They sing their dearest songs—
> He, she, all of them—yea,
> Treble and tenor and bass,
>   And one to play;
> With the candles mooning each face . . .
>   Ah, no; the years O!
> How the sick leaves reel down in throngs!
>
> They clear the creeping moss—
> Elders and juniors—aye,
> Making the pathway neat
>   And the garden gay;
> And they build a shady seat . . .
>   Ah, no; the years, the years;
> See, the white storm-birds wing across!
>
> They are blithely breakfasting all—
> Men and maidens—yea,
> Under the summer tree,
>   With a glimpse of the bay,
> While pet fowl come to the knee . . .
>   Ah, no; the year O!
> And the rotten rose is ript from the wall.

The change to a high new house,
He, she, all of them—aye,
Clocks and carpets and chairs,
   On the lawn all day,
And brightest things that are theirs . . .
   Ah, no; the years, the years;
Down their carved names the rain-drop ploughs.

The ostensible content is simple: "Families have good times to-
gether, but then people grow old and die. Times four." Yet read
the poem intimately, and the paraphrase is ridiculously trivial.
The paraphrase is conventional melancholy and the expression
of the poem is joyous. The expression derives from a language
which the top of our mind does not understand, but which
reaches through our mouths the country of wishes and fears. At
the center of the poem is the mystery. Hardy's poem is obscure,
like all good poems: Our minds cannot name the causes of our
response to it.

In the poem that leaves out the song and concentrates on ex-
pression, the obscurity is more candid. Here is a little poem by
Wallace Stevens:

Disillusionment of Ten O'Clock

The houses are haunted
By white night-gowns.
None are green,
Or purple with green rings,
Or green with yellow rings,
Or yellow with blue rings.
None of them are strange,
With socks of lace
And beaded ceintures.
People are not going
To dream of baboons and periwinkles.
Only, here and there, an old sailor,
Drunk and asleep in his boots,
Catches tigers
In red weather.

The paraphrase here is as banal as the paraphrase of Hardy's poem: "Folks around here don't have much imagination," or "These proper people are boring; improper people are more exciting." However you paraphrase it, you are not going to be adequate to a sailor who catches tigers in red weather. This poem is obscure, like Hardy's, in that the words move and delight us in our irrational selves. The poem dreams, asleep in its boots.

For most of the many years since Stevens wrote "Disillusionment of Ten O'Clock," American poets have written poems with ostensible contents fully visible. Sometimes they have written very well; Robert Frost is moving and mysterious, and always keeps up a surface. But many poets, in an opening-up of the imagination, have increasingly sought to discover and express their irrational selves. They have not followed any rigid program—the rule book hurt French surrealism—though they have learned much from modern European and Latin American poetry.

One of the methods of this poetry is to suppress old progressive forms like narrative or argument. The precise reverse—antinarrative is a story that makes no sense; illogic is useful if it is gross enough—can suppress trite associations, but of course takes some of its shapeliness from the order it is mocking. (An old example is "Jabberwocky.") There is also a poetry—more like the Wallace Stevens poem—in which the progress is fantastic, in which expression sings loud and clear, without a song. Here is a poem translated from the German by Christopher Middleton, Paul Celan's "Fugue of Death":

Black milk of daybreak we drink it at nightfall
we drink it at noon in the morning we drink it at night
drink it and drink it
we are digging a grave in the sky it is ample to lie there
A man in the house he plays with the serpents he writes
he writes when the night falls to Germany your golden
     hair Margarete
he writes it and walks from the house the stars glitter he
     whistles his dogs up
he whistles his Jews out and orders a grave to be dug in
     the earth
he commands us now on with the dance

Black milk of daybreak we drink you at night
we drink in the mornings at noon we drink you at
    nightfall
drink you and drink you
A man in the house he plays with the serpents he writes
he writes when the night falls to Germany your golden
    hair Margarete
Your ashen hair Shulamith we are digging a grave in the
    sky it is ample to lie there

He shouts stab deeper in the earth you there you others
    you sing and you play
he grabs at the iron in his belt and swings it and blue are
    his eyes
stab deeper your spades you there and you others play on
    for the dancing

Black milk of daybreak we drink you at night
we drink you at noon in the mornings we drink you at
    nightfall
drink you and drink you
a man in the house your golden hair Margarete
your ashen hair Shulamith he plays with the serpents

He shouts play sweeter death's music death comes as a
    master from Germany
he shouts stroke darker the strings and as smoke you shall
    climb to the sky
then you'll have a grave in the clouds it is ample to lie
    there

Black milk of daybreak we drink you at night
we drink you at noon death comes as a master from
    Germany
we drink you at nightfall and morning we drink you and
    drink you
a master from Germany death comes with eyes that are
    blue
with a bullet of lead he will hit the mark he will hit you
a man in the house your golden hair Margarete

he hunts us down with his dogs in the sky he gives us a
    grave
he plays with the serpents and dreams death comes as a
    master from Germany

your golden hair Margarete
your ashen hair Shulamith

The poem's eloquence is great, its expressiveness and power; but
it speaks in the second language, without an old surface, associ-
ating and inventing and amalgamating.

From the late 1950s, American poets have done some of their
best work in a mode that is inward, dreamlike, and fantastic. Po-
etry translated from the Spanish language—Lorca, Neruda—and
Trakl and Celan from the German have helped to show the way.
James Wright wrote "Miners":

1

The police are probing tonight for the bodies
Of children in black waters
Of the suburbs.

2

Below the chemical riffles of the Ohio River,
Grappling hooks
Drag delicately about, between skiff hulks and sand
    shoals,
Until they clasp
Fingers.

3

Somewhere in a vein of Bridgeport, Ohio;
Deep in a coal hill behind Hanna's name;
Below the tipples, and dark as a drowsy woodchuck;
A man, alone,
Stumbles upon the outside locks of a grave, whispering
Oh let me in.

4

Many American women mount long stairs
In the shafts of houses,
Fall asleep, and emerge suddenly into tottering palaces.

Nothing in this poem is reasonable. There is no daylight. By imagination's fertile dark, we search for downed bodies in the pools of nightmare. We understand a social landscape, an industrial waste of polluted waters that wrecks the possibilities of human joy. In the poem's characters, places, and actions, we have scenes but not a story. We have the foregone conclusions of poverty, and the longing for death felt in the deep places of darkness, the lust for repose of a miner who is not even identified as a miner. We end with the fragment of a woman's dream, where the nightmare finds its counterpart in a dream of palaces—and they are palaces which, appropriately, are tottering. Wright assembles these fragments by a coherence of feeling which is all the stronger for the purity of its expressiveness.

᪏

The Vatic Voice

The first moment of a poem's beginning is an excited flash of insight, coming in the shape of images and sounds, a rush of language before which one feels like a passive observer. Later comes elaboration—getting the words right, studying how to cross out the wrong words, stimulating the secondary inspiration of revision.

A premise: Within every human being there is the vatic voice. *Vates* was the Greek word for the inspired bard, speaking the words of a god. To most people, this voice speaks only in dream, often in unremembered dream. The voice may shout messages into the sleeping ear, but a guard at the horned gate prevents the waking mind from remembering, listening, interpreting. It is the vatic voice (which is not necessarily able to write good poetry, or even passable grammar) which rushes forth the words of ex-cited recognition, and which supplies what we call inspiration. And *inspiration,* a breathing-into, is a perfectly expressive meta-phor: "Not I, not I, but the wind that blows through me!" as Lawrence says. Or see Shelley's "Ode to the West Wind." We are passive to the vatic voice, as the cloud or the tree is passive to the wind.

Decades ago, when I did some teaching, I had an odd expe-rience with a student who was trying to write poems. I let him into a writing class, liking some of his examples but not con-vinced of his talent. The first poems he showed me were wordy, explanatory, sincere, and dull. Then I happened to tell the whole class an anecdote about Hart Crane, who sometimes stimulated first drafts by listening to Ravel, very loud, and about Gertrude Stein, who wrote while parked at Parisian intersections with all

From *Goatfoot Milktongue Twinbird: Interviews, Essays, and Notes on Poetry, 1970–76* (Ann Arbor: The University of Michigan Press, 1978).

the horns beeping. They were using noise to clear away the tops of their minds. A week later my student came to office hours excited. He had been trying something. He had been listening to music, earphones clapped to his head and volume turned way up, and writing, "whatever came into my head." He had a series of small fragments of new and original imagery. The lines weren't finished, the rhythm wasn't good, there were some clichés and dead metaphors. But there was originality in each fragment; some corner of new light, some imaginative intelligence. The apparatus of the ordinary intelligence had conspired to make his old poems pedestrian. When he was able to remove the top of his mind, by an external stimulus of noise, the vatic voice broke through.

I make up the phrase, "the vatic voice," not because I am in love with it—it is pretentious—but because I am trying to avoid using words that have acquired either more precise meanings, or more precise affectations of meaning, like "the unconscious mind." Two characteristics that distinguish the vatic voice from normal discourse are that it is always original, and that we feel passive to it. We are surprised by it, and we may very well, having uttered its words, not know what we mean. We must find ways to let this voice speak. We must get loose, we must regress in the service of the ego, we must become as children. We must do this not only to make poems, or to invent a new theory of linguistics, but because it feels good, because it is healthy and therapeutic, because it helps us to understand ourselves, and to be able to love other people. I think, I truly think, that to clear the passageway to the insides of ourselves, to allow the vatic voice to speak through us, is the ultimate goal to which people must address themselves. It is what to live for, it is what to live by.

Poetry is evidence of vatic speech, but it is also typically an exhortation toward the vatic condition. Never to hear this voice in remembered night dream, or in day dream, or in moments of transport, is to be a lamentable figure. Children hear the voice—a romantic commonplace, and an observable truth. "There is another world that lives in the air." Most bad poetry is bad because of fear of the imagination. That is, bad poetry is the result of being a lamentable figure.

Sometimes I have tried to keep in touch with this vatic voice by sleeping a lot. Taking short naps can be a great way to keep the channel open. There is that wonderful long, delicious slide or drift down heavy air to the bottom of sleep, which you need touch only for a moment, and then there is the floating up again, more swiftly, through a crazy world of images, sometimes in bright colors. I come out of these fifteen- or twenty-minute naps, not with phrases of poetry, but wholly refreshed, with the experience of losing control and entering a world of freedom. I wake with energy. On occasion, I remember phrases or scenes from dreams—nap dreams or night dreams, or waking dreams—and take these phrases or images directly into a poem, but these discoveries are not the only virtue of dream. Dream is the spirit dying into the underworld and being born again.

There is also the deliberate farming of daydream. You can learn to daydream loosely while you also observe yourself. You watch the strange associations, the movements. These associations frequently try to tell us something. Listen. When you hum a tune, remember the words that go with the tune and you will usually hear some part of your mind commenting on another part of your mind, or on some recent action.

There is something I want to call peripheral vision, and I don't mean anything optical. If you talk about a dream with an analyst, and there is an old unimportant battered table in the dream, he or she may well say, "What about this table? What did it look like?" Often these little details carry huge import. When I listen to something speaking out to me, I don't attempt to choose what is most important, I try to listen to all of it. I never know what is going to be the most important message until I have lived with it. Very frequently, the real subject matter is something only glimpsed, as if it were out of the corner of the eye. Often the association which at first glance appears crazy and irrelevant ultimately leads to the understanding, and tells what we did not know before. I don't know how to stimulate peripheral vision. But one can train the mind to observe the periphery rather than to ignore it. Remember: If you are thinking about something, and you have one really crazy, totally irrelevant, nutty, useless, unimaginable silly association, listen hard; it's probably the whole point.

Mostly, when the vatic voice speaks through me, I have not

stimulated its appearance. I do not know how to make it happen. I know that it comes frequently when I have been occupied with many matters. The way I live now, poetry is apt to come out of a busy schedule, as a kind of alternative to, relief from, or even infidelity to more conventional duties. I do know that as you grow older you can learn better how to listen to this vatic voice. You can learn better not to dismiss it, you can learn not to be frightened of it. You can learn to let it keep talking, learn how to remain attentive to it, to remember and record it. When the voice is silent you can only wait. You can only try to keep the channels open, to stay ready for the voice, which will come when it chooses to come. Staying ready for the voice involves not being mature, intellectual, frightened, reasonable, or otherwise neurotic.

⤸

Goatfoot, Milktongue, Twinbird

infantile origins of poetic form

When we pursue the psychic origins of poetic form, we come to the end of the trail. It is deep in the woods, and there is a fire; Twinbird sits quietly, absorbed in the play of flame that leaps and falls; Goatfoot dances by the fire, eyes reflecting the orange coals, as a lean foot taps the stone. Inside the fire there is a mother and child, made one, the universe of the red coal. This is Milktongue.

1. *Some Premises*

First, in connection with oppositions:

1. Any quality of poetry can be used for a number of purposes, including opposed purposes. Thus, concentration on technique has often been used to trivialize content, by poets afraid of what they will learn about themselves. But concentration on technique can absorb the attention while unacknowledged material enters the language; so technique can facilitate inspiration.

On the other hand, a poet can subscribe to an anti-technical doctrine of inspiration in a way that simply substitutes one technique for another. Surrealism can become as formulaic as pastoral elegy.

2. When a poet says he is doing *north,* look and see if he is not actually doing *south.* Chances are that his bent is so entirely *south* that he must swear total allegiance to *north* in order to include the globe.

From *Goatfoot Milktongue Twinbird: Interviews, Essays, and Notes on Poetry, 1970–76* (Ann Arbor: The University of Michigan Press, 1978).

31

3. Energy arises from conflict. Without conflict, no energy. Yin and yang. Dark and light. Pleasure and pain. No synthesis without thesis and antithesis. Conflict of course need not be binary but may include numerous terms.

4. Every present event that moves us deeply connects in our psyches with something (or things) in the past. The analogy is the two pieces of carbon that make an arc light. When they come close enough, the spark leaps across. The one mourning is all mourning; "After the first death, there is no other." This generalization applies to the composition of poems (writing) and to the recomposition of poems (reading).

5. The way out is the same as the way in. To investigate the process of making a poem is not merely an exercise in curiosity or gossip, but an attempt to understand the nature of literature. In the act of reading, the reader undergoes a process—largely without awareness, as the author was largely without intention—which resembles, like a slightly fainter copy of the original, the process of discovery or recovery that the poet went through in her madness or inspiration.

And then, more general:

6. A poem is one inside talking to another inside. It may *also* be reasonable tongue talking to reasonable ear, but if it is not inside talking to inside, it is not a poem. This inside speaks through the second language of poetry, the unintended language. Sometimes, as in surrealism, the second language is the only language. We have the expression without the song. It is the ancient prong of carbon in the arc light. We all share more when we are five years old than when we are twenty-five, more at five minutes than at fifty years. The second language allows poetry to be universal.

7. *Lyric poetry, typically, has one goal and one message, which is to urge the condition of inwardness, the inside from which its own structure derives.*

2. Form: the Sensual Body

There is the old distinction between *vates* and *poiein*. The *poiein*, from the Greek verb for making or doing, becomes the poet—

the master of craft, the maker of the labyrinth of epic or tragedy or lyric hymn, tale-teller and spell-binder. The *vates* is bound in a spell. He is the rhapsode Socrates patronizes in *Ion*. In his purest form he utters what he does not understand at all, be he oracle or André Breton. He is the visionary, divinely inspired, who like Blake may take dictation from voices.

But Blake's voices returned to dictate revisions. The more intimately we observe any poet who claims extremes of inspiration or of craftsmanship, the more we realize that such claims are a disguise. There is no *poiein* for the same reason that there is no *vates*. The claims may be serious (they may be the compensatory distortion which allows the poet to write at all) and the claims may affect the looks of the poem—a surrealist poem and a neo-classic imitation of Horace *look* different—but the distinction becomes trivial when we discover the psychic origins of poetic form.

I speak of the origins of poetic *form*. Psychologists have written convincingly of the origins of the *material* of arts, in wish-fulfillment and in the universality of myth. We need not go over ideas of the poet as daydreamer, or of the collective unconsciousness. Ernst Kris's "regression in the service of the ego" names an event but does not explain how it comes about. One bit of Freud's essay on the poet as daydreamer has provided a clue in the search for origins. At the end of his intelligent, snippy paper, Freud says that he lacks time now to deal with literary form, but that he suspects that formal pleasure is related to fore-pleasure. Then he ducks through the curtain and disappears. Suppose we consider the implications of his parting shot. Fore-pleasure develops out of the sensuality of the whole body which the infant experiences in the pleasure of the crib and of the breast. The connection between adult forepleasure and infancy is the motion from rationality to metaphor.

But to begin our search for the psychic origins of poetic form, we must first think of what is usually meant by the word *form,* and then we must look for the reality. So often form is looked upon only as the fulfillment of metrical expectations. Meter is nothing but a loose set of probabilities; it is a trick easily learned; anyone can arrange one hundred and forty syllables so that the even syllables are louder than the odd ones, and every tenth syllable rhymes according to a scheme: the object will be a sonnet. But only when you have forgotten the requirements of meter do you begin to write poetry in it. The resolutions of form which ultimately provide the wholeness of a poem—resolutions of syntax, metaphor, diction, and sound—are minute and subtle and vary from poem to poem. They vary from sonnet to sonnet, or, equally and not more greatly, from sonnet to free verse lyric.

Meter is no more seriously binding than the frame we put around a picture. But the *form* of free verse is as binding and as liberating as the *form* of a rondeau. Free verse is simply less predictable. Yeats said that the finished poem makes a sound like the click of the lid on a perfectly made box. One-hundred-and-forty syllables, organized into a sonnet, do not necessarily make a click; the same number of syllables, dispersed in asymmetric lines of free verse, will click like a lid if the poem is good enough. In the sonnet and in the free verse poem, the poet improvises toward that click, and achieves a resolution in unpredictable ways. The rhymes and line-lengths of the sonnet are too gross to contribute greatly to that sense of resolution. The click is our sense of lyric *form*. This pleasure in resolution is Twinbird.

The wholeness and identity of the completed poem, the poem as object in time, the sensual body of the poem—this wholeness depends upon a complex of unpredictable fulfillments. The satisfying resolutions in a sonnet are more subtle than rhyme and meter, and less predictable. The body of sound grows in resolutions like assonance and alliteration, and in near-misses of both; or in the alternations, the going-away and coming-back, of fast and slow, long and short, high and low. The poet—free verse or meter, whatever—may start with lines full of long vowels, glide on diphthong sounds like *eye* and *ay,* move to quick alternative lines of short vowels and clipped consonants, and return in a coda to the long vowels *eye* and *ay.* The assonance is shaped like a saucer.

The requirements of fixity are complex, and the conscious mind seldom deals with them. Any poet who has written metrically can write arithmetically correct iambic pentameter as fast as the hand can move. In improvising toward the click, the poet is mostly aware of what sounds right and what does not. When something persists in not sounding right, the poet can examine it bit by bit—can analyze it—in the attempt to consult knowledge and apply it.

This knowledge is habitual. It is usually not visible to the poet, but it is available for consultation. When you learn something so well that you forget it, you can begin to do it. You dance best when you forget that you are dancing. Athletics—a tennis stroke, swimming, a receiver catching a football—is full of examples of actions done as if by instinct, which are actually learned procedures, studied and practiced until they become second nature. So it is with poetry. The literary form of poems is created largely by learning—in collaboration with the unconscious by a process I will talk about later. Possible resolutions of metaphor, diction, and sound are coded into memory from our reading of other poets, from our talk with other poets, from our reading of criticism, and from our revisions of our own work, sometimes with the conscious analysis that revision may entail. New resolutions are combinations of parts of old ones, making new what may later be combined again and made new again.

When the experienced reader takes a poem in, the sense of fixity comes also from memory. The reader also has codes in her head. The new poem fulfills the old habits of expectation in some unexpected way. The reader does not know why—unless she bothers to analyze; then probably not fully—she is pleased by the sensual body of the poem. She does not need to know why. The pleasure is sufficient. Since the poet's madness is the reader's madness, the resolution of the mad material is the reader's resolution as well as the poet's. The way in is the same as the way out.

Whatever else we may say of a poem we admire, it exists as a sensual body. It is beautiful and pleasant, manifest content aside, like a worn stone that is good to touch, or like a shape of flowers arranged or accidental. This sensual body reaches us through our mouths, which are warm in the love of vowels held together, and in the muscles of our legs, which as in dance tap the motion and pause of linear and syntactic structure. These pleasures are Milktongue and Goatfoot.

There is a nonintellectual beauty in the moving together of words in phrases—"the music of diction"—and in resolution of image and metaphor. Sophisticated readers of poetry respond quickly to the sensual body of a poem, before they interrogate the poem at all. The pleasure we feel, reading a poem, is our assurance of its integrity. (So Pound said that technique is the test of sincerity.) We will glance through a poem rapidly and if it is a skillful fake we will feel repelled. If the poem is alive and honest, we will feel assent in our quickening pulse—though it may take us some time to explain what we are reacting to.

The *vates* feels that he speaks from the unconscious (or with the voice of the God), and the *poiein* that he makes all these wholenesses of shape on purpose. Both of them disguise the truth. All poets are *poiein* and *vates*. The *poiein* comes from the memory of reading, and the *vates* from the imprint of infancy. The sensual body of the poem derives most obviously from memory of reading, but ultimately leads us back further—to the most primitive psychic origins of poetic form.

3. Conflict Makes Energy

People notice that poetry concerns itself with unpleasant subjects: death, deprivation, loneliness, despair, abandonment—if love then the death of love. Of course there are happy poems, but in English poetry there are few which are happy through and through—and those few tend to be light, short, pleasant, and forgettable. Memorable happy poems have a portion of blackness in them. Over all—Keats, Blake, Donne, Yeats, Dickinson, Eliot, Shakespeare, Wordsworth—there is more dark than light, more elegy than celebration. There is no great poem in our language which is simply happy.

Noticing these facts, we reach for explanations: maybe to be happy is to be a simpleton; maybe poets are morbid; maybe life is darker than it is light; maybe when you are happy you are too busy being happy to write poems about it and when you are sad, you write poems in order to *do* something. There may be half-truths in these common ideas, but the true explanation lies in the structure of a poem; and, I suggest, in the structure of human reality.

Energy arises from conflict.

(a) The sensual body of a poem is a pleasure separate from any message the poem may contain.

(b) If the poem contains a message which is pleasurable (a word I have just substituted for *happy*), then the two pleasures walk agreeably together for a few feet, and collapse into a smiling lethargy. The happy poem sleeps in the sun.

(c) If the message of the poem, on the whole, is terrifying—that They flee from me, that one time did me seek; that I am sick, I must die; that On Margate Sands / I can connect / Nothing with nothing; that Things fall apart, the center will not hold—then pain of message and pleasure of senses copulate in a glorious conflict-dance and conflagration of energy. This alternation of pleasure and pain is so swift as to seem simultaneous, to *be* simultaneous in the complexity both of creation and reception, a fused circle of yin and yang, a oneness in diversity.

The pain is clear to anyone. The pleasure is clear (dear) to anyone who loves poems. If we acknowledge the pleasure of the sensual body of the poem, we can see why painful poems are best: Conflict makes energy and resolves our suffering into ambivalent living tissue. If human nature is necessarily ambivalent, then the structure of the energetic poem resembles the structure of human nature.

The sensual body, in poems, is not simply a compensation for the pain of the message. It is considerably more important, and more central to the nature of poetry. When we pursue the psychic origins of our satisfaction with poetic form, we come to the end of the trail. It is deep in the woods, and there is a fire; Twinbird sits quietly, absorbed in the play of flame that leaps and falls; Goatfoot dances by the fire, his eyes reflecting the orange coals, as his lean foot taps the stone. Inside the fire there is a mother and child, made one, the universe of the red coal. This is Milktongue.

4. Goatfoot, Milktongue, Twinbird

Once at a conference on creativity, a young linguist presented a model of language. Photocopied in outline, it was beautiful like a concrete poem. I looked for language as used in poems and looked a long time. Finally I found it, under "autistic utterance," with the note that this utterance might later be refined into lyric poetry. It reminded me of another conference I had attended a year or two earlier. A psychoanalyst delivered a paper on deriving biographical information about an author from reading his fiction. He distributed mimeographed copies of his paper, which his secretary had typed from his obscure handwriting; he began his remarks by presenting a list of errata. The first correction was, "For 'autistic,' read 'artistic' throughout."

The newborn infant cries, he sucks at the air until he finds the nipple. At first he finds his hand to suck by accident—fingers, thumb; then he learns to repeat that pleasure. Another mouth-pleasure is the autistic babble, the "goo-goo," the small cooing and purring and bubbling. These are sounds of pleasure; they are without message, except that a parent interprets them as "happy": Pleasure is happy. The baby's autistic murmur is the expression without the song. Her small tongue curls around the sounds, the way her tongue cherishes the tiny thread of milk that she pulls from her mother. This is Milktongue, and in poetry it is the deep and primitive pleasure of vowels in the mouth, of assonance and of holds on adjacent long vowels; of consonance, mmmm, and alliteration. It is Dylan Thomas and the curlew cry; it is That dolphin-torn, that gong-tormented sea; it is Then, in a wailful choir, the small gnats mourn.

As Milktongue mouths the noises it curls around, the rest of the infant's body plays in pleasure also. His fists open and close spasmodically. His small bowed legs, no good for walking, contract and expand in a rhythmic beat. He has begun the dance, his muscles move like his heartbeat, and Goatfoot improvises his circle around the fire. His whole body throbs and thrills with pleasure. The first parts of his body which he notices are his hands; then his feet. The strange birds fly at his head, waver, and pause. After a while he perceives that there are two of them. They begin to act when he wishes them to act, and since the *mental* creates the *physical,* Twinbird is the first magic he performs. He examines these independent/dependent twin birds. They are exactly alike. And they are exactly unalike, mirror images of each other, the perfection of opposite-same. Twinbird.

As an infant grows, the noises split off partly into messages.

"Mmm" can be milk and mother. "Da-da" belongs to another huge shape. The infant crawls and her muscles become useful to move her toward the toy and the soda cracker. Twinbird flies more and more at his will, as Milktongue speaks, and Goatfoot crawls. Still, she rolls on her back and her legs beat in the air. Still, sister hands flutter at her face. Still, noises without message fill the happy time of waking before hunger, and the softening down, Milktongue full, into sleep. The growing child skips rope, hops, dances to a music outside intelligence, rhymes to the hopscotch of jump rope, and listens to the sounds her parents please her with:

> Pease porridge hot
> Pease porridge cold
> Pease porridge in-the-pot
> Five days old.

The mouth-pleasure, the muscle-pleasure, the pleasure of match-unmatch.

But "Shades of the prison house begin to close / Upon the growing boy." Civilized humans gradually cut away the autistic component in their speech. Goatfoot survives in the dance, Twinbird in rhyme and resolution of dance and noise. Milktongue hides itself more. It ties us to the mother so obviously that men are ashamed of it. Tribal society was unashamed and worshipped Milktongue in religion and history. Among the outcast in modern society, Milktongue sometimes endures in language, as it does in some American black speech. In Ireland where the mother (and the Virgin) are still central, Milktongue prevails in the love of sweet speech. Probably, in most of the modern world, Milktongue exists largely in smoking, eating, and drinking; and in oral sexuality.

But Milktongue and Goatfoot and Twinbird have always lived in the lyric poem, for poet and for reader. They are the ancestors, and they remain the psychic origins of poetic form, primitive both personally (back to the crib) and historically (back to the fire in front of the cave). They keep pure the sensual pleasure that is the dark secret shape of the poem. We need an intermediary to deal with them, for a clear reason: Goatfoot and

Milktongue and Twinbird, like other figures that inhabit the forest, are wholly preverbal. They live before words.

They approach the edge of the clearing, able to come close because the Priestess has no eyes to frighten them with. The Priestess, built of the memory of old pleasures, knows only how to select and order. The Priestess does not know what she says, but she knows that she says it in dactylic hexameter. Goatfoot and Milktongue and Twinbird leave gifts at the edge of the forest. The Priestess picks up the gifts, and turns to the light, and speaks words that carry the dark mysterious memory of the forest and the pleasure.

The poet writing, and the reader reading, lulled by Goatfoot and Milktongue and Twinbird into the oldest world, become able to think as the infant thinks, with transformation and omnipotence and magic. The form of the poem, because it exists separately from messages, can act as trigger or catalyst or enzyme to activate not messages but types of mental behavior. Coleridge spoke of meter as effecting the willing suspension of disbelief. The three memories of the body are not only meter; and they are powerful magic, not only for the suspension of disbelief. The form of the poem unlocks the mind to old pleasures. Pleasure leaves the mind vulnerable to the content of experience before we have intellectualized the experience and made it acceptable to the civilized consciousness. The form allows the mind to encounter uncensored experience but only because the figures in the forest, untouched by messages, have danced and crooned and shaped.

The release of power and sweetness! Milktongue also remembers hunger, and the cry without answer. Goatfoot remembers falling, and the ache that bent the night. Twinbird remembers the loss of the sister, convictions of abandonment forever. From the earliest times, poetry has existed in order to retrieve, to find again, and to release. In the poet who writes the poem, in the reader who lives it again, in the ideas, the wit, the images, the doctrines, the exhortations, the laments and the cries of joy, the lost forest struggles to be born again inside the word. The life of urge and instinct, that rages and coos, kicks and frolics, as it chooses only without choosing—this life is the life the poem grows from and reconstitutes.

ॐ

Journal Notes

In literature much that passes for technique really derives from the structure of the psyche. Critics who are able to discern structure in works of literature—but who know nothing of the psychic life—perpetuate the notion that formal discoveries in literature are gimmicks. There has never been a formal innovation in writing which did not represent, in the outer and conscious world of language, a shape of the inner and unconscious and wordless process.

A great innovation in modernist English and American literature was the multiple protagonist. *The Waste Land* has one character and one character only but that character changes his sex, his name, his history. He is Tiresias, Fisher King, a woman in a pub, a Roman. Eliot virtually copied the shape from Joyce's *Ulysses,* where one character is an Everyman, a Noman, an Emperor, and a masochistic cuckold.

The multiple protagonist is a psychic fact not a literary device. We are aware of our own multiplicity—I am not a person, I am a boarding house—not only, and most intimately, in dreams but also in our emotional lives. If there is any deep commitment to another person, *the other person always becomes a cast of characters.* If you love a woman she is daughter, mother, wife, sibling, death's head, and valley grass.

The poetry of serious fantasy is poetry which recalls a psychic event of considerable disturbance, as if one put the well down deep enough, not just to get water, but to start the rocks moving under the ground.

Portions of *Journal Notes* have appeared in *Death to the Death of Poetry: Essays, Reviews, Notes, Interviews* (Ann Arbor: The University of Michigan Press, 1995) and *Poetry and Ambition: Essays 1982–88* (Ann Arbor: The University of Michigan Press, 1988).

Coming back from five weeks in England, I understand that I love the country and that I could not live there. My speech goes crazy. After seventy-two hours there, I say (of a proposed journey): "It will be difficult to obtain a conveyance." My companion understands; I mean that it will be hard to get a taxi.

English poets don't have to write such diction. (Some do.) I pick up this precise polysyllabic argot because I am absorbed by its strangeness—just as a newcomer to the United States may collect idioms until she sounds like a slang dictionary. If I lived in England I would rewrite Williams's wheelbarrow:

> Such an extraordinary degree of importance
> is attached
>
> to a crimson-hued conveyance
> for waste material
>
> which has accumulated particles of liquid
> emanating from the skies
>
> in the approximate vicinity
> of the albino poultry

I think I'll stay here.

Poets read poems better than actors. All poets know this. Actors disagree.

Poets read poetry better than actors because they pay no attention to what the poems mean. Because they know that "meaning" is more complicated than some damned explication or interpretation. The actor looks for "the motivation of the speaker." (The actor sounds like an English teacher.) When he finds it, he *characterizes* the speaker of the poem by the voice he uses. Poets speak the voice of the poem, which is the voice of the noise, all the wild inward stuff of sounds. The noise comes from the mouth and is heard by the mouth, and from the listening mouth it travels directly to the stomach, the bowels, and the genitals.

Vowels do this mostly, and resemble volume in sculpture.

Consonants are more intellectual, travel to the eye, and resemble painting.

Poets can read their contemporaries for confirmation or for contradiction.

Some good poets don't read their contemporaries at all. They read mystics or Marxists, anthropology or ecclesiastical history—but never poetry. Others read old poetry, or poetry in a foreign language, but never their contemporaries. Some avoid contemporaries because they feel contempt for them. Others are afraid that they will pick up the manners of anybody they admire, that enthusiasm may lead to ventriloquism. Yet other poets *never* sound like the poets they have been reading, even when they want to. When they try to write parody or pastiche, they fail ignominiously; they always sound weirdly themselves, like people who cannot shake an accent.

For better or worse, many poets read poetry incessantly: for pleasure, for spite, to see what's happening, and to guess what will happen next.

Poets can read either for confirmation (finding and liking poems which resemble their own, in ambition, scope, and tone) or for contradiction (finding poems alien to their own, founded in wholly different wishes for poetry—but which they like anyway). Confirmation is useful when a poet is feeling his way toward a kind of poem that is new to him. Most of the time, contradiction is more useful still.

The trouble with reading for contradiction is that your taste is likely to be bad. It is easier to judge the kind of poem you know about—from trying to make it. Reading for contradiction, you can fool yourself into admiring something because it is your opposite. But reading for contradiction, you open yourself to the possibilities of dialectic. And the dialectic keeps you moving, and moving is what you have to do.

To the poet, the pleasure and value of writing poetry occur in the act of writing.

When the poet is young, he or she takes pleasure in publication; this pleasure remains when the poet is older, but diminishes a thousandfold; it blows away like dandelions. The pleasure of being praised fades less; and at a poetry reading, there are the pleasures of performance and the rewards of applause. I don't need to say that these various pleasures have a counterpart in pain; today I am talking of the pleasures.

All these rewards are nothing compared to the process of writing itself. Failure frustrates, blockage bouleverses; the act of writing—all writing is action-writing—is recompense for whatever miseries occur with impediment.

Writing poems is not like writing an editorial for a newspaper, or telling how to knit a sweater. In these activities, we search for words to implement an argument or to name an activity already known (known either as inferior or incomplete words, or as images that encode rote action). Much bad writing (or bad reading) results from the confusion of poetry with the use of words in other connections, as if words remained the same material when used as art and as information. Writing poems is more like making sculpture than like making speeches. Poems are objects which we manipulate with the fingers of our tongues. Sculpture is a useful analogy, either carving or modeling, though these methods are different. Sculpture creates *volume.* Poems have volume as editorials do not. Rodin said that a sculptor must never think of a surface except as the extension of a volume. In a good poem everything pushes up from under, against the taut surface of the word.

When a young poet says that she wants to walk in the field and love the field, without making words about the field—to stand there in happiness, without hearing "How beautiful!" speak itself inside her head—I can understand her battle. Sometimes she uses words to keep the world away, the way ancient men waved fire at elephants. But in the poem the words are not real weapons. Instead, they resemble the weapons ancient men so carved and decorated that they stopped being weapons and became sculpture. In the act of making a poem, the words for the field do not become the field. They remain words but they become material we walk into and lie down in.

The notion of action-writing seems to me to destroy a distinction commonly made between seekers and makers. Of course there are seekers who make nothing sensual. (A poem is *for the senses* before it can be for anything else.) And of course there are poets wholly unconscious of seeking; but even for these poets, poetry is not merely some metier or craft, like accounting or telegraphy, because a poem (seekers' poems also) is *never about anything.* The poem is the monument of its moment; it is the surface presenting (present-ing) the volume which is the whole life lived, the psyche's farming harvested, and the history of the race.

Such a complexity is far too multiple to be managed by the consciousness. Only an unacknowledged intelligence can handle so many things at once, and only at certain inexplicable moments can the vast system of our synapses provide metaphor and sound. This is the moment's action which is writing, and it is the moment of the pleasure and the value and the reward.

There are the moments of assemblage, moments when you feel so good that you want to live a thousand years. They happen when the present and the past fuse in a sudden imagination, and the real Troy becomes visible as the layered wholeness: Only the all is the one. Memory flared into the senses of the moment makes the poem. And the boy who walks down the street, in 1942, is the man of this moment, who is seventy-four years old.

The Line most obviously bodies forth the dance—the pause, balance, and sudden motion—that is Goatfoot. At line-end—by altering pitch or lengthening the hold of a vowel or of a consonant—the Line is Milktongue. By giving us units which we hold against each other, different and the same—and by isolating the syllable which rhymes, different and the same—the Line is Twinbird.

By invoking Goatfoot, Milktongue, and Twinbird, the Line is wholly serious, because it allows us to use parts of the mind usually asleep. When we take a lined poem and put it into paragraphs, we remove imagination and energy, we create banality. When a critic takes a lined poem and prints it as prose, in order to show that the poem is inferior, he tells us nothing about the poem. A reviewer in the *Hudson Review* tried to denigrate poems by Charles Simic and John Haines by printing them as prose. Such a critic reveals that he is ignorant or disingenuous. Back in the silly wars about free verse, toward the end of the First World

War, American critics who wished to prove that free verse was only prose took poems by Ezra Pound (or Amy Lowell) and printed them as prose. "See," they said triumphantly, like the man in the *Hudson Review,* "it's only prose." They proved only that they had no sense of the Line.

A sense of the Line disappeared from common knowledge some time ago. In 1765, an English critic proposed breaking Milton's lines according to sense, and not according to the pentameter, presumably changing:

> Of man's first disobedience, and the fruit
> Of that forbidden tree, whose mortal taste
> Brought death into the world, and all our woe,
> With loss of Eden, till one greater man
> Restore us, and regain the blissful seat,
> Sing heavenly muse. . . .

into:

> Of man's first disobedience
> And the fruit
> Of that forbidden tree
> Whose mortal taste
> Brought death into the world
> And all our woe
> With loss of Eden
> Till one greater man
> Restore us
> And regain the blissful seat,
> Sing heavenly muse. . . .

This rewriting of Milton resembles bad free verse, which is often rhythmically bad *because* the poet has no sense of the line as a melodic unit. The lines are short, coincidentally semantic and phonic. But Milton—need I say—is not damaged by this crude rearrangement. Damage only occurs to the critic who thinks that line structure does not matter, or to the reviewer who thinks that the poem must prove itself apart from its lineation— which is to propose that line structure does not matter.

A hundred years earlier than his 1765, the critic's ear would have been more reliable. With the increase of literacy, and the vast increase in printed books of prose, people began to read poetry without pausing at the ends of lines. As far as I can tell, actors indicated line-structure by pause and pitch at least through Shakespeare's time, probably until the closing of the theatres. Complaints from old-fashioned play-goers—that upstart actors like David Garrick no longer paused where the poet indicated that they should pause—occur in the eighteenth century. It is possible to connect literacy, capitalism, and puritanism with this insult to Goatfoot. Of course the Line has continued to exist, even among certain actors, and among all good poets.

You cannot read Keats or Hardy or Pound or Shakespeare or Williams as if they were prose without losing a connection to the unconscious mind, a connection made by sound. Maybe the reason people *want* to speak poetry as prose, and therefore to belittle the Line, is that they are frightened of the psychic interior to which the Line, inhabiting mouth and muscle, may lead them.

To speak with such seriousness of the Line is not to deny the frequency in poetry of other things: metaphor, image, thought, and whatever people mean by "tension" or "density." But Williams writes without metaphor on occasion, Creeley writes sometimes without images, and Mother Goose writes poems with little thought. Mother Goose is all mouth and muscle.

Back to the sources of poetic form and the process from sources to poems:

Of course Goatfoot, Milktongue, Twinbird, and the Priestess all inhabit the same poet. The poet can be defined as the innkeeper who entertains all these creatures, and watches them, and makes sure that they don't watch each other. But there is at least one further character essential to poetic form. He is not one of the psychic *sources,* which is why I didn't speak of him when I wrote "Goatfoot, Milktongue, Twinbird." But neither is the Priestess. Both of them are links that connect the sources to the written poem. After the Priestess speaks her dactyls, there is a further process. The Maker listens, copies down (the Priestess can speak, but she is illiterate), puzzles, scratches his head, wonders if he heard wrong, tries a new word for an old one he might have misheard, returns to the Priestess to listen some more, sighs again, closes his book, cannot sleep, opens it again, puts things together, takes things apart, scratches his head again, decides when to begin and when to end, speaks the words aloud, copies them over—and burns a million candles trying to get the words right.

The Maker has a beard, many wrinkles, wears a long black gown, and often does not hear his own name when he is spoken to. He is the Rabbi who examines the Talmud. He is the theologian of the middle ages who puzzles for forty years over the meaning of a single pluperfect which may have been spoken by the cousin of a saint.

Goatfoot and Milktongue come from the first day of birth, Twinbird comes from a week or two later. The Priestess is one-and-a-half years old, maybe two. The Maker is ten or eleven or even twelve. In racial rather than in personal time, Milktongue and Goatfoot begin as early as mammals begin; Twinbird is a hundred thousand years further along; the Priestess uses sharp stones at the edge of the savannah; the Maker remembers how the old men conspired to kill an elephant.

And the Maker is priest, wiseman, seer, rememberer, shaman, bard. He interprets lightning and goats' entrails. He keeps the journal of the tribes' wandering. He carries the book in his head. He goes over and over the texts he received from the makers before him. After a long time, he makes his decision. He comes out of his tent, out of the monastery, out of the library; he makes his decisions known.

Every good poem is innovative. Some people would invert the order: Every innovative poem is good. I agree, so long as I define innovation. There is gross innovation and there is minute innovation. In *Lyrical Ballads* Wordsworth was grossly innovative; so was Apollinaire in *Calligrammes;* and each poet was minutely innovative as well, making not only obvious breaks with convention but continually inventing on the cellular level of language—sub-cellular, atomic, even particular. They combined what seemed impossible of combination; they resolved the unresolvable. On the other hand E. E. Cummings's gross innovations, mostly typographical, were genuine so long as they were obvious, but worked to disguise stale romantic language, weary old metaphors and symbols—goatfooted balloon men, for goodness sake—and clichés of Victorian and Edwardian magazine verse. If we take a cliché—"basic assumption," for example, or "Yankees clash with archrival Red Sox," or "mud wonderful"—and print it in red ink on blue paper in Germanic script with perfume on it and project it from four projectors on four walls at once, with four people speaking it at four levels of pitch and volume—we still use a cliché; as well, we may have a nice party going.

And on the other hand Robert Frost, with sonnets and blank verse and quatrains, with conventional signs, with familiar syntax, innovated minutely and genuinely in his particular syntax and diction, in the relationship of sentence and line structure. Or, say: Thomas Hardy's poetry is weird, innovative, unlike anyone's before him, and largely inimitable; the same is true of his contemporary Hopkins, with the difference that it is obvious in Hopkins.

Which does not make the one better than the other.

Eric Gill: "Work is sacred, leisure is secular." Georgia O'Keeffe: "The days you work are the best days." Matisse: "Work is paradise." Rodin: "To work is to live without dying." And then Flaubert, to keep us honest: "It passes the time."

If you find yourself telling an anecdote or a fantasy, to illustrate something, more than seven times in your life, try writing it out and see what happens.

The pleasure of writing is that the mind does not wander, any more than it does in orgasm—and writing takes longer than orgasm. Trying to watch movies, often I cannot pay close continual attention. Watching baseball I read magazines between pitches. Even reading a good book—which is the third-best thing—my mind sometimes wanders; or I watch myself reading. When I write I *never* watch myself writing; I only *am* the struggle to find or make the words. I am fundamentally boring with a boring mind until, I hope, the word with its sounds and associations becomes a texture in front of me for working over, for shaping, for cutting, and for flying on.

It's the medium not the matter which affords this concentration. If I am working on a headnote for an anthology, I am engulfed by concentration on the rhythm and phrase, syntax and pitch, though I write nothing more than "John McPhee (b. 1930) writes. . . ." It is the grain of the wood, not the symbol of the Pieta, that concentrates the mind.

The poetry's in the redundancy. Reduction to message is reduction to concept, the abstract fallacy. Essence of Vanilla! So redundancy is never redundant (the nominalist's self-contradiction) but minutely varied in ways both visual and audible—the thousand tongues of style.

Work is style, and there is style without thought—not in theory, only in fact. When I take a sentence in my hand, raise it to the light, rub my hand across it, disjoin it, put it back together again with a comma added, raising the pitch in the front part; when I rub the grain of it, comb the fur of it, reassemble the bones of it, I am making something that carries with it the sound of a voice, the firmness of a hand. Maybe little more.

On the other hand there is no thought without style. Unless language taps chisel into stone, nothing is being thought. By itself the stone is only the blunt opacity of an area for thinking in; the stylus does the thinking—by cutting, by making clean corners, by incising. When we attempt translation into concepts, philosophy or poetry, we do not really think. Of course, when we use the stylus we are not necessarily thinking. But unless we use the stylus we are certainly not thinking. It is not always necessary to think. When it is necessary to think, poetry, because it most controls the stylus—because it makes more facets to control—is the ideal instrument of thought.

I understand that this notion is not generally accepted. "Poetry is for decoration and prose is for thought." Piss on that. Some philosophers know better, like Cavell, not to mention Wittgenstein or Heraclitus. The stylus cuts word into stone, therefore the apothegm and the fragment. Emerson carved in stone; they were small stones and hard to build with but they were carved stones as Nietzsche understood.

Sometimes when I read my poems at a college, a teacher has distributed photocopies to the students. While I am saying stanza four, at a long-studied line-break, I hear a sound like ten thousand crickets scraping their hindlegs; we are turning the page.

If I am warned in advance, I discourage this practice, and not because of page-turning. Reading and hearing are different processes, and the two channels of receiving interfere with each other, almost cancel each other out. Seen print distracts from heard word, and heard from seen. Visual shape, the black marks on the page, line length and white space—the eye perceives these matters with its own receptors. The obvious analogies— white space with silence or pause, for instance—remark imprecise equivalents, not identities. Experienced listeners become skillful in following performance, in hearing form and shape. Skill in silent reading is another matter. Doubtless a third skill, with sufficient experience, could combine the two sorts of receiving; but it is a skill we rarely require.

When a form dominates, we no longer see the possibility of alternate forms. The contemporary poetry anthology exists in *one* form, which prints large representative samples of a limited number of poets. I speak of the anthologies by which poetry is mostly taught in schools or represented in living rooms. (I do not speak of thematic collections, gift books of love poetry or poetry about Christmas.) Thus the *New Oxford Book of American Verse* prints thirty-three pages of Robert Frost, a small selected poems, and forty-six pages of Emerson. We have fourteen poems by A. R. Ammons and none by Kenneth Rexroth. We have seven by Yvor Winters and none by J. V. Cunningham, fifteen by Sylvia Plath and none by W. D. Snodgrass, nine by Ed Dorn and none by William Stafford.

This anthology-form gives us poetry by the Star System. So do the Norton Anthologies, and anthologies of the contemporary: A Penguin I once edited did it, as does the *Contemporary American Poetry* of A. Poulin, Jr.

It is not the *only* way to make an anthology. We used to make anthologies not of poets but of poems. The most famous is Palgrave's *Golden Treasury,* which intended to cull the best examples of the short English lyric from the centuries—and naturally enough chiefly represented its own age. Some anthologies show forth a particular period by its poems not its poets, like Norman Ault's *Elizabethan Lyrics,* and Oscar Williams's *Little Treasury of Modern Poetry.* Even the old Quiller-Couch *Oxford Book of English Verse,* which organized itself by poet and by date of birth, had room for many poets with one or two poems only, and included Anthony Munday (1553–1633) as well as Sir Philip Sidney, and William Bell Scott (1812–90) as well as Robert Browning.

There are faults to this form, most especially the enshrining of the Anthology Piece, like Yeats's "Lake Isle"; Robert Graves and Laura Riding, when they made their pamphlet against anthologies, made a good case against this kind of collection. If we deride the contemporary form as *The Star System,* we may mock the Palgrave method as *Poetical Gems.*

Still, let me praise collecting poems rather than poets. Oscar Williams printed some poets in quantity but he scattered a poet's poems throughout the book instead of printing them all together. By isolating the poem, he drew attention to its own qualities, rather than its position in the poet's *oeuvre.* Scattery organization allowed shocking juxtapositions, setting Dylan Thomas against William Carlos Williams—confrontations of style, High Noon at the Old Diction Corral. In such organization we ignore the poet's character and chronology; we do not watch one major figure after another strut his hour from youth to age; we do not observe lifetimes, careers, and developments; instead we discover poems by the one-poem poet and we discover one poem at a time, isolating the poems from the name.

The *Little Treasure of Modern Poetry* begins, making a statement, with seven poems by Gerard Manley Hopkins. But then it moves by contrast to Housman, quickly to Hardy, on to Delmore Schwartz, Vernon Watkins, Stephen Spender, Conrad Aiken, Henry Treece, George Barker, Elizabeth Bishop . . . In the Star System anthology, Elizabeth Bishop exists in multiplicity— and George Barker may be omitted. Few contemporaries read the fine poetry of Vernon Watkins, while his friend Dylan Thomas remains a Star.

Going along in Oscar Williams, one sees single poems by

Leonie Adams, Yvor Winters, Edwin Muir, W. R. Rogers, W. J. Turner, W. H. Davies . . . There is room for one poem by Maxwell Bodenheim; here are Elinor Wylie, Mark Van Doren, John Peale Bishop, Frederic Prokosch, Dunstan Thompson, F. T. Prince, Winfield Townley Scott, and the great Isaac Rosenberg. Now, because of the vogue of the Star System anthology, most of these poets go unread. Many of these poems here are by Major Figures . . . but thirty percent are not. There is a spirit of generosity here that is absent from our major-figure anthologies, a sense of possibility . . . For it is simply not true, in our era or any other, that the best poems are all the products of a few major poets. I remember a Poetical Gems anthology put together by Edmund Blunden and Bernard Mellor for the Hong Kong University Press, *Wayside Poems of the Seventeenth Century.* The editors organize alphabetically by author, printing lesser-known poets, the unusual and the good—or maybe, in a sense, the *usual* and the good instead of the atypical John Donne. Seventeenth-century wayside poets include Charles Cotton and Aphra Behn, Philip Ayers, George Wither, and Edward Thimbleby. Here are great poems which are never taught in school.

And there's the rub. We could make, I think, a fine anthology of American poetry from the last three decades which included no poems by poets who had won a Pulitzer Prize or been nominated for a National Book Award or printed in a major anthology or won a Guggenheim or served on an NEA panel or been front-paged by *APR.* This book is not collected because it will not sell; and publishing is not an eleemosynary industry. This book would have no life as a textbook. Teachers need heroes and courses need focusing. Courses like "Introduction to Modern Poetry" or "Contemporary Poetry" or "English Poets of the Nineteenth Century" usually work on the Major Authors plan—which is to say the Star System. It is far easier to teach a *poet*—her life, her development, influences upon her and coming from her, her place in the era—than it is to teach good *poems* one at a time.

If we live in an age which distorts the body of literature, it is the conventions of the academy—class size and semester length as well as focus on author instead of work—that do the most distorting.

When we hear the complaint that Americans write the same poem, we are listening to people who read the same magazines. Looking at Clayton Eshleman's *Sulfur*—rather eclectic, but not to be confused with any other contemporary quarterly—I find a review by Eliot Weinberger that speaks of poetry's overpopulation and of the exclusiveness of poetic camps: "One effect of the poetry pandemic," he writes, "has surely been the elimination of exogamous reading."

> It has become so hectic in one's own longhouse that one rarely has the time or stamina for visits to the other clans. Twenty years ago, in the ardent days of the anthology battles, even diehard Beat or Black Mountain partisans could, at the least, recognize the insignia of the opposing troops. . . . Today, who among *Sulfur* readers (which I take as the progressive, but not radical, flank) can spot the ear of Alfred Corn, or distinguish between Howard and Stanley Mosses? . . .

He then proceeds to devastate Frederick Seidel—"our latest most important American poet"—with a wit and acuity that admits no diffidence to accompany its alienation. It is rough and solid stuff.

"Exogamous reading" is a necessity, occasionally for the harsh and accurate criticism it can provide. Mostly we need it just to shake ourselves up. As I mentioned earlier, most poets and critics seem to read not for contradiction but for confirmation; not to be jolted and shocked out of their complacency but to build walls around it. The sameness within the fortified positions is timid and self-protective, restrictive to personal growth and the possibilities of poetry. Contradiction may be sought in a thousand places. Late in the 1950s, with Robert Bly's help and the help of others, contradiction came from foreign sources overlooked for decades. American poetry moved into an international modernism, not Bauhaus constructivist formalism but an expressionist or surrealist use of fantasy. And this movement hardened into a received style—"the way to write poems." (Black Mountain's third generation hardened just as obdurately.) So where do we find our contradiction now? Doubtless other foreign poetries wait for translators, and will nourish us again. Doubtless contradictions from experimentalists, Language Poets, and Slammers may help us change and grow.

But there's another source of contradiction arising from a radical place: I mean English literature of the past. After years of attending to American speech and surreal images, to the private confessions of true feeling, to virtuous grief in unambiguous syntax that cats and dogs can read, young poets may begin to mention the name of John Milton, and speak of such eccentric figures as Chaucer, Spenser, Shakespeare, Wordsworth.

In the history of literature, most poets have been so saturated in their own language's poetry that they have used it without knowing what they were doing. Doubtless this is The Tradition, and it provides us with models of greatness that we have the temerity to take as measures for our endeavors. Of course if we are so foolish as to imitate Milton's syntax or Spenser's crazy diction, we write pastiche. But if we abandon ourselves to the old greatness, submerge ourselves in the superb art of our own language's poetry—while our egos require us to remain Americans now—we will find ourselves altered and enhanced.

It is a wonderful thing for poets growing older, with some skills acquired, to discover a source of renewal which they had been ignorant of. Or which they dismissed or overlooked when young because of fashion. When I was growing up in the new-critical 1940s and 1950s, I could not read Walt Whitman. He seemed silly, pretentious, gushy, artless. How fortunate for me that I followed the herd!—for willy-nilly I saved *Leaves of Grass* for middle-age. I discovered Whitman's noise and spiritual largeness in my thirties when I needed a new start, a new place for departure.

And a poet who grew up on Whitman may need Pope and John Donne and Thomas Wyatt. Obviously some poets have loved them all along, but many looked past them and saw only Tu Fu and Zbigniew Herbert . . . wonderful, but not of our language, unable to sing to us in the language of our own word-centuries. Younger poets now have the good fortune to be able to discover, with new eyes, the poems of Ben Jonson and Thomas Campion.

If we try to regard our own literary culture from a Stuart or Cromwellian perspective, things that had seemed dissimilar reveal their cousinship. During the late 1950s, when some of us manned (accurate sexist verb) the barricades in the war of the anthologies, Allen Ginsberg and Frank O'Hara belonged to the Red Army; across no man's land were the White Guards of Robert Lowell and, for instance, W. D. Snodgrass. The high, angry Ginsberg of *Howl* served alongside the chatty and ironic O'Hara, who wrote poems during his lunchbreak from the Museum of Modern Art; and across the way were Lowell's decasyllabic drumbeats and Snodgrass's poignant elegies of private loss.

Viewed from the side of *Paradise Lost,* or the "Exequy". . . Well, I do not claim that *Life Studies* is indistinguishable from *Kaddish,* or "The Day Lady Died" from *Heart's Needle,* but surely they resemble each other more clearly than any of them resembles Michael Drayton or John Dryden. And what does Lowell say, in those late *History* poems about Jarrell and Schwartz and Berryman, but "I saw the best minds of my generation destroyed by madness"?

When my writer friends talk about revision, most of them sound as if they were speaking of gum surgery. For me, it's the part of writing I like most. With my first drafts, I would rather shield my eyes than read the wretched lines I put on the page. Second drafts are not much better. If I get to a fifth or seventh draft, there's a point when I sense—although my words and moves and line-breaks are all wrong—that a poem may lurk behind the scrim of boring epithets and dead metaphors. I just need to keep at it.

Early drafts pursue *something*—or there would be no first drafts. Words arrive, wanting to embody something urgent but nameless. The body of the poem will be its name, which I will discover only by going over a manuscript again and again. Sometimes the lines that begin the poem really belong at the end. Sometimes a stanza is missing, and writes itself after a month and twenty drafts. Sometimes I need to cut half my lines, and what I cut may become another poem. Always I discover redundancies, repetitions, useless explanation. One morning I think I have solved the poem; the next morning I realize that I have come closer but that the poem has not yet arrived to the page. Cross out; try something new.

If I feel frustrated, often I feel more pleasure than I do frustration. Maybe crossing out is the most pleasure, and it's certainly the first. The No is as crucial as the Yes, and you can't have the second without the first. Revising is perpetual repeated waves of the negative and the positive. When I find an error—for thirty-seven drafts I have neglected to notice that my metaphor "harbor" decomposes before me—I am happy to have discovered the corpse, so that I can fill the dead space with a word that may walk and talk. Twenty years ago I spent four or five years on "Great Day in the Cows' House," and for most of that time it was a poem (as I said at the time) "with no words in it." In the last twenty drafts the words started to arrive. They picked up or repeated images and vowels that had been there all along, waiting to be resolved. With this poem, I had found its bodily structure early, and much detail, but I needed to wait for poetry blood to flow in the veins.

Revision is gay, and gayer as it proceeds. The impetus to so many poems—look at any anthology—derives from misery: elegy, loss, rejection, a cloudburst of grief. Whatever the subject matter, the language of revision seeks for pleasure. The first time I remember noticing this apparent conflict—pleasure in working with painful material—happened long ago. I was dejected after breaking up with a girlfriend. Over months, I thought of good days and was immediately overcome by memory of rejection. The pain was thick. During these months, words arrived—notes of images and actions—but I could not *work* on poems. Then one morning I returned to the desk and lost myself. For three hours or more, I felt again the bliss of time passing unnoticed; I had no identity; there was nothing except desk, paper, and pen. For the first time in weeks I was happy. Then I laughed: Working from my isolated scribbles, I was happy writing miserable poems about *her*. Revising, I was thinking not about loss but about metaphors, line-breaks, punctuation; I made images fit together; I crossed out empty epithets and clichés. I used the materials of rapture and despair as a sculptor uses clay.

In a question period somebody asks: "When you revise so much, don't you lose the feeling you began with?" If you want to make art, you had better. It's not heartless. The heart supplies armature and plaster for the hands to work on. If the hands are good enough, they make art. If the art is good enough, it speaks to others. When my wife was sick I sat by her side writing about her sickness. I could not read; no book could hold my attention. Only working at words, about her suffering, could give me respite from the scene of suffering. After she died, only writing poems of grief provided respite from grief.

Not all poems serve such purposes. These notions would not apply to *The Faerie Queene,* or an epic by William Morris, or *King Lear,* or "Casey at the Bat." They apply to poems that speak out of personal feeling, poems that people call confessional, poems that confess to confusion and despair. Revision moves me from the raw, formless suffering of the poem's impetus to the expressed suffering of the poem. If the reader were to observe the mere scream of pain—first draft—the reader could sympathize but not empathize, could take inside only the sound of screaming. It's art that carries intense, articulated feeling from writer to reader. No art, no transport.

At a poetry reading, the listener receives the poem as if the poet's feelings happened *now.* The poet's private past seems a public present. If the poet has revised doggedly, over years, a new book derives from events long ago. By months of revision, the poems have become for the poet made things, sensual objects for the mouth and the tapping foot. Someone asks, "How can you say these poems aloud?" For the poet the reading does not reconstitute the suffering of five years before (that gushed out a welter of inchoate despair in flaccid language) but embodies suffering revised into an object of art. The words recited are not the pain but the poem.

❧

Marvell's Manyness

During the question period they ask: "Who's your favorite poet?" When I was young and sophisticated I explained that I could not have one favorite; now I answer Thomas Hardy one day and Marianne Moore the next—or, more often than not, Andrew Marvell. Only Marvell would have made my short list forty-five years ago and all the years between. Of course Marvell's poetry has *altered* over the years. Without a doubt he has produced, during my decades, much more work, most especially "An Horatian Ode upon Cromwel's Return from Ireland," which becomes available only when we have read a little history. "Upon Appleton House" eluded us when we were young and lazy because of its length; now its length is a luxury. It is also true that the range and import of the old poems have enlarged: Their scale has grown greater while their miniature size—pastoral conventions, carpe diem—has remained the same.

The analogy of scale and size comes from sculpture, which provides another analogy: When we look at a bronze or stone Henry Moore reclining figure, sited outdoors in a sculpture park, it changes every few inches as we walk around it. New lines-of-sight make new combinations, configurations, connections. If we continue to read a complex and multiple poem, as we grow older, it alters each time we return to it. The greater the poem the more it changes; we cannot read the same great poem twice. Thus "To His Coy Mistress" veers over the years from flesh to bone. Universality gathers upon "The Garden" as youth's gregariousness proves shallow, and as solitude enhances meditation or the pleasures of imagination. Conviction of historical ambiguity, or of human diversity within the ostensibly

From *Principal Products of Portugal* (Boston: Beacon Press, 1995).

single self, illuminates and deepens "An Horatian Ode upon Cromwel's Return from Ireland."

We know about Andrew Marvell's life because of his politics, not because of his poetry. He was a lively controversialist during the Restoration, satirizing the court from his republican vantage. He was also the dutiful and assiduous Member of Parliament who represented the city of Hull. What we know of Marvell's life frustrates us, for the poet inside the Member remains elusive.

The poet's father, also Andrew Marvell, was born in Meldreth, eight miles south of Cambridge, educated at Emmanuel College, Cambridge, and in 1614 took the living at Winestead, in Holderness, where the poet was born seven years later. When Andrew *fils* was three years old, his father became preacher at Holy Trinity Church in Hull, as well as master of its grammar school; the poet was associated with the city for the rest of his life. (Three centuries later Philip Larkin lived and died there, librarian at the University.) Marvell's mother, whose name was Anne Pease, died in 1638, and his father remarried six months later—only to be drowned in 1640 while crossing the Humber. Thomas Fuller in his *Worthies,* who describes the elder Marvell as "most facetious in his discourse, yet grave in his carriage," apportions blame: The preacher "drowned . . . by the carelessness (not to say drunkenness) of the boat-men." Apparently father and son had suffered a contretemps a year before the father drowned. Scholars suggest that the poet left Trinity College, Cambridge (where he matriculated in 1633), in the company of Jesuits, a brief flirtation with the popery of which as satirist he became enemy. His father rooted him out of London—discovering him at a bookseller's—and brought him back to Trinity College and Puritan values.

When Marvell took his degree from Trinity he spent some years traveling on the continent, possibly as a tutor, during the onset of the civil wars. He left England in 1642 and returned probably in 1646, master of Dutch, Italian, French, and Spanish. Presumably his Latin and Greek were in place before he left. He wrote many Latin poems; at least one Greek poem survives. His Latin, both spoken and written, was fluent even for a seventeenth-century man of learning; he employed his languages in office under Cromwell and later on diplomatic missions during the Restoration.

Returned to England, he tutored Mary Fairfax, daughter of a Cromwellian general who had left the field, at Appleton House in Yorkshire from 1650 to 1653. There he probably wrote much of his best poetry. Later John Milton (Latin secretary to Cromwell; the office corresponded with foreign governments) recommended Marvell to Cromwell as tutor for a ward of the Lord Protector's living in Eton. Later still—in 1657—Marvell was appointed to assist Milton as Latin secretary. Another helper was the young John Dryden, many years later a Royalist antagonist of Andrew Marvell.

Marvell was first elected to Parliament in 1660. Like his father he was a moderate Puritan, Church of England; yet like many another Cromwelliam, he welcomed the Restoration for stability's sake. Marvell used his relative political security to free Milton from jail; he may have saved Milton's life. Elected to Parliament, he served his constituents until his death. Many of his letters to the corporation of Hull are preserved in the Oxford University Press volumes of Marvell's *Poems and Letters,* meat for students of seventeenth-century English political life. These official letters frequently lament that taxes must be raised. Private notes to his nephew William Popple contain gossip and even scurrilous jokes about the king; but Marvell was no fervent anti-Royalist: He deplored courtly corruption but tolerated or perhaps indulged Charles the rake.

Marvell's political career was not without event. During his first Parliament he engaged in a public fistfight. From 1663 to 1665 he traveled on a trade embassy to Russia, with stops in Denmark and Sweden, an extraordinary adventure in the seventeenth century. Although we hear little about the journey in Marvell's own words, from other sources we understand that he was secretary to the mission and scripted letters home on behalf of the embassy's leader, the Earl of Carlisle. Czar Alexis professed dissatisfaction with Marvell's initial Latin address because Marvell called him *Illustrissimus* instead of *Serenissimus.* The embassy, which failed in its purpose, included a long series of aggravations. Early on, Marvell apparently pulled a gun on a recalcitrant teamster. On February 19, 1664, Czar Alexis provided his English visitors a banquet that lasted for nine hours and consisted of five hundred dishes. Marvell received the special attention of a sturgeon's head. We are told that the banquet ended early because the czar suffered a nosebleed.

In the last decade of his life, the public Marvell was quiet, representing Hull and reporting by regular letter to the corporation. Privately, or at any rate anonymously, Marvell was noisy: He occupied himself with political satire—anticourt, antipapist—in favor of toleration and liberty. When he died suddenly in 1678, perhaps of a stroke, it was rumored that Jesuits had poisoned him; he had recently satirized the Roman church.

Andrew Marvell never married. After his death his housekeeper Mary Palmer represented herself as Mary Marvell. (The poet's widow stood to receive some monies owed the poet's estate.) While he was alive, his political adversaries denounced Marvell as homosexual. Although his poems are full of pastoral love, no reader has ever discerned in his work tenderness toward a particular woman. The strongest erotic suggestion arises in "The Garden," where Marvell's vegetal eroticism exaggerates a convention. "The Definition of Love" can be read as an ironic description of the difficulties of homosexual love. Maybe it provides a rueful account of unfulfilled homoerotic desire:

> As Lines so Love *oblique* may well
> Themselves in every Angle greet:
> But ours so truly *Parallel,*
> Though infinite can never meet.

But we merely speculate.

Of his politics we may say more. From the start Marvell was political. In the seventeenth century who could be apolitical? From time to time he appears to stand on both sides of a question: His attack on the Cromwellian Tom May was written during Cromwell's time—when he also wrote Cromwellian panegyrics. At the same time one may discern consistencies in Marvell: He favored religious toleration, whether its opponents were low church or high; he attacked corruption in the Long Parliament—and again in the court of Charles II. Stories are told of Marvell's incorruptibility, of his refusal to take a bribe. If he seems at times to stand on both sides of a question, we must ask how many issues limited themselves to two sides. The seventeenth century was politically many-sided, more complex than our own age, and one need not have been the Vicar of Bray to appear inconsistent. To divide England into parties of Cavalier and Roundhead is to preclude understanding. One could stand to the Parliament side on a dozen issues, and to the Court side on a dozen others—at the same time and without inconsistency, much less hypocrisy.

Mixed loyalties were standard. Some rebels of the Long Parliament considered themselves loyal subjects who wished to save the king from wicked advisers. (Decapitation seems an extreme measure of correction.) Take Marvell's employer Fairfax, a great general for Cromwell against the king. (Milton addressed a sonnet to the parliamentary hero, "To My Lord Fairfax," "whose name in arms through Europe rings.") Fairfax resigned his command when he disagreed with the Lord Protector; a Presbyterian himself, he would not invade Scotland. His wife was aghast at the execution of Charles I; it was rumored that My Lord Fairfax shared her opinion. Retired from combat, Fairfax returned to his country seat in Yorkshire, and later corresponded with Charles II from Appleton House. This old Cromwellian general helped to restore Charles II in 1660.

Ambivalence wove its texture into details of all private and practical arrangements. The boy whom Marvell had tutored at Eton—Cromwell's ward William Dutton—was son of a Cavalier who died in 1646 fighting in the Royalist forces, but his uncle arranged that William marry Cromwell's youngest daughter. Of course, when ambivalence tries to act, it finds itself incapable. That Cromwell's ward was Royalist did not keep the king's head on his shoulders. To take part in the life of their times, Fairfax or Marvell or Milton needed perforce at times to take sides, Milton without wavering. From time to time, throughout his life, Marvell in his satires could sound dogmatic and singleminded. Only when he writes great poetry does Marvell's language embody ambivalence or manyness. If ambivalence makes for paralyzed politics and anarchic governance, it makes for poetry complex enough to mimic human complexity; in Marvell, it made for great poetry.

It is a mark of Marvell's honorable manyness that, if he had published the "Horatian Ode" in his lifetime, he would have been in trouble with both regicide and loyalist. He published little in his lifetime—poems printed in anthologies—and none of the poems for which we honor him. After his death, in 1681, his nephew William Popple issued *Miscellaneous Poems*. Only in small measure may we attribute this absence of publication to politics. Marvell was not a professional poet, as the young John Dryden was. Marvell's attitude toward himself as a poet was old-fashioned: He resembles not Ben Jonson but Sir Walter Raleigh, or his own contemporary John Wilmot, Earl of Rochester, who was poet among his other roles—gentleman and rake, for instance. Marvell was a poet while he was tutor, Latinist, bureaucrat, and M.P.

Marvell was also old-fashioned in poetic style, which helps to account for the strange history of his reputation. Usually he hoed his tetrameter garden, instead of going avant-garde with the heroic couplet that Dryden spent his life exploring and extending. Marvell also cultivated the old metaphoric extravagance associated with John Donne, the out-of-fashion, faintly fusty metaphysical style. To someone reading his work late in the seventeenth century, Marvell must have seemed reactionary—like Thomas Hardy writing rhymed lyrics in the heyday of 1920s modernism.

When Popple published *Miscellaneous Poems,* no one celebrated a great poet. For that matter readers lacked Marvell's greatest work: "An Horatian Ode" was suppressed until a century after his death. (Popple at first seems to have included it: This poem and the lesser verses on Cromwell's death turn up in two surviving copies; in all other copies they have been removed.) It was not until 1776 that Marvell's Cromwellian poems reached print to remain there.

Meanwhile Marvell the lyric poet lacked an audience. When English booksellers picked the poets for Samuel Johnson to write about in *Lives of the Poets,* Marvell's name went unlisted: At the time, his name would not have occurred to anyone. Other seventeenth-century poets, like Robert Herrick and Thomas Campion, also remained forgotten until the Romantics found them, but Marvell had the misfortune to be remembered for something other than his poetry. All through the eighteenth century, his was a name to conjure with, for Whigs and lovers of liberty. Jonathan Swift praised and learned from Marvell's satirical prose, especially *The Rehearsal Transpros'd*. When Wordsworth thought of Marvell it was as a son of liberty: "Great men have been among us . . . Sydney, Marvell, Harrington."

It took a later generation of Romantics to discover the poetry. At first they considered him merely a poet of nature, but once he was reprinted, the limits of this discovery could expand. The antiquarian Charles Lamb found him, read him, and praised him. William Hazlitt reprinted some of the best work in an 1825 collection. Palgrave treasury'd him. Tennyson recited him to friends. Ward in *English Poets* (1880) left out "To His Coy Mistress" (perhaps as distressing in 1880 as praise for Cromwell in 1681) but included "An Horatian Ode," "The Bermudas," and "The Garden."

One would think the battle won. But, if we had learned to admire the poetry, we had not credited its greatness. When Augustine Birrell wrote about Marvell in 1905, for the *English Men of Letters* series, he was modest or scrupulous to limit his praise. "A finished master of his art," Birrell says, "he never was." He compares Marvell's skill unfavorably with the poetry of Lovelace, Cowley, and Waller. "He is often clumsy," Birrell writes, "and sometimes almost babyish."

In 1922 the Oxford University Press published *Andrew Marvell*, tercentenary tributes by eight critics including mossbacks like Edmund Gosse and J. C. Squire—and the young turk T. S. Eliot. We consult this volume to read the Tercentenary Sermon at Holy Trinity Church and the Tercentenary Address at the Guild Hall in Hull, or to read about "The Marvell Tramcars" and to study photographs of a Hull trolley repainted in honor of the city's poet and parliamentarian. But it was Eliot's great essay, reprinted from the *Times Literary Supplement*, which especially fixed our attention on Marvell's excellence: After being neglected for two centuries, and condescended to for another, he was at last discovered.

When you love a poet's poems, it is annoying to feel required to adduce reasons. But if you are to move a skeptic you need to try. For at least a hundred years people have used

> Annihilating all that's made
> To a green Thought in a green Shade

as an example of poetry or even the poetic. In the seventeenth century this couplet would have been an example of wit; by history's revisionary magic two centuries later its wit vanished in romantic smoke. Its thoughtful trope—an exaggeration of concentration, the inward defining itself as outward—came to seem mystic: a moment of pantheistic ego-loss or Freud's oceanic feeling. Why not both at once?

Surely this couplet is poetry at its most condensed. Keats advised Shelley, "Load every rift with ore," and Marvell was expert at this endeavor. Rift-and-ore is never mere quantity, more midgets in the Volkswagen; rifts are most ore'd when number is not merely multiple but various. The smoothly rolling polysyllabic Latin of "annihilating," with its densely syntax'd accusative English monosyllabic "all that's made," contrasts with (and completes itself in) a monosyllabic line absolutely balanced—preposition / article / adjective / noun // preposition / article / adjective / noun—in which four out of eight monosyllables appear twice. Wit and grammar together serve to embody a pleasurable and mildly scary vaguening of consciousness: both at once. Three hundred years of consciousness about consciousness hook together in these lines.

Marvell's banner reads: *Both at Once.* The simultaneous affirmation of opposing forces—by no means limited to two items—requires compression. By this compression we not only acknowledge ambivalence, we embody it.

His couplets accommodate a vast range of tone and of pacing. If the beginning of "To His Coy Mistress" is old-fashioned and metaphysical—hyperbolic-witty, slow in its performance of slowness—the end of the poem is modern, streamlined, and speeds like little else in English poetry: and all, perforce, to the same octosyllabic tune. Barbara Everett alludes to the "Horatian Ode" when she observes that "Marvell is using a metre for thinking aloud in"—but in his great poems he always uses meter to think aloud in. The tetrameter couplet balanced four against four, and each four balanced two against two—except when enjambment and eccentric caesura saw that it didn't, which was shocking or outrageous:

> Thus, though we cannot make our Sun
> Stand still, yet we will make him run.

Poetry is a language for thinking aloud in—and not for putting thoughts into words, although the philosophical heresy is almost universal among critics. (Everett provides an exception.) Metaphor, syntax, image, meter, and rhythm are means-of-thought; so is overall construction. "To His Coy Mistress" has been well observed: its logical structure, its combinations of flesh and bone, time and space, eros and thanatos, its use of poetic conventions two thousand years old. It is a culminating poem in a millennial sequence that affirms: *Make love because you die.* In the process this theme combines in one poem the two subjects of human discourse: *both at once.*

Poetry exists, not only Marvell's, to say and do *both at once.* Philosophical discourse dedicates itself to find, to set forth, and to decide what's first or best or true. Only poetry admits (proclaims, insists, shouts): *both at once!* or even *all at once!* (Therefore I need call Heraclitus, Emerson, and Nietzsche poets.) Surely Marvell is foremost among the manysayers. Manyness is ineluctably human, and poetry (among human artifacts) best embodies manyness.

Although we need from time to time to make a choice—Marvell voted, Marvell advocated and denounced—choices are always *faute de mieux.* To pretend otherwise is to lie, an activity deplored by the Muse. Utterly captured by the mixed political life of seventeenth-century England, housed with many-sided Fairfax at Nun Appleton, Marvell found in the expression of ambivalence his poetic form and power.

If Marvell made the octosyllabic couplet his own, using the modern pentameter couplet only for lighter work, he experimented in his greatest single work by marrying the tetrameter couplet to a trimeter, constructing the eloquent, heartbreaking stanza of "An Horatian Ode." The Cromwell who appears in Marvell's poem is massive, violent, and willful:

> Then burning through the Air he went,
> And Palaces and Temples rent:
>   And *Caesar's* head at last:
>   Did through his Laurels blast.

The last line trembles the scale, as we sort its syntax out and watch "blast" perform its possibilities. We must reconstruct Marvell's Cromwell away from normative leaders like Napoleon and Hitler, who have been praised in similar terms, because on the other hand, "Much to the man is due . . ."

> Who, from his private Gardens, where
> He liv'd reserved and austere,
>   As if his highest plot
>   To plant the Bergamot,
>
> Could by industrious Valour climbe
> To ruine the great Work of Time,
>   And cast the Kingdome old
>   Into another Mold.

Meter, consonants, and syntax mimic strength, embody phallic masculine muscularity and determination. In the great couplet, "Could by industrious Valour climbe / To ruine the great Work of Time," Marvell clearly values both "valour" and "the great work." Emotions conflict, values conflict, and "valour" destroys "great work" as an army lays waste to a castle. I think of Yeats's oxymoron, "terrible beauty," in "Easter, 1916"—where "is born" gives narrow victory to beauty over terror.

Marvell the traditionalist poet is not unmoved by tradition. The poem continues directly:

> Though Justice against Fate complain,
> And plead the antient Rights in vain:
>   But those do hold or break
>   As Men are strong or weak.

> Nature that hateth emptiness,
> Allows of penetration less:
>   And therefore must make room
>   Where greater Spirits come.

The most eloquent and touching stanzas describe the execution of Charles, written by the poet later described by Royalists as a "bitter Republican":

> *He* nothing common did or mean
> Upon that memorable Scene:
>   But with his keener Eye
>   The Axe's edge did try:

> Nor call'd the *Gods* with vulgar spite
> To vindicate his helpless Right,
>   But bow'd his comely Head,
>   Down, as upon a Bed.

Everett remarks, "Everything is beautiful, and something is betrayed." There's nothing greater in English poetry than this beautiful betrayal—but Marvell does not end with this passage that would have ended most poets' poems. Praise for Cromwell continues to find glory in the power, and yet the poem ends in the prophetic aside that shades itself back over the hundred and eighteen lines before:

> The same *Arts* that did Gain
> A *Pow'r*, must it *maintain*.

The poise of Marvell's judgment wavers, but it concludes, as it does in his other great poems, with an appropriately complex justice. Such conclusions are neither simple nor comforting—except that the existence of honest, difficult, human intelligence consoles us: Poetry's thinking consoles us.

Long Robinson

In 1869, Edwin Arlington Robinson was born in the village of Head Tide in Maine, third son and final child of Edward and Mary Robinson; his brothers Dean and Herman were twelve and four. Because his mother had wanted a daughter, Robinson began life as a disappointment; he went unnamed for half a year. When a summer visitor insisted that the six-month-old baby be named, "Edwin" was chosen by lot; the poet's middle name remembered the provenance of the visitor. As he grew up in Gardiner, where the family moved shortly after his birth, this poet of failure and defeat was known as "Win"; he preferred "Long Robinson" himself—at six foot two, he was tall for his generation—but his friends later settled for "E.A.R.," which was appropriate enough: The near anonymity of initials fitted the shadowy silence of his character; and he had a beautiful ear.

Perhaps because she never welcomed him, Robinson doted on his mother. His father prospered while the Union did—storekeeper, small-time banker, investor—and favored his second son, Herman, businessman and entrepreneur. Robinson loathed Herman (not coincidentally, he adored Herman's wife, Emma) while he admired his elder brother Dean, who became a doctor. Then the family fell apart in a rapid series of disasters: Dean became addicted to morphine; the 1893 panic destroyed Herman's fortunes and Edward's investments in Herman's schemes; Edward took to drink and died; not much later, Mary died of diphtheria. Remnants of the Robinson fortune bought a Gardiner drugstore, at least partly as a source for Dean's morphine. Then Dean died, probably by deliberate overdose, and Herman turned alcoholic, hawking lobsters in Gardiner's streets

From *Principal Products of Portugal* (Boston: Beacon Press, 1995).

while Emma took in sewing. Herman later died in the public ward of a Massachusetts hospital.

E.A.R. never took a college degree; but to graduate from a good high school in the 1890s was to know history and languages. He made close friends at Harvard, where he spent two years as a special student, and where he first published his work, in undergraduate magazines. He studied philosophy, English literature, and languages, without distinguishing himself unduly. Harvard was his entry into a larger world, his release from provincialism; he indulged himself happily in bibulous Cambridge talk. Robinson loved cities; all his life, he doted on theatre, opera, and orchestral music.

By his mid-twenties the character had emerged that endured until death. E.A.R. refused with few exceptions to hold down a job or to work for a living. With a calling for solitude, he was "a confirmed bachelor," as the cliché has it. The phrase was not a euphemism for homosexuality. Like other males of his time, Robinson presumably sought professional relief when he was young—he wrote poems about prostitutes—but his erotic experience was probably limited. A frequently repeated story has him rejecting an offer from Isadora Duncan. Some of his friends in their reminiscences hint at love affairs; certainly he cherished unacceptable love for his brother's wife and widow. It is clear that several times in his life he thought about marriage, especially to the beautiful Emma after Herman's death; but we may doubt that he came close.

E.A.R. was affectionate, as his letters show, but in person he was shy and often dumb. Many anecdotes illustrate his silence, or immense silences terminated by monosyllables. Only late at night, after considerable whiskey, did Robinson become voluble; if he was an alcoholic, like his father and brother, surely his drinking began as self-medication for shyness, melancholy, and silence. When he finally found readers, when summers at the MacDowell Colony added structure and society to his year, he stopped drinking—only to resume later in response to the Volstead Act, which he considered "fundamentally evil and arbitrary."

When he was not married to whiskey he was married to art. If he read Yeats's poem about choosing perfection of the life or of the work, he never doubted the choice. He wrote in a letter,

"Do you know I have a theory that Browning's life-long happiness with his wife is all humbug? The man's life was in his art." Maybe his concentration on the art of poetry compensated for love's loss: both his mother's love and Emma's. Whatever its irrational source, his devotion to making poetry remained fundamental. All his life, he characterized himself as someone who could do only one thing.

In Gardiner after he had graduated from high school, staying at home except for his two years at Harvard, he lived with his family as a sort of servant or hired man, tending the garden and doing odd jobs, working at his poetry as he could. After his mother died he moved to fin-de-siècle New York. For twenty years he survived on a tiny inheritance, on the charity of others, and on free lunches in saloons; he turned down the journalistic opportunities that largely supported rival poets. He labored for a while as timekeeper for workers constructing the subway. Back in Massachusetts, he failed as an office boy at Harvard. Returned to New York he continued the old Bohemian life of furnished rooms and patched clothing. "I starved twenty years," he said late in life, "and in my opinion no one should write poetry unless he is willing to starve for it." Once he laboriously accumulated nickels toward a new pair of trousers, then plunged his saving into a Metropolitan Opera ticket for *Tristan und Isolde*. Continually he worked at his verses, sitting in a rocking chair in a bare room high over a New York street, solitary and industrious, revising his lines over and over again. On several occasions he worked on stories and plays, trying to earn a living with his pen, but failed utterly. He was right, however much he fulfilled his own prophecy: Poetry was the one thing he could do.

Which made it a pity that no one thought he could do it.

E.A.R. published his first book at his own expense in 1896: He mailed out many copies, receiving letters of praise but no significant attention. His second and third books—many essential poems derive from the early volumes—appeared because of subsidies or guarantees from more affluent friends. Magazine editors rejected his best work—at a time when many magazines printed poems, or what passed for poems—because they were realistic. (Robinson admired Zola; remember that he wrote at a time when *Jude* was obscene.) In the 1890s and the 1900s, magazine poems told cheerful lies in words considered pretty. As Robinson bragged of his first book (1896), "there is not a red-bellied robin in the whole collection." It was daring, shocking, and unacceptable to write sonnets about butchers overcome with grief or about hired men who spoke the common language. After a decade of assiduous labor and continual discouragement, Robinson sank into alcoholic depression. "For seven years," he told a friend late in his life, over a tumbler of whiskey, "I had *ab-so-lute-ly* nothing but the bottle." His friend reports that E.A.R. loved to say "*ab-so-lute-ly.*"

Then, early in the century, before the Great War, several things happened almost at once. The first event was most astonishing—the arrival of a letter with a White House frank. Theodore Roosevelt's son Kermit attended Groton, where an English master from Gardiner, Maine, showed him the unknown poet's poems; impressed, Kermit showed the book to his father in the White House—who was dazzled, and who found Robinson in New York and offered to help: Would the poet take a consular position in Mexico or Canada? Robinson settled for a sinecure in Customs in New York—he loved New York—which allowed him to help Herman's widow and daughters when they needed it. T. R. then bullied his own publisher into reissuing a Robinson volume and reviewed Robinson's poems from the presidential desk; of course, opposition newspapers ridiculed the incumbent's taste.

Two further miracles were required. First was the MacDowell Colony in Peterborough, New Hampshire—just beginning—which E.A.R. visited reluctantly and was amazed to enjoy. MacDowell provided a structure for the remainder of his structureless life; every summer from 1911 on E.A.R. rocking-chaired in a MacDowell studio. He visited Massachusetts friends in spring and fall, and spent his winters in New York, but Peterborough was the frame for his year's house. For most colonists, MacDowell is a release from family life into creative solitude; for E.A.R. the Colony *was* family life. He sat in his own chair for dinner, indulging his "idiom of silence," as a friend called it, among a knot of artists year after year.

The third miracle was the gradual emergence of an American literary and artistic culture or community, of which MacDowell itself was a sign. America had already produced great artists, but some had lived much of the time in Europe; some had been learned and provincial in Massachusetts (Emerson, Longfellow, Thoreau, Hawthorne); and some had been the magnificent eccentrics (Whitman, Dickinson, Melville) who were our greatest writers—masters or mistresses of separation, who lived at the brilliant margin of the national life.

Then, in 1912, Harriet Monroe started *Poetry* in Chicago (poetry in *Chicago!*) and Ezra Pound corresponding from London supplied her with T. S. Eliot, H. D. Imagiste—and Robert Frost. Pound, Eliot, and H. D. still required Europe but now *Poetry* (also: *Broom; Secession; The Dial; Others; The Little Review;* also: the Armory Show; Stieglitz) and its ambiance rendered the United States possible for poets who worked in a community, like most artists over history. Wallace Stevens, Marianne Moore, and William Carlos Williams did not need to carry their sensibilities to England or France or Italy. Instead, they argued about linebreaks and Marcel Duchamp at weekend picnics in New Jersey.

When E.A.R. finally turned famous, the monthlies that had rejected him for decades started to court him (the way the *Atlantic,* played like a fiddle by Robert Frost, printed Frost poems that they had earlier rejected). E.A.R.'s personal fortunes began to improve when he was fifty: prizes, honorary degrees, and money (*Tristram* sold almost sixty thousand copies in its first year). The old Bohemian, with indecent speed, became a figure of respectable eminence. It is seldom observed that E.A.R. also published in *Poetry*—with Eliot's "Love Song of J. Alfred Prufrock," with Pound and Stevens and Moore. In one issue—March 1914—Harriet Monroe published Carl Sandburg's most famous poem, "Chicago" ("Hog butcher to the world," etc.), and the poem "Eros Turannos," which is perhaps Robinson's best.

"Eros Turannos" tells about a marriage, in a Maine coastal town, between a fortune hunter and a woman of old family who marries to avoid solitary old age. Robinson catches the man's opportunism and the woman's desperation:

She fears him, and will always ask
    What fated her to choose him;
She meets in his engaging mask
    All reasons to refuse him;
But what she meets and what she fears
Are less than are the downward years,
Drawn slowly to the foamless weirs
    Of age, were she to lose him.

. . . .

A sense of ocean and old trees
    Envelopes and allures him;
Tradition, touching all he sees,
    Beguiles and reassures him;
And all her doubts of what he says
Are dimmed with what she knows of days—
Till even prejudice delays
    And fades, and she secures him.

It does not take long before she understands her error; she se-
cludes herself while townspeople gossip about her eccentricity
or madness:

The falling leaf inaugurates
    The reign of her confusion;
The pounding wave reverberates
    The dirge of her illusion;
And home, where passion lived and died,
Becomes a place where she can hide,
While all the town and harbor side
    Vibrate with her seclusion.

There follows a stanza of padding and needless qualification.
Such wasted motion often annoys us in Robinson; we learn to
scan such passages quickly, bored but anticipatory, to reach his
constructed conclusion:

Meanwhile we do no harm; for they
    That with a god have striven,
Not hearing much of what we say,

Take what the god has given;
Though like waves breaking it may be,
Or like a changed familiar tree,
Or like a stairway to the sea
Where down the blind are driven.

Here, the first four lines reaffirm the title: Her struggle, not with a secular king but with a divine tyrant, achieves nothing but madness and dysphoria.

Robinson tells his story in a stanza form that might seem fitted to light verse. (Yvor Winters noted that Robinson's prosody borrows from W. M. Praed's.) He constructs his stanza out of a quatrain made of tetrameters and trimeters, the B-rhymes disyllabic, followed by a tetrameter tercet and concluded by a trimeter, the last line rhyming with lines two and four. How can such a jingle render feeling?

Here's how: His similes are structural, not decorative, as "like waves breaking" embodies the relentless dolor of a featureless daily life in a house by the ocean; as "like a changed familiar tree" alludes to the "family tree" and combines ancestral pride with debasement; as "like a stairway to the sea" (ocean, again) foreshadows inevitable descent into death, recalls the "foamless weirs / Of age," and suggests possible suicide by drowning—tyrannical Love driving its victim into the sea. These similes conclude the poem with a passage that is tragic, ironic, and gorgeous.

But the poem cannot be ironic in its metrical form—or gorgeous in its compressed and witty style—unless the reader's ear is conditioned by the glorious tradition of meter in English: another reason for the diminishment of this poet's reputation.

The best of Robinson's poems are rhymed and brief, although he wrote creditable book-length poems in blank verse. There are shorter narratives like "Isaac and Archibald," a wonderful poem in a blank verse derived—like Frost's—from Wordsworth; slightly less valuable shorter blank verse narratives are "Ben Jonson Entertains a Man from Stratford" and "Rembrandt to Rembrandt." For glories in a more Tennysonian blank verse, look at the lush conclusions to the book-length poems *Merlin* and *Tristram*.

A few fine lyrics describe the natural world, existing for their own sweet sakes, for the joy or ecstasy of their saying or singing:

> Dark hills at evening in the west,
> Where sunset hovers like a sound
> Of golden horns that sang to rest
> Old bones of warriors under ground,
> Far now from all the bannered ways
> Where flash the legions of the sun,
> You fade—as if the last of days
> Were fading, and all wars were done.

"The Dark Hills" compares landscape to romance, and Robinson is more moved by Roman legionaries or King Arthur than by Mount Monadnock.

But most of his rhymed lyrics are narrative. Usually, by Heraclitean paradox, the man of silence and solitude wrote poems about people, poems of character and story. His narrative sonnets provide a characteristic signature: usually a bizarre or extraordinary story. A prostitute's sonnet ("The Growth of 'Lorraine'") ends: "'I'm going to the devil.'—And she went." We read of a dying blind man ("Ben Trovato") whose mistress has fled, whose wife wears the mistress's fur so that he will die mistaken (and content) over whose hand he holds. Again and again we read of suicide ("The Mill") and failure, of business as greed and ruin, of capitulation to twin devils of drugs and alcohol. Or we read of the butcher's grief:

REUBEN BRIGHT

Because he was a butcher and thereby
Did earn an honest living (and did right),
I would not have you think that Reuben Bright
Was any more a brute than you or I;
For when they told him that his wife must die,
He stared at them, and shook with grief and fright,
And cried like a great baby half the night,
And made the women cry to see him cry.

And after she was dead, and he had paid
The singers and the sexton and the rest,
He packed a lot of things that she had made
Most mournfully away in an old chest
Of hers, and put some chopped-up cedar boughs
In with them, and tore down the slaughter-house.

Robinson's octave ends with wild grief; but the active imagination of the sestet is his genius—the cow-killer converted.

(This sonnet's beauty is not diminished by an anecdote of accident: In its initial printing, a magnificent proof hack changed the last phrase to: "tore down to the slaughter house.")

For other narratives of character read *passim,* not forgetting early work; "Luke Havergal," from the Harvard years, captivated T. R. Few of Robinson's philosophical poems succeed: "The Man Against the Sky" and "Octaves" do not think so well; an exception is "Hillcrest," dour and fierce, relentlessly intelligent. Here are the last three stanzas:

> Who sees unchastened here the soul
> Triumphant has no other sight
> Than has a child who sees the whole
> World radiant with his own delight.
>
> Far journeys and hard wandering
> Await him in whose crude surmise
> Peace, like a mask, hides everything
> That is and has been from his eyes;
>
> And all his wisdom is unfound,
> Or like a web that error weaves
> On airy looms that have a sound
> No louder now than falling leaves.

The best work remains anecdotal and ethical, like "The Poor Relation," "Isaac and Archibald," "Eros Turannos," and—why not?—"Mr. Flood's Party," which is funny and miserable with an appropriate misery. With a subject—loneliness in old age—suggesting sentimentality, Robinson mocks himself and his old man protagonist by an overreaching reference to Roland's horn, and by a triple-switch that goes the necessary step beyond expectation: He set us up with a sentimental simile—

> Then, as a mother lays her sleeping child
> Down tenderly, fearing it may awake,

and then swoops the chair from beneath our descendant backsides—

> He set the jug down slowly at his feet
> With trembling care,

so that, with a gross vaudeville humor, we laugh at the joke— his baby is the jug!—until Robinson takes genius's third step:

> knowing that most things break; . . .

This lesson Robinson knew from his family and from Gardiner, Maine.

If we are old enough, we grew up learning that modern poetry *has* to be difficult; therefore, "Mr. Flood's Party" cannot be modern poetry, or maybe (by idiotic extension) poetry at all. According to this requirement, neither Frost nor Hardy can be poets either—and indeed I remember the 1940s when the poems of Frost and Hardy were inadmissible or at least embarrassing and awkward of admission. By the end of the twentieth century, we had brought Hardy and Frost back without (let me hope) needing to expel Eliot, Stevens, Moore, Williams, and Pound.

We must bring Robinson back. Although he remains among the best American poets, Robinson now goes largely unread. An insidious form of neglect enshrines one minor effort, genuflects, and bypasses the best work. Robinson is remembered chiefly for a brief story in quatrains, punchy as a television ad, in which the protagonist surprises us (once) by putting a bullet through his head.

Robinson was the poet chosen as sacrifice to modernism. The poetic enemy, addressed at the turn of the century by the young

T. S. Eliot and Ezra Pound, was someone like Richard Watson Gilder—not Robinson—but by the 1930s no one knew Gilder's name; and Robinson was momentarily notorious for multiple Pulitzers and for writing a best-selling blank verse Arthurian narrative. When he was young Robinson sounded like no one else—and paid the price; but to the unhistoric ear of a later era, Robinson's poetry, when set beside *The Waste Land,* sounded Victorian. If the combative Eliot needed to dismiss Robinson as "negligible," it is understandable. But surely we need no longer dismiss the author of "Eros Turannos" and "Reuben Bright" because he wrote iambics in a coherent syntax.

The generation of great poets, after the magnificent solitaries Dickinson and Whitman, begins with Robinson and Frost before it moves to Pound, Stevens, Moore, Williams, and Eliot. Robinson was essential to this motion, in his realism or honesty, and in his relentless care for the art of poetic language. Reading his letters or his sparse table-talk, one encounters his dour, unforgiving professionalism. Woe to the poet-friend who counts "fire" as two syllables or who heaps one preposition on top of another.

Robinson was master of verse and poetry, of metric and diction, syntax and tone, rhyme and understanding, ethics, metaphor, and the exposure of greed. The last nouns in this series are not disconnected from the first: Dead metaphors are unethical, and forced rhymes are corrupt. In monkish solitude, with painstaking and moral attention, in long hours of revision, he made great poems. Once at MacDowell, at an evening meal, he was outraged to hear someone boast of having written hundreds of lines that day. Speaking slowly, or stingily, he told how he had spent four hours in the morning placing a hyphen between two words—and four hours in the afternoon taking it out.

❧

Robert Frost Corrupted

In 1974 it was discovered that works by the American sculptor David Smith had been altered after the artist's death. One of the executors of his estate, acting on his own initiative, changed the patina on some of Smith's metal work. A friend of Smith's reported that the sculptor had "painted 'Primo Piano III' with a yellow undercoat something like twenty times. Then he painted it three times with white paint. Then he died." An art critic who was executor of Smith's estate stripped the paint from "Primo Piano III" and varnished it brown.

The Poetry of Robert Frost, edited by Edward Connery Lathem, is the only full collection of Frost's poems in print*—but the text is corrupt; the editor altered the rhythm of Frost's poems by re-punctuating them throughout. Although several of Frost's critics complained of these alterations, no one noted their full extent and nature; most anthologists and many critics now reprint the corrupt text. Lathem removed commas, added commas, removed hyphens, added hyphens, made words compound, added question marks, and altered dashes. Besides regularizing quotation marks—double quotes for single seems a tolerable change—the editor makes by my count 1,364 emendations, of which his notes justify 247 by reference to earlier printings. Thus he makes 1,117 changes for which he offers no textual sources, an average of 3.39 for each poem.

Frost wrote the line:

From *The Weather for Poetry: Essays, Reviews, and Notes on Poetry, 1977–81* (Ann Arbor: The University of Michigan Press, 1982).
* In 1995, the Library of America published Frost's poems as he wrote them, together with essays, plays, and selected letters. The corrupted *Poetry of Robert Frost,* however, remains in print. I reprint this essay chiefly for its attention to punctuation and sound.

The woods are lovely, dark and deep. . . .

We do not find this line in *The Poetry of Robert Frost;* instead we find:

The woods are lovely, dark, and deep. . . .

To say that the woods are (1) lovely, (2) dark, and (3) deep differs considerably from claiming that they are lovely *in that* they are dark and deep. In Frost's line, the general adjective "lovely" is explained by the more particular modifiers "dark" and "deep." In the editor's altered line, the egalitarian threesome is nonparallel—as if we proclaimed that a farmer grew apples, McIntoshes, and Northern Spies.

Before *The Poetry of Robert Frost* our texts were the books that Frost saw into print during his lifetime, individual volumes added serially to a collected volume. While the poet lived, he reprinted most of these poems without change. At his death in 1963 they were available in *Complete Poems of Robert Frost* and the 1962 collection *In the Clearing.* In 1969 Lathem published his edition with Holt, Rinehart and Winston.

It would seem axiomatic that an editor's task is to represent the author's intent insofar as the editor can establish it. When the author is long dead, when manuscript or printed sources are absent, when a variety of evidence lacks single authority, an editor must rely on historical scholarship to inspire guesses of authenticity and to mediate a readable, probable text. The matter of Robert Frost, however, differs from the matter of Shakespeare or Keats. Frost lived long and spoke his poems aloud on thousands of occasions, reading from one of his printed texts. If he had wished to sprinkle his lines with new commas, as one might salt a roast, he could have penciled them into his reading copy. If he had wished to add a question mark, or to delete a hyphen, it would have been simple to do so. In the absence of alterations, his repeatedly printed texts suggest intention—almost as clearly as twenty undercoats of yellow.

Frost's inconsistencies in punctuation and his deviations from standard practice bother a tidy mind. A tidy mind will find relief in Lathem's revision, which insists on consistency to the exclusion of other criteria. But poets are notoriously innovative in punctuation, inventing combinations like "—:" and ";—?". E. E. Cummings would make an extreme example, but we need not go so far. William Butler Yeats arranged colons and dashes and semicolons among his lines, not according to the conventions of prose but as notation for pause and pitch; T. S. Eliot's punctuation and capitalization were eccentric and expressive; among Frost's American contemporaries, Wallace Stevens most nearly abided by conventions of punctuation, but was partial to an unorthodox colon; Marianne Moore was both scrupulous and inventive. Even E. A. Robinson, the one contemporary whom Frost praised, was given to coinages like ",—".

We await a history of punctuation in modern poetry. In the meantime we may suggest that eccentric punctuation has been purposeful. Possibly some punctuation fails its purpose, but deliberate intent remains clear—to serve as notation to sound, the pale cousin of musical notation. In the last essay, I repeated a story about E. A. Robinson at the MacDowell Colony, who told how he spent four hours in the morning placing a hyphen between two words and four hours in the afternoon taking it out. Frost's editor removed one hundred and one of Robert Frost's hyphens, usually compounding two words into one, sometimes dividing them into two separate words. In other places he added eighty-one hyphens to word-pairs Frost left uncoupled. On one hundred and eighty-two occasions he did to Robert Frost's text what Robinson took a day to do and undo.

Poetic practice supports the notion of expressive improvisation in punctuation, rather than consistency of editorial rule. Most magazines, the better newspapers, and some publishers have house rules by which copy-editors try to standardize practice, but these rules tend to change every few years as one party or the other gets the upper hand. For instance there is the habit sometimes called the Harvard comma. Should it be "Holt, Rinehart and Winston," or "Holt, Rinehart, and Winston"? The publishing company uses the first formula. American academic practice frequently follows the second. Frost usually omits the second comma, but not always. For a careful stylist, this comma has become optional, depending on pace and import. If commas be our servants not our masters, we vary them to represent the sounds of speech; by commas we may control pitch and the groupings of words. Or by omitting punctuation an author may leave much to his readers, controlling pace and pitch by word-choice alone. Hemingway was a master of the omitted comma. In his letters and in much of his prose, Frost punctuates like Hemingway. When someone wrote Frost in 1930, criticizing details of a book, his reply included the boast: "One of my prides is that I can write a fifty word telegram without having to use a single 'Stop' for the sense." (He refers to the old requirement of telegraphy; the word "stop" indicated a period or full-stop.) He prided himself on so arranging words, on so mastering spoken syntax, that he needed few marks of punctuation to indicate relationships among words, or to fix pace and pitch. Frost admired self-reliance even in sentences.

Frost cared for the sound of verse. He went so far as to claim that words existed in order to make noises: "Words are only valuable in writing as they serve to indicate particular sentence sounds. . . ." Frost seems not to have cared much for assonance, lush vowels rubbing against each other. He cared most for the cadence of talk, with the nudge and thrust of intelligence in pace and pitch. Continually he refers to a semantics of noise. "Remember," he told us, "that the sentence sound often says more than the words. . . ." "There are tones of voice that mean more than words." Another phrase he liked was "the sound of sense," the way cadence makes sense and sense makes cadence: "[I]f one is to be a poet he must learn to get cadences by skillfully breaking the sounds of sense with all their irregularity of accent across the regular beat of the metre."

Anyone who has read Frost's letters and essays becomes familiar with the theme of "sentence sounds" and "the sound of sense," Frost's contribution to modern poetics. Doubtless both critical idea and poetic practice derive from Wordsworth, an extension of the desire to write with the material of the spoken idiom. And in his best poems Frost exemplifies again and again the miraculous wedding of speech and metrical line. If ever one feels puzzled by a phrase like "breaking the sounds of sense . . . across the regular beat," one can refresh one's understanding by listening to a stanza like this one, from "A Patch of Old Snow":

There's a patch of old snow in a corner
That I should have guessed
Was a blow-away paper the wind
Had brought to rest.

Frost listens to speech and repeats it like a mimic. Breaking the line, a poet expects some indication by the voice (almost always a slight pause; a hold on the last vowel; often pitch-change) to match the line-structure visible on the printed page. Set as prose Frost's lines make a sentence without tension: "There's a patch of old snow in the corner that I should have guessed was a blow-away paper the wind had brought to rest." Breaking the sounds of sense across the regular beat, Frost gives us "the wind / Had brought," making a pause both unnatural and wonderful, raising pitch on "wind" and hesitating between subject and verb.

With this poem, Mr. Lathem was largely merciful; but he puts a comma at the end of the first line, after "corner," where the line-ending pause is all the pause Frost wanted. (For that matter, the added comma is conventionally incorrect.) Put a comma after "corner" and you pile Pelion-pause on Ossa-pause, slowing the poem down, leaving Frost's cadence sluggish.

I cite this alteration not because it destroys the poem but because it is typical of the editor. Unlike the comma in "lovely, dark, and deep," it is not confusing; it does not alter Frost's thought. Lathem merely adds punctuation that Frost chose to omit—and by so doing he slows things down. In the second line of "Stopping by Woods," Lathem changes Frost's "His house is in the village though" into "His house is in the village, though." Besides adding pause Lathem adds pitch variety because we drop our voices when the comma isolates "though." It is no calamity, perhaps, to drop the voice—but we have Frost's word for it that "The living part of a poem is the intonation entangled somehow in the syntax idiom and meaning of a sentence." By intonation we may know character. Maybe the speaker who runs over the pause—"His house is in the village though"— tosses away his notion more lightly than the speaker who pauses and lowers pitch: "His house is in the village, though." This latter fellow seems more calculating.

Doubtless many readers will find these objections quibbles, as if they resemble the discomfort of the princess troubled by a single pea under a dozen mattresses. These readers find a poem's identity in its paraphrase or summary, "what the poet is trying to say," instead of its articulate body, its bulk and its shapely dance, its speech and color and tone and resolution, its wholeness of which meaning is part. But a poem resembles a Henry Moore reclining figure at least as much as it resembles philosophical disquisition. Frost defined poetry as what gets lost in translation; mere meaning is what gets translated. When you change the movement of a poem by adding pause, you alter the reclining figure's dimensions or you use paint-remover on David Smith's metalwork. The 1,364 peas under these mattresses add much pause: Lathem adds 443 commas to Robert Frost's poems, thirteen colons, 156 long dashes (some replacing short dashes), and twenty-two semi-colons. He adds three parentheses; he adds ellipses three times and deletes them twice. On occasion he deletes a punctuation mark; but when he deletes one mark he often adds another which provides greater pause—a semi-colon or a long dash replaces a comma.

Lathem also adds twelve question marks, altering not time but pitch and sense. On many occasions, especially in narrative poems, Frost wrote sentences in the grammatical form of questions, but concluded with periods instead of question marks. If we assume that Frost is aware of this mark of punctuation, we may suspect that he omitted it on purpose. In "Home Burial" the wife gazes out a window from which she can see her son's grave; Frost has the husband say:

> "What is it you see
> From up there always—for I want to know."

The idiom, grammar, pace, and pitch embody the husband's state of mind. He feels his wife estranged and he wants the sensitivity he lacks. As Frost punctuated it, the husband begins the speech as a question which he interrupts with a demand: "—for I want to know." Lathem alters and diminishes Frost's characterization of the husband by supplying the question mark:

> "What is it you see
> From up there always?—for I want to know."

Of course if a reader charges through "Home Burial" as if it were *Newsweek*, Lathem's question mark does little harm; but if the reader hears the poem in the mind's ear, then the question mark raises the pitch of "From up there always," sentence-sound is altered, and the husband's voice becomes gentler and less demanding.

Later in the poem the wife remembers that her husband, after digging their child's grave, remarked casually how little time it took a birch fence to rot. She cannot forgive "talk like that at such a time!"

> What had how long it takes a birch to rot
> To do with what was in the darkened parlor.

Her sentence is not a question inviting an answer but a statement of outrage. Lathem's question mark raises pitch and diffuses anger:

> What had how long it takes a birch to rot
> To do with what was in the darkened parlor?

Correctness makes politeness. For one more example, "The Witch of Coos" cackles at her son, "We'll never let them, will we, son! We'll never!" For Frost the exclamation is the thing. Lathem has the witch inquire: "We'll never let them, will we, son?"

When Lathem adds eighty-one hyphens and deletes a hundred and one, these alterations are as destructive as added commas and question marks, but the changes are more various and more difficult to describe. In E. A. Robinson's phrase, which he revised over eight hours, there could be three forms, not only his alternatives—"hell-hound" and "hell hound"—but the further possibility "hellhound." When Lathem removes a hyphen he usually makes a single compound word out of it; but sometimes he turns it into two words and sometimes he takes two separate words and makes a compound; more rarely he takes a compound word and divides it again, either into a hyphenated pair or into two separate words.

In our language, the compounding of words is variable and practice changes rapidly. As Theodore Bernstein puts it, "The world of the hyphen is anarchic." A *Chicago Manual of Style* advocates compounds; it usually favors omitting hyphens and running any two words together, with the result that we find monstrosities like "antiintellectual." Perhaps this contemporary fashion influences Lathem. I question the editorial practice which imposes new habits on old poems; I would not expect Yeats's editor to change the line into

That dolphintorn, that gongtormented sea.

Take "uphill," "up hill," and "up-hill." Let me assert that there are three possible ways to spell this place or direction. Each is permissible; each differs to the eye; each can be pronounced so that audible difference represents visual difference. Therefore, each spelling affects the sound of the sentence that contains it. In "uphill" the first syllable is louder than the second; in "up hill" the volume of the two syllables is virtually identical; in "up-hill" (less common) the relationship of loud and soft falls between the other two; and its eccentricity calls attention to the linkage.

When Lathem emends "lower chamber" in "Storm Fear" into "lower-chamber" he alters the rhythm of the line because "low-" becomes louder than "chamb-." In "The Trial by Existence," Lathem turns "cliff-top" into "cliff top," slowing the line down by adding the percussion of more equal volume. When Lathem changes "sun-burned" into "sunburned" ("Pan with Us") and "tip-toe" into "tiptoe" ("The Death of the Hired Man") he follows modern usage but he does not represent the sentence-sounds of *A Boy's Will* and *North of Boston*. In the "Hired Man," "barn-door" becomes "barn door" and "harp-like" becomes "harplike"—and on the other hand, "college boy" becomes "college-boy." For Frost's "pocket-money" we have Lathem's "pocket money." Frost's "up hill" becomes Lathem's "uphill" and Frost's "down-hill" becomes Lathem's "downhill." In "A Lone Striker," "many, many eyed" travels a long distance to become "many-many-eyed," and Frost's pace is considerably quickened. In "Birches," Lathem removed five hyphens from Frost's fifty-nine lines. "Ice-storm" and "ice-storms" become "ice storm" and "ice storms," and "snow-crust" becomes "snow crust." One line loses three hyphens; "With all her matter-of-fact about the ice-storm" becomes "With all her matter of fact about the ice storm," with considerable change to the sentence sound; "matter-of-fact" speeded the line up. In "The Last Mowing" Frost wrote the touching lines,

> There's a place called Far-away Meadow
> We never shall mow in again,

which are destroyed in this edition. Surely that hesitation, that mini-mini-pause of the hyphen in "Far-away," makes delicate mimickry of emotion. Lathem's "Faraway Meadow" sounds like a real estate agent's name for a subdivision.

Often Lathem has changed dashes, commas, and hyphens within the same few lines. It is most upsetting, of course, when alterations hurt the best poems. In "To Earthward" there is a new comma which extends the pause at the end of a line—and which, as it happens, destroys the paralleling of syntax and therefore the sense of a stanza. Frost wrote:

> Now no joy but lacks salt
> That is not dashed with pain
> And weariness and fault. . . .

Frost hurtles passionately from line to line, making this poem as overtly emotional as anything in his work. Feeling is diminished by Lathem's comma after "salt"—and the sense vanishes:

> Now no joy but lacks salt,
> That is not dashed with pain
> And weariness and fault. . . .

Frank Bidart wrote in *Partisan Review*: "Suddenly 'is' becomes parallel to 'lacks,' and the lines say that *every* joy is 'dashed with pain.' This is not only wrong, but self-contradictory: if every joy '*lacks* salt' it cannot also be 'dashed with pain.' . . . [I]n the name of 'textual clarity' Lathem has ruined a crucial stanza."

Almost as bad, in this wonderful poem, is an earlier editorial revision. Frost wrote this swooping cadence:

> The flow of—was it musk
> From hidden grapevine springs
> Down hill at dusk?

Here the enjambed swoop of the question—Frost employed a question mark when he wanted to—hurtles over two lines into the two monosyllables beginning the last line—two loud words with a slight pause between them. But you will not find this effect in *The Poetry of Robert Frost,* where the last line begins with the single trochaic word, "Downhill."

For one more example let me cite a small change in a poem which some critics consider Frost's best work. "The Most of It" does not escape revision. "And then in the far distant water splashed" finds itself changed into "And then in the far-distant water splashed." Doubtless this addition of a hyphen is a small matter; its alteration of sound is slight. But if the hyphen does *not* change the sound of the line, why bother to add it? If it *does* change the sound of the line, how dare we alter Frost's sentence-sound?

I argue with a two-headed coin.

Edward Connery Lathem was graduated from Dartmouth College in 1951, took a D. Phil. at Oxford in 1961, and was Librarian of Dartmouth College from 1968 through 1978. A friend of Robert Frost's for many years, he is author or co-author of several publications connected with Frost, beginning with *Robert Frost: Farm-Poultry-Man,* edited with Lawrance Thompson in 1963. With Frost's biographer Thompson he also edited *Robert Frost and the Lawrence, Mass. High School Bulletin,* in 1966. Also in 1966 he and Hyde Coxe edited the useful *Selected Prose of Robert Frost.* Frost's frequent omission of expected commas goes uncorrected in his prose. In the same year Lathem collected *Interviews with Robert Frost* and in 1969 the edition under discussion.

It should be acknowledged that Lathem's notes, at the back of the text, record his emendations. Some changes are justified. Lathem discovers that broken type in an old edition deleted a comma, a deletion scrupulously followed in subsequent editions; he restores this comma, which was surely intended by the author. Lathem replaces English spelling with American; evidently Frost had expressed annoyance at the English spellings surviving in some of his poems. These alterations are the editor's proper business.

In 1971, two years after his edition was greeted with some criticism, Lathem defended himself in an introduction to the Imprint Society's reprint of *The Poetry of Robert Frost*. He began with the statement that Frost requested Lathem's help toward a new collected edition which the poet did not live to make. "Following the appearance of *In the Clearing* in 1962," Lathem tells us, "Mr. Frost spoke with the current editor about such an undertaking and requested his assistance with parts of the overall task." When Frost died early in 1963, "the responsibility [for the undertaking] devolved upon his publishers and estate." (Executor of the Frost estate was Alfred Edwards, who was Frost's publisher at Holt, Rinehart and Winston. It was understood that Lathem would succeed him as executor.) Chosen to be editor, Lathem arrived at the decision that "the general reader would oftentimes be helpfully served by some degree of editorial attention to the poems. . . . Thus, the desired objective could be attained of editorially enhancing textual clarity. . . ."

It would be difficult to object to the motives acknowledged in these passive sentences; but looking back from the perspective of the completed text, "enhancing textual clarity" seems understatement and "some degree of editorial attention" gross euphemism. Lathem nowhere alleges that Frost authorized him to change the punctuation of his poetry. He quotes from the letter I cited earlier, in which Frost spoke of his pride in omitting punctuation. As Lathem puts it: "[Frost] replied disarmingly [to the correspondent who complained about the 1930 *Collected Poems*], 'I indulge a sort of indifference to punctuation. I don't mean I despise it. I value it. But I seem rather willing to let other people look after it for me.'" At first glance these sentences seem almost the permission Lathem requires. But the whole letter is not so much disarming as enraged. Leonidas W. Payne, Jr., Chairman of the English Department at the University of Texas, had sent Frost a list of "errors" in the 1930 volume. After speaking of his indifference, Frost makes his boast about being able to write a telegram without using the word "stop," and continues: "I'll have these commas and hyphens tended to though, if only for your peace of mind." Enjoying his sarcasm he goes on: "You must remember I am not writing schoolgirl English"; defending an inversion he says, "[T]he order should remind you of a very ancient figure of speech. Your friends of the Classical Department will tell you about it." If I had received this letter, I would not have characterized it as "disarming."

Although Frost appears to give way to Payne on punctuation—"Fortunately it turned out you were wrong in all your findings of errors except the punctuational"—it is noteworthy that he lived thirty-three years after writing this letter without "[having those] commas and hyphens tended to."

Acknowledging that Frost hated to be corrected, Lathem tells of three occasions on which Frost accepted correction during his lifetime, two of these suggestions offered by Lathem himself. These corrections add commas to remove ambiguity. Because of George Whicher's puzzlement, Frost altered "To err is human, not to animal" into "To err is human, not to, animal." Lathem's two suggestions are similar—but if Lathem, after years of association with Robert Frost, has only two corrected commas to tell us about, how can we accept his addition of 441 others? If we cannot accept these revisions we may at least understand why Lathem hesitated to propose them to the living poet. As Lathem puts it, " . . . Frost did not actually relish having individuals challenge him regarding the punctuation of his verse. . . ."

The great majority of Lathem's changes do not remove ambiguity. Lathem's unauthorized re-punctuations exist for the purpose of consistency—and they impose a consistency on Frost's poems that Frost gave no evidence of desiring. "Mr. Frost was," says Lathem, "in many ways, a very inconsistent person—as Emerson proclaims great souls are wont to be. (It was, withal, one of the myriad fascinating aspects of his personality.)" Fascinating as Lathem found Frost, surely the two men differed in character as thoroughly as they differed in prose style. One observes that

Mr. Lathem is, in many ways, a very consistent person—one for whom consistency, order, and regularity are primary virtues. Perhaps they are—but I regret that a consistent editor should enforce his passion on an inconsistent poet.

For Lathem is passionate on the subject of the consistency which his friend lacked. Consistency is his pride, as Frost's pride was self-reliance. Although Lathem acknowledges that "Diverse spellings and irregularity of practice in punctuation" are not "apt to render a text unintelligible," he insists that "they can distract, puzzle, and indeed annoy readers, undesirably intruding upon an assimilation of what the author has wished to communicate."

Here I must object. The inconsistency of omitting question marks in "Home Burial" was itself communicative; the inconsistency of grouping "dark and deep" together rather than separating them by a comma was itself communicative. The poet who argued that sentence-sounds carried the thrust of meaning would not agree that altering these sounds facilitated communication: *These sentence-sounds were themselves the communication.*

We need no proof that Frost was inconsistent. When Lathem defends the comma added to "His house is in the village though," he quotes six lines in which Frost used the comma that he omitted here:

It's seldom I get down except for meals, though.

That's always the way with the blueberries, though. . . .

You can see what is troubling Granny, though.

I tell them they can't get through the door, though. . . .

This is not sorrow, though. . . .

Unfortunately all of one kind, though.

In these lines Frost used the comma because he heard the pause. But when he did not hear the pause he omitted the comma— and not only in "Stopping by Woods." In "Death of the Hired Man," when the husband claims that the hired man had a rich brother, the wife responds, "He never told us that"; quick as a wink the husband returns, "We know it though." It is a snappy reply, and Lathem's "We know it, though," with its pause and lowered pitch, falsifies Frost's "sound of sense." Again, in "The Witch of Coos," the witch speaking of the ghost hisses, "It's with us in the room though." Be-Lathem'd, she says, "It's with us in the room, though." "What the author wished to communicate," with its observant notation of speech, is what the editor removes.

Lathem's defense has another component. As evidence supporting his revision of Frost's punctuation, Lathem cites Frost's performance of the poems preserved on records and tapes. He uses this device to support only "lovely, dark, and deep": "[L]iterally scores of voice recordings exist of Frost saying his poems. Over and over again he is heard to give the three adjectives approximately equal stress, with no vocal suggestion that punctuation [might be otherwise]." Well, I also have listened to Frost and I do not agree; perhaps we hear what we want to hear. As a reader of his poems, Frost was as inconsistent as he was in other matters, and often hurried through them as if he wanted to get the reading done with. He kept to the meter, usually kept to the line-break—but he would sometimes rush through the pauses his punctuation indicated; if we were to punctuate according to Frost's performance we would find ourselves omitting many commas in his true text—and omitting periods as well. His performance recalls another Frost comment on punctuation, quoted by Lathem: "I hate to depend on punctuation at all. I hate to end with a word in one sentence that might well belong to the next sentence."

But editors must not punctuate by performance. In "Ash Wednesday" Eliot's text omits expected commas in "my legs my heart my liver." But in performance he paused where we would expect commas in ordinary punctuation; perhaps the unaided ear needs help the eye does not require. Should Eliot's future editor add commas to "Ash Wednesday"? Wallace Stevens has a consistently beautiful ear, equally skilled in meter and free verse; but if his editor relied on his ghastly poetry readings, we could find periods between words in a single phrase, or the lines broken after every word, to represent the rhythm-destroying pauses of his speaking voice.

Of course I raise an old question, never to be answered: What *is* a text? If a text is the product of consistent copy-editing designated as official by the poet's estate, then Lathem's Frost is Frost's text. But I would rather a poet's text represented a poet's *probable intentions,* even if these intentions are inconsistent. An editor's task is picayune, difficult, and humble; it serves the poet and the poetry. I would have an editor repair broken letters, examine manuscripts to discover proof hacks and printer's unauthorized emendations, and study the poet's own texts and correspondence for clues to intended revision. Perhaps I would have him perform mechanical (preferably mandated) changes like making English spelling American. Perhaps I would have him repair the spellings of proper names, and footnote the original misspellings. To discover an author's intentions is often difficult, the evidence contradictory; we are grateful to editors who serve reader and poet in the cause of authenticity.

Editors of other modern poets make contrast with Lathem's practice. There is the *Variorum Edition* of Yeats, which includes all printed versions of Yeats's poems, monumentally useful for readers of this poet who revised so frequently. The editors print the poet's latest known version at the top of each page and footnote earlier variants. This poet's punctuation was eccentric and inconsistent. The editor's note that "in later years W. B. had become very irate several times with a publisher who had taken it upon himself to change the poet's punctuation." Acknowledging Yeats's irregularities, the editors "decided it was not their concern to resolve this matter" but to discern and follow the poet's latest intention.

Perhaps the 1981 edition of Marianne's Moore's *Complete Poems* is even closer to the point. Superficially it resembles her collection of 1967; but that volume was a mess: Miss Moore was alive at the time, ill, and could not pay scrupulous attention to proofing. Clive E. Driver edited the 1981 volume, with Patricia C. Willis as his consultant. Driver's "Note" on the edition reports that

> The text conforms as closely as is now possible to the author's final intention. Late authorized corrections, and earlier corrections authorized but not made, have been

incorporated. Punctuation, hyphens, and line arrangements silently changed by editor, proofreader, or typesetter have been restored.

Ms. Willis adds in a letter:

> We worked from proofs, MS, corrected books, correspondence, searching for MM's intent until we were satisfied that the text met her standards. The cleaning up meant about five hundred changes in the text. . . . [Someone] had failed to query changes, and had failed in several cases to follow instructions from the poet.

In the case of Moore, a variorum edition like Yeats's will be useful because she revised her poems throughout her lifetime, and because many readers prefer early versions of some poems. But the careful editors of the current volume are bound to her latest intentions only.

It seems strange that there has not been more complaint about Lathem's Frost. However, some voices have been raised. Richard Poirier is perhaps Frost's best critic; in *Robert Frost: The Work of Knowing* (Oxford University Press, 1977), he complains of Lathem. He cites examples from "Home Burial" and "Stopping by Woods" which I have used. ("Without the question mark [in 'Home Burial'], there is the implication that the husband has learned, after many trying experiences, not to expect an answer to his questions.") William Pritchard, who teaches at Amherst and was acquainted with Frost, has spoken out on several occasions. ("Aside from what seems to me the needless and presumptuous fiddling involved in such emendations, what happens when the amusing line from 'Fireflies in the Garden' about how though the fireflies aren't stars they 'Achieve at times a very starlike start' now becomes 'starlike'?") Gerald Burns in the *Southwest Review* complained of "Lathem's hyperconservative commas, largely unnecessary in a poet who prided himself on writing lines you *couldn't* misread. . . ." The most outraged commentary on this edition was Frank Bidart's in *Partisan Review*. Bidart is a poet whose control of speech tempo depends on ingenious, expressive, and eccentric punctuation. "Lathem has re-punctuated about half of Frost's poems," Bidart complains, as he calls this edition "a grotesquely corrupt text" and a "betrayal of Frost." Bidart's small prose ode to punctuation deserves quotation:

> Lathem ... doesn't understand the way punctuation works in poetry. Basically, I think, a poet punctuates not simply for "meaning" or some notion of grammatical "correctness," but for rhythm and dramatic accent. Confronted with Lathem's "regularizing" of Frost's punctuation, one realizes how genuinely strange and adventuresome Frost often is. . . . Obviously, "punctuation" doesn't exist in isolation: it is only part of the difficult process of trying to put the poem on the page, of trying to make written lines correspond to the complex rhythms and accents in the poet's head. When it succeeds usually it is invisible; one doesn't notice commas and semi-colons, but hears pauses and accents.

Richard Wilbur writes poems as different from Frank Bidart's as may be, but shows the same attitude toward punctuation. He writes in a letter:

> We all know that poets punctuate—or leave out punctuation—in deliberate personal ways, and not only for meaning but for timing. . . . If memory doesn't deceive me, Frost once said to me, "The less punctuation the better." If he did say that, and I think he did, he was saying that the right words can govern one's tone and placing well enough to make full standard punctuation redundant. Or inauthentic, a finical obscuration.

In Lathem's defensive "Introduction," cited earlier, he quotes a line from John Benbow's *Manuscript and Proof* (Oxford University Press, 1937), evidently in mockery: "Poets, however, are to spell, capitalize, and punctuate (or not) as fancy moves them." There is little doubt of Frost's opinion on the question: He wished to do his own work. As an old friend of the poet says in a letter: "He was stubborn and adamant about leaving the poems as writ." Another writes: "He would be much disturbed if any of the sounds of his poems were altered." It is ironic that this edit-ing-revision should happen to Robert Frost, of all modern poets; for of all the modern *genus irritabile vatum,* he was the most determinedly self-reliant.

This corrupted text of Robert Frost is increasingly taken as the true text. When a critic or anthologist writes Holt for permis-sion now, permission is granted to reprint from Lathem's edi-tion. Not everyone does as he is told. Poirier quoted the old text, as did Pritchard in *The Lives of the Modern Poets,* and Robert Pinsky in *The Situation of Poetry.* The first volume of Thompson's biography, published in 1966, uses Frost's punctu-ation; the second volume (dedicated to Lathem) and the third use Lathem's punctuation. Anthologists by and large do poorly. William Harmon's *Oxford Book of American Light Verse* preserves the corrupt Lathem text. Richard Ellmann's *New Oxford Book of American Verse* prints thirty-three poems, almost thirty pages, and uses Lathem's versions every time. These books seem espe-cially regrettable, because Oxford books have the half-life of Strontium 90; it is as if the historian, not of Dada but of the Renaissance, illustrated the Mona Lisa complete with mous-tache. Ellmann's *Norton Anthology of Modern Poetry* (edited in collaboration with Robert O'Clair) is possibly worse: Here the text follows Lathem most of the time but occasionally follows both, as when "Stopping by Woods" has the "though" comma but not the "dark and deep" comma, and occasionally provides punctuation that neither Frost nor Lathem anticipated. In time, if we do nothing, the sounds which are not Frost's sounds will be the only sounds one can hear—and Frost's own punctua-tion, when it turns up in an eccentric edition, will look like a misprint.

Lathem's edition should be allowed to go out of print. Holt should commission a responsible literary scholar to edit a vari-orum edition of Frost's poems. It would not be nearly such an undertaking as the Yeats volume, for Frost revised little and there are few uncollected poems. A variorum Frost should re-establish Frost's intended punctuation, while a sub-text records variations—including broken letters, English spellings, single or double quotes, and even Lathem's corruptions for all I care. But the poet's sentence-sounds should live on the poet's page. If David Smith's "Primo Piano III" were repainted with twenty coats of yellow, we would never be sure we had it quite the way the sculptor wanted it. It is easier to ascertain the authentic Robert Frost.

Pound's Sounds

In his early poetry, which the *Cantos* extends and replicates, Ezra Pound discovered a thousand ways to make a noise. Although he was not innovative as an iambic poet, on the whole Pound's ear is the most inventive in modern literature. With *Cathay* he invented a lyrical flatness developed by Rexroth, Snyder, Bly, and Wright; powered by an illusion of simplicity, this sound (which is also a diction) erects itself as plain, clear, lucid; and stylelessness is always a style. In addition to the sound and diction of *Cathay*, the young Pound developed the related tone of Imagism, and the free verse epigram style of the *Blast* poems. This flat sarcasm can contain or transmit social notes, literary judgments, cultural observations, moral outrage, and erotic feeling. Then, in his "Propertius" Pound invented a discursive narrative noise which can fly to lyric touchstone-lines and accommodate stories and reflective passages together. Useful to the *Cantos*, this sound accommodates and includes, can turn ironic *or* ecstatic, without altering itself to the point of indecorum. By the time of "Propertius" and "Mauberley," Pound's sounds can move with swift sureness from tones at one end of the scale to the other.

But there is one special Poundian sound-figure, starting in *Personae* earlier than *Cathay* and running through the *Cantos*, which I find most breath-taking. It bunches adjacent loud syllables, as in Canto II:

> Ear, ear for the sea-surge, murmur of old men's voices. . . .

(The words are almost repeated later in Canto VII; Pound substitutes "rattle" for "murmur," and the line breaks in two, dropping down after a semi-colon instead of the comma.) The beat

---

From *Poetry and Ambition: Essays 1982–88* (Ann Arbor: The University of Michigan Press, 1988).

is slow: percussive monosyllables, often hyphenated compounds, caesuras pronounced, loud syllables usually long as well as loud. This frequently percussive figure softens to a falling rhythm, often for its coda, and it runs all through the *Cantos*. Here it is again in Canto II:

> Seal sports in the spray-whited circles of cliff-wash,
> Sleek head, daughter of Lir,
> > > eyes of Picasso
> Under black fur-hood, lithe daughter of Ocean. . . .

His ear repeats the cadence decades later in Canto LXXIV from the *Pisan Cantos:*

> and olive tree blown white in the wind
> washed in the Kiang and Han
> what whiteness will you add to this whiteness,
> > > > what candor?

Here it is in a line from LXII, a patch where such examples are fewer:

> > Ice, broken ice, icy water. . . .

The middle *Cantos* for long stretches use a documentary flatness, rarely attempting this sound-figure, but the noise returns in the *Pisan Cantos* accompanied by the most Shakespearean blank verse since John Keats's. This sound-figure shows again in the wonderful bits and pieces Pound assembled toward his unreachable Paradiso in *Drafts and Fragments:*

> A blown husk that is finished
> > but the light sings eternal
> a pale flare over marshes
> > where the salt hay whispers to tide's change.

My examples assemble a small variation of tunes, Pound's sounds at their most erotic. These quotations refer to nothing in common; they exist in the mouth, then outward to muscle and skin in bodily sensuousness.

The sensuousness belongs to the real sound, not to idea or to the visual image or (sometimes) a sound referred to in content. Anybody knows that the word *food* fills no bellies, but the word *food* is for chewing on all the same: *ef* that sets lip to tooth, *ou* that rounds the lips as if for kissing, *deh* that smacks tongue onto mouth-top. The word carries no calories but in a receptive mouth the juices flow. In this Poundian sound-figure, the syllables are often long in the saying and delicious in the chewing, either through length of vowel or of vowel in combination with extended consonants, long sounds adjacent and percussive: *ear, ear; sea-surge; old men's voice-; Seal sports; spray-white-; cliff-wash; Sleek head, daught-; Lir, / eyes; black fur-hood; lithe daught-; tree blown white; wind / washed; ice, broke-; ice, ic- . . . blown husk; light sings; pale flare; salt hay whisp-; tide's change.* The mouth holds or sucks on those long syllables, and the adjacent bang-bang-bang slows rhythm down and concentrates mouth-sensations.

Other devices enforce more connections. Alliteration links these clusters: See the first, second, and fourth examples above. Assonance or near-assonance makes further linkage. Caesura's slowness enforces the thud of adjacent monosyllables. Like Ben Jonson, Pound experiments with the multiple caesura. If we reset these lines by dropping the line down the page at the caesura (as Pound sometimes does) we have:

> sleek head,
> daughter of Lir,
> eyes of Picasso. . . .

Or:

> where the salt hay
> whispers
> to tide's change.

Or:

> ice,
> broken ice,
> icy water. . . .

Surely this rhythm resembles the triadic foot of late William Carlos Williams.

When Pound in this figure moves away from adjacent stress, he tends (daughter of Lir, eyes of Picasso) toward something like the trisyllabic foot in English meter. I avoid reference to the dactyl, as I avoid saying spondee for adjacent stress. Pound is not making classical meter—or meter at all. Meter is measure; meter is what we count. Prosody is the larger subject and study: rhythm, alternations of volume, euphony, pitch—what we count as well as what exists uncounted. In Greek meter, we count the length of time syllables take to pronounce, and by convention syllables are either short or long, a short syllable half the duration of a long one. Variations in pitch and volume of course occur, and they may be controlled and beautiful—but the poet does not *count* them.

This sound-figure of Ezra Pound's makes the happiest mouth-occasion since "To Autumn" but it does not derive from anything in the iambic tradition. The few words above try to describe some of its characteristics. Another way to talk about this figure is to speculate on its sources. What in Pound's eclectic reading allowed him to invent this tune? Breaking the pentameter, we were told, was the first thing. If Pound's sounds broke the pentameter by a dozen innovations, most of his sound-innovations derive from his study of the alien—from reading Anglo-Saxon, Greek, Chinese, Provençal. The sound-figure I describe, in particular, is Pound's fortuitous combination of two different, one might think unassimilable, sources.

Let me quote some pre-Canto Poundian chestnuts from *Ripostes* (1912). For one thing, there is the alliterative, percussive, falling-rhythm'd, be-caesura'd "Seafarer," translated from the Anglo-Saxon and mimicking its rhythm:

> May I for my own self song's truth reckon,
> Journey's jargon, how I in harsh days
> Hardship endured oft.
> Bitter breast-cares have I abided. . . .

Repetition of sound is rhythmic and consonantal, drumbeats of loudness separated by pronounced caesura, muscle- or dance-rhythms. And on the other hand there is "Apparuit," in which

Pound tried writing Sapphics in English, imitating Greek prosody with its longs and shorts, with its emphasis on the connections of repeated vowels and consonants—mouth-sound rather than the leg's pounding beat. Surely "Apparuit" fails as quantitative meter: In the English tradition loud is more noticeable than long because by tradition *louder* is what we count, and Pound makes long and loud coincide. But in its concentration on long vowels and mouth-connections, "Apparuit" moves toward the later sound-figure: "Golden rose the house," it begins, and goes on to speak of "a marvel, carven. . . ."

Later, Pound wrote that "progress lies rather in an attempt to approximate classical quantitative meters (NOT to copy them). . . ." I think the approximation was not to classical meter but to a Greek or classical notion of euphony. This approximation shows itself in "The Return," also from *Ripostes:*

> Haie! Haie!
> These were the swift to harry;
> These the keen-scented;
> These were the souls of blood.
>
> Slow on the leash,
> pallid the leash-men!

There are eight long *e*'s here, and the last broken line is characteristic of the cadence of the sound-figure I have been noting.

Now Anglo-Saxon metric and Greek metric do not resemble each other, and neither of them resembles traditional English meter. Anglo-Saxon verse measures caesura and the number and placement of loud sounds. It does not count relatively louder sounds, as in the relative-stress verse which is traditional from Chaucer's pentameter to Wilbur's, nor does it count quantity like the Greeks nor approach Greek euphony.

The most mouth-luscious, limb-erotic of Pound's sounds derive from the implausible combination of Sappho's euphony and a Viking drumbeat. To the Greek sweetness of assonance (the first line of the *Iliad* includes six occasions of the *ay* diphthong) Pound adds the bang-bang of North Sea alliteration and warrior drum-pounding. From the quantitative dactyl (in our misread-

ing of long for loud) he takes his falling-rhythm. In his percus-
sive repetition of long vowels he brings the northern thudding
of alliterative accents together with the southern mouth-hold of
two, three, four, and even five *long* syllables together—like the
true quantitative spondees of classical metrics, sometimes two
spondees in a row followed by the initial long syllable of the
quantitative dactyl. North is muscle, south is mouth, and the
combination is "Ear, ear, for the sea-surge; murmur of old men's
voices."

Kenneth Rexroth

In December of this year (1981), Kenneth Rexroth will turn seventy-five. Among his lesser accomplishments, he has appeared as a character in two famous novels: James T. Farrell put him in *Studs Lonigan,* a kid named Kenny who works in a drug store; with more creative denomination, Jack Kerouac called him Rheinhold Cacoethes in *The Dharma Bums,* that 1958 Beat Generation testament, where he is a figure we recognize: anarchist, leader of San Francisco's literary community, and poet.

For decades he has written lines like these, setting human life in a context of stone:

> Our campfire is a single light
> Amongst a hundred peaks and waterfalls
> The manifold voices of falling water
> Talk all night.
> Wrapped in your down bag
> Starlight on your cheeks and eyelids
> Your breath comes and goes
> In a tiny cloud in the frosty night.
> Ten thousand birds sing in the sunrise.
> Ten thousand years revolve without change.
> All this will never be again.

One thing that is without change is that everything changes. Like many of the greatest poets—Wordsworth, Keats, Frost, Eliot—Rexroth returns continually to one inescapable perception. Maybe this elegiac vision of permanent stone and vanish-

---

From *The Weather for Poetry: Essays, Reviews, and Notes on Poetry, 1977–81* (Ann Arbor: The University of Michigan Press, 1982).

ing flesh derives from the great private event of his middle years—the death of his first wife, Andree, in 1940 after thirteen years of marriage. Her name and image return decades after her death.

But Rexroth is not limited to elegy; he is the most erotic of modern American poets, and one of the most political. The great public event of his young life was the execution of Sacco and Vanzetti. Years after the electrocution he wrote "Climbing Milestone Mountain, August 22, 1937":

> In the morning
> We swam in the cold transparent lake, the blue
> Damsel flies on all the reeds like millions
> Of narrow metallic flowers, and I thought
> Of you behind the grill in Dedham, Vanzetti,
> Saying, "Who would ever have thought we would make
>   this history?"
> Crossing the brilliant mile-square meadow
> Illuminated with asters and cyclamen,
> The pollen of the lodgepole pines drifting
> With the shifting wind over it and the blue
> And sulphur butterflies drifting with the wind,
> I saw you in the sour prison light, saying,
> "Goodbye comrade."

In Rexroth's poems the natural world, unchanged and changing, remains background to history and love, to enormity and bliss.

When a young man, Rexroth was a Wobbly and studied Marxism as a member of a John Reed Club. Later he moved into anarchism and pacifism, ideologies which his mature philosophic poems support with passion and argument. His politics of the individual separates him from the mass of Americans— and obviously from Stalinists of the left—and yet joins him to all human beings; it is a politics of love—and Rexroth is the poet of devoted eroticism. "When We With Sappho" begins by translating from a Greek fragment, then continues into a personal present:

".... about the cool water
the wind sounds through sprays
of apple, and from the quivering leaves
slumber pours down ..."

We lie here in the bee filled, ruinous
Orchard of a decayed New England farm.
Summer in our hair, and the smell
Of summer in our twined bodies,
Summer in our mouths, and summer
In the luminous, fragmentary words
Of this dead Greek woman.
Stop reading. Lean back. Give me your mouth.
Your grace is as beautiful as sleep.
You move against me like a wave
That moves in sleep.
Your body spreads across my brain
Like a bird filled summer;
Not like a body, not like a separate thing,
But like a nimbus that hovers
Over every other thing in all the world.
Lean back. You are beautiful,
As beautiful as the folding
Of your hands in sleep.

This passionate tenderness has not diminished as Rexroth has aged. His latest book includes the beautiful "Love Poems of Marichiko," which he calls a translation from the Japanese. However, a recent bibliography lists a translation of Rexroth's Marichiko *into* Japanese: Rexroth *is* Marichiko, and in the middle of his eighth decade, the poet published his most erotic poem.

His work for forty years has moved among his passions for the flesh, for human justice, for the natural world. He integrates these loves in the long poems, and sometimes in briefer ones. "The Signature of All Things" may be the best of all:

My head and shoulders, and my book
In the cool shade, and my body

Stretched bathing in the sun, I lie
Reading beside the waterfall—
Boehme's "Signature of all Things."
Through the deep July days the leaves
Of the laurel, all the colors
Of gold, spin down through the moving
Deep laurel shade all day. They float
On the mirrored sky and forest
For a while, and then, still slowly
Spinning, sink through the crystal deep
Of the pool to its leaf gold floor.
The saint saw the world as streaming
In the electrolysis of love.
I put him by and gaze through shade
Folded into shade of slender
Laurel trunks and leaves filled with sun.
The wren broods in her moss domed nest.
A newt struggles with a white moth
Drowning in the pool. The hawks scream,
Playing together on the ceiling
Of heaven. The long hours go by.
I think of those who have loved me,
Of all the mountains I have climbed,
Of all the seas I have swum in.
The evil of the world sinks.
My own sin and trouble fall away
Like Christian's bundle, and I watch
My forty summers fall like falling
Leaves and falling water held
Eternally in summer air.

Deer are stamping in the glades,
Under the full July moon.
There is a smell of dry grass
In the air, and more faintly,
The scent of a far off skunk.
As I stand at the wood's edge,
Watching the darkness, listening
To the stillness, a small owl

Comes to the branch above me,
On wings more still than my breath.
When I turn my light on him,
His eyes glow like drops of iron,
And he perks his head at me,
Like a curious kitten.
The meadow is bright as snow.
My dog prowls the grass, a dark
Blur in the blur of brightness.
I walk to the oak grove where
The Indian village was once.
There, in blotched and cobwebbed light
And dark, dim in the blue haze,
Are twenty Holstein heifers,
Black and white, all lying down,
Quietly together, under
The huge trees rooted in the graves.

When I dragged the rotten log
From the bottom of the pool,
It seemed heavy as stone.
I let it lie in the sun
For a month; and then chopped it
Into sections, and split them
For kindling, and spread them out
To dry some more. Late that night,
After reading for hours,
While moths rattled at the lamp—
The saints and the philosophers
On the destiny of man—
I went out on my cabin porch,
And looked up through the black forest
At the swaying islands of stars.
Suddenly I saw at my feet,
Spread on the floor of night, ingots
Of quivering phosphorescence,
And all about were scattered chips
Of pale cold light that was alive.

It is the strength of Rexroth's language that it proscribes nothing. Starting from his reading in a Christian mystic (Jakob Boehme, 1575–1624) he writes vividly of the natural world; he refers to *Pilgrim's Progress;* he ranges out into the universe of stars and focuses back upon the world of heifers and minute phosphorescent organisms. It is a poetry of experience and observation, of knowledge—and finally a poetry of wisdom. Nothing is alien to him.

Rexroth's characteristic rhythm moves from the swift and urgent to the slow and meditative, remaining continually powerful; his line hovers around three accents mostly deployed over seven or eight syllables. It is remarkable how little his line has changed over forty years, in a world of changing poetic fashion. This steadfastness or stubbornness recalls his patience over publication: He did not publish a book of poems until 1940, when he was thirty-five years old, although he had been writing since the early 1920s. Later, in *The Art of Worldly Wisdom* (1949), he collected and published work from his cubist youth. Some poems had appeared in Louis Zukofsky's *An Objectivists' Anthology* (1932).

When we try to describe a poet's style, it can be useful to name starting points, but it is not easy with Kenneth Rexroth. He has said that Tu Fu was the greatest influence on him; fair enough, but there is no analogy between the Chinese line, end-stopped, with its count of characters, and Rexroth's run-on accentual and syllabic line. In temperament and idea Rexroth is close to D. H. Lawrence, about whom he wrote his first major essay in 1947; but Lawrence's best poems take off from Whitman's line—and Rexroth's prosody is as far from Whitman's as it can get. Perhaps there is a bit of William Carlos Williams in his enjambed lines; maybe Louis Zukofsky. We could say, throwing up our hands, that he is a synthesis of Tu Fu, Lawrence, and Mallarmé. To an unusual extent, Rexroth has made Rexroth up.

He was born in Indiana in 1905 and spent most of the 1920s in Chicago's Bohemia—poet, painter, and auto-didact. Late in the decade he moved to San Francisco where he has lived much of his life, traveling down the coast to Santa Barbara only in 1968. He was the poet of San Francisco even before Robert Duncan,

Philip Lamantia, Kenneth Patchen, and William Everson (Brother Antoninus). For decades he advocated the poetry of the West, the elder literary figure of the city where poetry came to happen: Jack Spicer, Philip Whalen, Michael McClure, Lawrence Ferlinghetti, Lew Welch, Joanne Kyger . . . His influence on the young is obvious, clearest in Gary Snyder, who is worthy of his master. When young writers from the East arrived in the 1950s—Allen Ginsberg, Jack Kerouac, Gregory Corso—they attended gatherings at Rexroth's house, and it was Rexroth who was catalyst for the 1955 Six Gallery reading that was the public birth of the Beat Generation.

Later, alliances altered . . . Talking about Kenneth Rexroth, it is easy to wander into the history of factionalism, for he has been partisan, and few polemicists have had a sharper tongue. Inventor of the *Vaticide Review* (apparently *Partisan,* but it could have stood in for any quarterlies) he wrote in 1957 of poet-professors, "Ninety-nine per cent of them don't even exist but are androids manufactured from molds, cast from Randall Jarrell by the lost wax process." On the West Coast he has been a constant, grumpy presence. If the West has taken him for granted, the East has chosen to ignore him, perhaps because he has taken potshots at the provincial East forever and ever. The *Harvard Guide to Contemporary American Writing* (1979), which purports to cover the scene since 1945, will do for an example; the poetry critic quotes *none* of Rexroth's poetry but sputters about his "intemperate diatribes." Nor does Rexroth make the *New York Review of Books* shortlist of Approved Contemporaries.

Which is a pity, because he is better than anyone on it.

Taste is always a fool—the consensus of any moment. Contemporary taste is the agreement of diffident people to quote each other's opinions. It reaffirms with complacency reputations which are perceived as immemorial, but which are actually constructed of rumor, laziness, and fear. As a writer ages and issues new volumes, he or she is reviewed as if the writing has remained the same, because it would require brains and effort to alter not only one's past opinion but the current professional assessment.

Perhaps the consensus of our moment, product largely of the East and the academy, is especially ignorant, especially gullible. Or perhaps it is only—in the matter of Kenneth Rexroth—

that the tastemakers are offended by Rexroth's morals. In fact they *ought* to be, because the ethical ideas that Rexroth puts forward with such acerbity are old-fashioned and individual—anathema to the suburban, Volvo-driving, conformist liberalism of the academy. He stands firm against technocracy and its bureaus, of which the university is as devoted an institution as General Electric. Rexroth's morals derive in part from Indiana before the First World War, in part from centuries of oriental thought, and in part from the radical non-Marxist thinking of late nineteenth-century Europe.

James Laughlin of *New Directions* has been his loyal publisher, and keeps his poetry in print, including paperback editions of the *Collected Shorter Poems* (1967) and the *Collected Longer Poems* (1968).* The long poems are five in number, including "The Phoenix and the Tortoise," a thirty-page meditative philosophic poem from the early 1940s, and "The Dragon and the Unicorn," from the second half of the same decade, which describes European travel and argues on a high level of abstraction. Best of the long poems is the latest, "The Heart's Garden, the Garden's Heart" (1967).

There are many volumes of prose: *An Autobiographical Novel* (1966), several collections of essays both literary and political, and a rapid, polemical literary history called *American Poetry in the Twentieth Century* (1971). There are volumes of translations; Rexroth has translated from Latin, Greek, French, German, Spanish, Swedish, but it is his work in Chinese and Japanese which is deservedly best known—beginning with *One Hundred Poems from the Chinese* (1956). His verse translations remain among the best in an age of translation.

However, if we look for his best work, we look to his own poems. To end with, here is a lyric from his *New Poems* of 1974:

YOUR BIRTHDAY IN THE CALIFORNIA MOUNTAINS

A broken moon on the cold water,
And wild geese crying high overhead,
The smoke of the campfire rises

---

* In 2003, Copper Canyon Press published *The Complete Poems of Kenneth Rexroth*.

Toward the geometry of heaven—
Points of light in the infinite blackness.
I watch across the narrow inlet
Your dark figure comes and goes before the fire.
A loon cries out on the night bound lake.
Then all the world is silent with the
Silence of autumn waiting for
The coming of winter. I enter
The ring of firelight, bringing to you
A string of trout for our dinner.
As we eat by the whispering lake,
I say, "Many years from now we will
Remember this night and talk of it."
Many years have gone by since then, and
Many years again. I remember
That night as though it was last night,
But you have been dead for thirty years.

᪐

James Wright: Lament for a Maker

I that in heill wes and gladnes,
Am trublit now with gret seiknes,
And feblit with infermitie;
 Timor mortis conturbat me.

He hes done petuously devour
The noble Chaucer, of makaris flour,
The Monk of Bery, and Gower, all thre;
 Timor mortis conturbat me.

He hes Blind Hary and Sandy Traill
Slaine with his schour of mortall haill,
Quhilk Pauik Johnestoun might nocht fle;
 Timor mortis conturbat me.
    —William Dunbar, *from*
    "Lament for the Makaris"

It is a mystery, how poetry will thrive in an age or a country, then fade out only to appear elsewhere. Between Chaucer (dead in 1400) and Wyatt (born 1503), poetry was sparse in England and copious north of the border in William Dunbar's Scotland. When he lamented the dead and dying poets, William Dunbar listed "The noble Chaucer, of poets the flower, / The Monk of Bery, and Gower, all three; / *Timor mortis conturbat me*" (The fear of death confounds me). Gower died just after Chaucer, and Lydgate in a Bury St. Edmunds monastery half a century later. Mostly, Dunbar mourns the Scots makers, naming twenty-five dead and dying poets in twenty-five stanzas; with most of the poets he names, not a line of their poetry survives. When Dunbar complains that "Gud Maister Walter Kennedy / In point of

---

From *Principal Products of Portugal* (Boston: Beacon Press, 1995).

dede lyes veraly, / Gret reuth it wer that so sould be; / *Timor mortis conturbat me,*" he must speak of a dear friend, for "The Flyting of Dunbar and Kennedie" survives. (A *flyting* is a poets' fight or slanging match.) In another stanza, Dunbar mourns the genius of his age, author of "The Testament of Cresseid" which is the great work between Chaucer and Shakespeare: "In Dumfermelyne he hes done roune / With Maister Robert Henrysoun."

Dunbar's "Lament" is a universal elegy for the dead poets. James Wright, who loved it, recited this poem in my hearing half a dozen times, in what passed with us for a Scots accent. His mouth relished the names: "Blind Harry," "Sandy Traill," "Sir Mungo Lockhart of the Lee." Jim died in 1980 and many friends have lamented this maker. Has any American poet been subject to so many elegies? He was born (Martins Ferry, Ohio) on December 13, 1927, and belonged like Dunbar to a numerous and varied generation of poets—makers of James Wright's moment—and this poetic community of friends and rivals was central to his life and work.

(Also born in 1927 were John Ashbery, Galway Kinnell, and W. S. Merwin. Maybe 1926 was the annus mirabilis—Robert Bly, Robert Creeley, Allen Ginsberg, James Merrill, Frank O'Hara, A. R. Ammons, W. D. Snodgrass, David Wagoner—unless it was 1923: Denise Levertov, James Dickey, Richard Hugo, James Schuyler, Anthony Hecht, Alan Dugan, John Logan, Louis Simpson. There was also 1924: John Haines, Jane Cooper, Edgar Bowers; 1925: Donald Justice, Gerald Stern, Carolyn Kizer, Maxine Kumin, Philip Booth, Kenneth Koch; 1928: Philip Levine, Anne Sexton, L. E. Sissman, Peter Davison, me; 1929: Adrienne Rich, X. J. Kennedy, Ed Dorn, John Hollander, Richard Howard; 1930: Gary Snyder, Gregory Corso. In 1931 came Etheridge Knight, in 1932 Sylvia Plath—but as we stray outside the decade, the numbers diminish.)

We were aware of each other. At Harvard College I argued poetry with Bly, Rich, Creeley, O'Hara, Ashbery, and Koch; at the same time Merwin and Kinnell read Yeats at Princeton; Louis Simpson returned from the war to the Columbia of Allen Ginsberg, where the young would soon include Hollander and Howard. Wright studied under John Crowe Ransom at Kenyon College, overlapping with Robert Mezey and the novelist E. L.

Doctorow. Philip Whalen and Gary Snyder roomed together at Reed College. A little later, Iowa collected Philip Levine, Donald Justice, and W. D. Snodgrass. Never had so many American poets crowded into one decade to be born. Then in 1966 Frank O'Hara died of injuries suffered in an accident; Paul Blackburn died in 1971, Anne Sexton in 1974, L. E. Sissman in 1976, James Wright in 1980, Richard Hugo in 1982, John Logan in 1987 . . . *Timor mortis* . . .

Why were so many poets born in the 1920s? This generation emerged blinking into the American Century—which lasted from 1945 to 1963—as the first literary generation in American history for whom envy of Europe was not a problem. (James Wright's love of Italy and France implied no diffidence about American poetry. His love was like Goethe's, the northerner's discovery of sun and flesh; he burrowed in the sweet meat of the Italian pear.) This generation grew up alienated adolescents in milltowns and suburbs, in California, on the great plains, in factory cities, and in Palm Beach. Like all generations of American artists, this generation was largely middle class—but these childhoods endured the Depression. In Martins Ferry, across the river from West Virginia, James Wright's father, Dudley, worked in the Hazel-Atlas Glass factory all his life, laid off during bad times. Although Jim admired and praised his father—who never surrendered to adversity—the family lived through hardships, enduring the 1930s under threat of poverty in a succession of rented houses. Jim's whole life was compelled by his necessity to leave the blighted valley, to escape his father's fate—and *never* to work at Hazel-Atlas Glass. In his poems, Martins Ferry and its sibling valley towns blacken with Satanic mills along the river and under the green hill.

When he graduated from high school and joined the army at eighteen, he planned to avoid the factories by means of the G.I. Bill and a college education. Once he wrote me about his army paydays in Japan: "I was paid $120 on the first day of each month. And I remember walking, every single time, from the end of the payline to the Fort post office, two blocks away, and writing a money order for exactly $110 . . . sending it home to Ohio for banking. . . . At the time I thought of nothing but the Ohio Valley (i.e., death, real death of soul) on the one side and life (escape to my own life . . .) on the other." For no one more than James Wright was literature so much the choice of life over death: Thomas Hardy and Beethoven on the one hand; on the other hand Martins Ferry and Hazel-Atlas Glass. Life was *art,* poetry as paradise or at least as refuge—for the free and natural expression of feeling, for delight in the wit and sensuousness of words, and for sensitivity or receptivity to the world's pleasures. At the same time, most importantly for James Wright, poetry expressed and enacted compassion over the world's suffering.

He was fifteen when he started to write his poems. Words in the mouth must have pleased him always; when you heard him tell a story, or say a poem, you felt his joy in saying the words, the words in his mouth. There was also for Jim the desire to make in art an alternate and improved universe. If he reviled his Ohio, he understood that Ohio made him; and he understood that Ohio remained his material. We choose exile as a vantage point; from exile we look back on the rejected, rejecting place—to make our poems both out of it *and* against it. Wright's poems, alternatives to Ohio, are populated with people who never left the valley—factory workers and fullbacks, executed murderers, drunks, and down-and-outs. If some of his *maudits* derive from other milieux—from the Pacific Northwest, from Minneapolis, from New York—they live the life Jim intended to abandon by leaving the Ohio Valley. Withdrawing from his desolate internal Ohio, he observed and preserved. He is like Yeats's musician in "Lapis Lazuli," privileged to observe the "tragic scene" and to make, with the skill of his "accomplished fingers," "mournful melodies."

The "mournful" began early on the fifty-two-year journey. In 1943, when he turned sixteen, Jim lost a year of high school to a nervous breakdown. There would be more breakdowns—but he struggled against breakage, as later when the branch inclined to break, and graduated from high school. When he mustered out of the army in 1947, he entered Kenyon College—the most literary enclave in the state of Ohio, with its poet Ransom, its tradition of student-writers, and the *Kenyon Review,* which was the journal of its national literary moment. Older than his classmates, he would graduate at twenty-three in January 1952. Attending Kenyon, Jim must have felt at home for the first time in his life—among teachers like Charles Coffin and Philip Timberlake as well as Ransom; and with literary and even writerly friends among the undergraduates. At the same time, he must have felt the scholarship boy's guilt, living for the first time among people largely middle class. It could not have been easy, and his G.I. Bill ran out after his third year. When he made Phi Beta Kappa as a junior, Kenyon gave him a full scholarship for his senior year.

As an undergraduate poet, Wright wrote poems with fierce patience and dedicated haste. The undergraduate magazine *Hika* published many; then, when Wright was a senior, John Crowe Ransom printed two poems in the *Kenyon Review:* "Lonely" and "Father." The latter poem is especially strong and tender. It is also curious: In its dreaminess, it resembles the poetry that Wright wrote fifteen or twenty years later—and not the narrative and reasonable iambic with which "Father" surrounded itself at the time; so often, in a poet's life, today's anomaly foreshadows tomorrow's invention.

A month after graduation Jim married his high school sweetheart Liberty Kardules, who had become a nurse. Jim taught for a few months at a school in Texas, then spent the next year in Austria, on a Fulbright to study at the University of Vienna. He worked on the poems of Georg Trakl and the stories of Theodore Storm—both of whom he translated, both of whom contributed to his mature work. In the same year, Liberty gave birth to their first child, Franz.

Jim and I became acquainted in the autumn of 1954 and we were friends until he died. Although our friendship was crucial to us, each of us had closer friends within our generation. There were times when we became irritated with each other, and we had bad luck in getting together; mostly we connected by letter. Like any friendship among artists, ours was based on rivalry combined with admiration. I became aware of "James Wright" as early as 1952. When I was a senior at college an undergraduate literary magazine called *Coraddi* (from the Women's College of North Carolina, now the University of North Carolina at Greensboro) solicited work for an issue devoted to undergraduate writing everywhere. They printed a poem I sent them, and a year later mailed me the 1952 issue, which included James

Wright from Kenyon College, with a poem called "Oenone to Paris . . .". It was a sonnet, pretty nifty, referring to

> Some buttons made of artificial gold,
> These ordinary pumps, and rarely sheer
> Stockings to celebrate the turning year.
> I need an aspirin. My eyes are old.

Soon I began to see other Wright poems in good magazines. I looked at published work with an acquisitive eye, because I had become poetry editor of the upstarting *Paris Review,* which wanted to be the magazine of a generation. One day in the autumn of 1954, I solicited poetry from James Wright. Jim's answering letter (with poems) came from Seattle, December 2, 1954. ("Dear Mr. Hall, / Thank you very much for your extremely kind letter.") I knew of the University of Washington because Theodore Roethke taught there. By this time in the history of the American academy, poets had begun to make their livings as teachers—but they did not yet spend their lives teaching only Line-breaks 101. When Roethke taught his famous class in writing, he brought old poetry into it—whereby he filled the cistern as much as he emptied it. Deciding to support himself as a teacher, Jim pursued a conventional Ph.D. in English and wrote a thesis about Charles Dickens. In his academic career, by preference, Jim taught literature rather than creative writing.

The older poet resembled the younger. Roethke came from a background more prosperous than Wright's (Otto Roethke owned a greenhouse) but from the milltown of Saginaw in Michigan; Ann Arbor was Roethke's Kenyon. Both men were provincial, literary, and shy; both relied on comic routines to get them through social situations; both enjoyed sports, and when Jim took his Ph.D., Roethke's graduation present was a ticket to the world heavyweight championship bout of 1957 between Floyd Patterson and Pete Rademacher in Seattle. They attended the bout together. (Jim described that fight for me round-by-round.) And both men drank too much. Roethke was manic-depressive, delusional—suffering from a thought-disorder, not merely a mood-disorder—and several times hospitalized. If James was delusional, I do not know it, but like most poets he suffered from a bipolar mood-disorder. Some alcoholics start from bipolarity; they drink to relieve depression (and become more depressed) or in mania drink to calm down (and induce depression). In the letters that we wrote each other—sometimes multipage single-spaced letters like manic monologues—the bravado about drink was continuous.

More than drink, of course, our letters talked *poetry*. We talked about old poets—we both loved E. A. Robinson and Thomas Hardy; not everyone did—and we talked about our friends and contemporaries. We worked over each other's things. Poets work together more than most people suppose, not institutionally in workshops but privately as friends and rivals; many poets act as if they share a common endeavor. Competition between artists can be fierce but benign, dedicated to the art rather than to the artist, as when older athletes (sometimes) help younger ones who will succeed them. I remember a trivial gesture that may stand in for the serious generosity of many people. About the time my first book came out, Jim planned to submit *The Green Wall* to the Yale Younger Poets competition. I was visiting my parents' house outside New Haven. Jim wanted me to see the manuscript—and so I offered to deliver the book to the Yale University Press when I had read it. I handed his prizewinner to the receptionist.

Over the years, Jim's letters were full of Robert Bly, John Logan, Theodore Roethke, Galway Kinnell, Carolyn Kizer, Anne Sexton, Jean Valentine, Jane Cooper, Bill Merwin, Vassar Miller, Phil Levine, Dick Hugo, and . . . In our letters we talked prosody, enthralled by iambic; most of the old poetry we loved was metrical. We were so saturated with iambic that later we needed to jettison both meter and rhyme—most of our generation did—in favor of other tunes and musics. In *The Green Wall* Jim shows joyous skill in rhyme, line-breaks, and caesurae. His learning comes not from workshops but from love of Pope, Keats, Dunbar, Robinson, Hardy, Herrick, Marvell, and company. He takes pleasure in being champion of the socially unacceptable, as in "A Gesture by a Lady with an Assumed Name"—and, in the same words and without contradiction, he takes pleasure in rhyme and metrical inversion:

Whether or not, how could she love so many,
Then turn away to die as though for none?
I saw the last offer a child a penny
To creep outside and see the cops were gone.

Jim's medial inversion, third line, third foot, in those days would have us clapping our hands: "Get a load of *that!*"

His metrical style perfected itself in *Saint Judas,* for instance in the sonnet that supplies the title, which ends in a classic single line of resolution; only one ictus keeps it from the almost-rare fulfillment of the iambic paradigm: "I held the man for nothing in my arms." Many of us, if we had written the poem, would have wrecked the ending, diction and rhythm both, by a slack metaphor and an extra syllable: "I cradled the man for nothing in my arms." Jim's diction was as pure as his metric was resourceful and exact.

If *Saint Judas* was the best he could attain to, in the old mode, it was also the end of it. In 1958, in July, he wrote me a letter (I'm sure similar letters went to others) in which he announced that he was through writing poems. Another poet had mildly assaulted Jim in a review of the first *New Poets* anthology; Jim's first reaction had been thirty scurrilous epigrams and an insulting letter addressed to the reviewer . . . but now he turned his anger upon himself. In this letter he spoke of "denying the darker and wilder side of myself for the sake of subsisting on mere comfort—both academic and poetic." The first issue of Robert Bly's magazine *The Fifties,* which Jim read at this crucial point, arrived like a reproach. (He did not yet know Bly.) He told me: "So I quit. I have been betraying whatever was true and courageous . . . in myself and in everyone else for so long, that I am still fairly convinced that I have killed it. So I quit." In the letter he called himself "a literary operator (and one of the slickest, cleverest, most 'charming' concoctors of the do-it-yourself *New Yorker* verse among all current failures)."

A day later he wrote again, admitting that "I can't quit and go straight. I'm too deep in debt to the Olympian syndicate. They'd rub me out." (This was Roethke-talk, who during mania often talked what he considered mob-talk.) Later he said, "It was my old, shriveling, iambic self that struck." He continued to write iambic, as he attacked his old iambic self; he was at the same time the fox and the hounds, turned upon himself in the corrosive iambics of "At the Executed Murderer's Grave," neatly berating himself for neatness—and beginning to find his way out. It was a way out, not really from iambic—arrangements of softer and louder syllables are guiltless—but from diction and thought he associated with iambic.

Jim visited Ann Arbor that August, an intense moment of talk and merriment. In these years we met several times—at an MLA convention, where we both looked for work; at a poetry do at Wayne State in Detroit—and I discovered the pleasures of his companionship. He liked to laugh—a good storyteller, a fine mimic. With children he was especially inventive, playing little magic tricks; children could never get enough of him. For grown-ups he had another repertoire, mostly borrowed from comedians he admired. Like Roethke he did an exemplary W. C. Fields. He had yards of Jonathan Winters by heart. One brief bit I especially admired, and asked him to perform a thousand times. He stood assuming a humble, even pathetic posture—head tilted, arms akimbo—and crooned in his handsome voice, "By day, a humble butcher . . ." Then manic energy leapt into his face, he smiled broadly, his fingers clicked at his sides, and he gave a three-second impression of Bojangles, while his lit-up voice announced: "By night, a *fabulous tap-dancer!*" Thinking of him now, long after his death, I remember what Ezra Pound said about his friend the sculptor Gaudier-Brzeska, killed in France in 1915: "He was the best fun in the world."

On his quick August visit, we planned that he would return with his family in the autumn, after the birth of their second child. They would come for the weekend when the University of Minnesota played Michigan in football. I would get tickets. They would drive—or Liberty would; Jim never learned to drive—for a long weekend of football and poetry. But the visit was a disaster. The drive to Ann Arbor seemed interminable, as Liberty parked at the side of the road when she needed to nurse the baby, a new son named Marshall. Then their car broke down; they bought another used car and arrived late, exhausted, with Jim intensely nervous. He talked without stopping. He quoted page after page of prose and poetry, Dunbar's

"Lament" at least twice. At one point, at a cocktail party we took them to, Jim recited German poetry for twenty minutes to an assembly of mathematicians. Jim and I sat at the football game for perhaps four hours, getting there early to watch the warm-ups, but I'm not sure I spoke at all. Jim talked about free verse, iambic, wit, images, Dickens, Dickinson, Pope, James Stephens, football, Robert Bly, James Dickey, Ted Roethke, boxing, Liberty, Franz, Marshall, Jonathan Winters, basketball . . . His voice was like the sea, when you stand at the rail of a ship watching the waves all day.

Maybe that night, maybe the next, Jim's good-natured, affable, unstoppable tirade suddenly turned black. Late at night he decided that *they* wanted him to go back to the mills. He made a speech about how he would never go back to the mills, no matter how much *they* tried to push him there; he had fought *them* all his life. And he stormed upstairs to bed. In the morning, he walked outside in the frost of early morning without eating or speaking. He leaned against an old oak tree and smoked Pall Malls for two hours, while Liberty ate breakfast, fed Franz and Marshall, packed, and loaded the car. Continually I slipped outside to try to talk with him; he mumbled and shook his head. He did not seem angry; he would not talk now, but he would write a letter. It was cold, and the white of his cigarette smoke mingled with the white of his breath. Feeling the cold, I would go back inside to warm up; then I would look out the window, see him there alone, and go back. When Liberty finished her chores they drove away.

A few days later, letters began arriving from Minneapolis. He remembered seeing me "forlorn and troubled in the wet leaves, both of you seeing us vanish." It was in one of these letters that he told me about saving his soldier's pay while he was in Japan. "I knew musicians and possible poets and even ordinary lovable human beings, and I saw them with brutal regularity going into Wheeling Steel, turning into stupid and resigned slobs with beer bellies and glassy eyes." Every now and then, he said, this madness flashed over him.

Although Jim had been drinking over the weekend, the problem did not begin with alcohol. When he returned to Minneapolis, the considerable torment of his life turned worse. He entered a mental hospital where he received electroshock for depression. In the new year, he and Liberty separated for the first time. They went back together, then parted again. Psychotherapy helped; it didn't cure. And—I suppose especially when separated from his family—the drinking turned worse. Once in a letter he told me about attempting suicide (years earlier) by walking into the water near Seattle. His letters, like his poems, gave testimony to the day-to-day struggle of his life, which lasted—with restful respites, especially after his marriage to Annie—until he died, a struggle to live and make art, a struggle that the branch should not break.

Above the River, James Wright's "Complete Poems" of 1990, is testimony that it didn't. However beaten he was—some poems record defeat—James Wright was resilient. Even in the letters of 1959, the struggle to make poetry continued; it was identical to the struggle to live at all. Working away from his iambic, which for a while seemed to him glib or complacent, he asked me for instructions in making syllabics, which had been my own first alternative metric. Other poets excited him. He wrote enthusiastically about John Logan, Robert Bly, and Geoffrey Hill, whom he had come greatly to admire. Then there were terrible setbacks: on September 3, 1960, a woeful letter: "I really am sick this time."

In July of 1961, my family and I spent a week at Robert and Carol Bly's Minnesota farmhouse, visiting with Louis and Dorothy Simpson and their two children. Jim was living alone, teaching summer school; he came out to join us for two weekends. From April on, his letters dwelt upon this possible getting-together, and in June he was writing agendas, numbered paragraphs of questions that we must take up with Robert when we were all together. He conspired with me against Robert because of Robert's perceived dogmatism about meter. (In his formal ambivalence, Jim was always sneaking off to write an iambic poem, showing it to me, and asking me not to tell Robert.) Out at the farm, Robert and Carol, Louis and Dorothy, and my wife and I lived an ebullient holiday, competing in badminton and swimming as well as in poetry and jokes. Jim came out from Minneapolis on the bus, a three- or four-hour ride. He was sad and lonesome, living a little to the side of the rest of us: He was divorced, without his children, and drinking too much.

A few years earlier, Jim and I had added another facet to our relationship. I became a member of the poetry board for the Wesleyan University Press, which took Jim's *Saint Judas* for its beginning poetry series. When we accepted Jim's book, I became his editor, which meant that I gave him my opinions—as we had always done—and also passed him advice from the other editors. After *Saint Judas,* James submitted a collection of poems called *Amenities of Stone* that included old-style James Wright iambic poems as well as early expressionist free verse. The book was perhaps confused but it was powerful: Wesleyan's board was unanimous in accepting it. Then, just after the Minnesota gathering—on July 29, 1961, with *Amenities of Stone* already scheduled for publication—Jim withdrew the book from publication. If it had appeared, it would have shown Wright's transformation in process, almost in slow motion. Because he withdrew *Amenities,* James Wright's metamorphosis shocked his readers when *The Branch Will Not Break* came out in 1963. Many reviewers disparaged it; but the new style gathered its own constituency. "The cool master of iambic," said the critical caricature, "sheds his costume and walks naked." It is still difficult for many readers to love both sides of James Wright—Neruda and Robinson, Hardy and Trakl.

The critical caricature is distorted not only because it makes a stick figure but because of an invalid image: Nakedness is always a new costume. The many sides of James Wright are not nearly so discontinuous as they first appear. If we ignore either the discontinuities or the continuities, we ignore matters large in his poems. For my taste, there are three high moments in Wright's work. First came the height of traditional sound and structure, already handsome in *The Green Wall,* achieving its zenith in the poems of *Saint Judas*—including "At the Executed Murderer's Grave," which derides its own tradition and achievement. The second height was *The Branch Will Not Break,* an apparent opposite, where simple images embody almost unbearable tension between deathward suffering and the desire to endure, to love, and to enjoy the world's pleasures. At best, the opposites come together, as in a famous enjambment: "I would break / into blossom." Sometimes the insistence on blossoming is contradicted (or even mocked) by a clear evidence of breakage. Always the battle (conflict makes energy) takes place before us in these poems—as it takes place within us.

The third height, and best poetry of all, turns up in the last two books, but before he could reach this final eminence his work went through a lesser moment. Fine poems in *Shall We Gather at the River* mingle with slackness, which increases in the new poems of *Collected Poems* and in *Two Citizens*. This essay is no place for dwelling on failures—all poets fail—but let me suggest that in his slack patches, Wright abandons oxymoronic images, often to rely on a storyteller's voice which rambles, and, proclaiming certainty, seems uncertain. Sometimes when he fails he insists not on beauty (which is conflicted) but on prettiness (which isn't) against his own ugly experience.

At his best, from *The Green Wall* through the posthumous *This Journey,* Wright gathers true feeling—often feeling for the oppressed (internal and external)—into lines of great sensuous beauty; at his best, he had the finest ear of his generation. In *To a Blossoming Pear Tree* and *This Journey,* the stance of the storyteller or performer (awkward in *Two Citizens*) energizes the page in prose poems like "The Wheeling Gospel Tabernacle." Better still, in a poem like "The Best Days," or even more "The First Days," everything comes together—vision and vowel, ineluctable suffering and the capacity for joy, even Ohio and Italy. Each of these latter poems begins with the epigraph from Virgil, *optima dies prima fugit,* and by the end of "The First Days," when the poet rescues a bee drowning in the sweet juice of a pear, James Wright has found his Ohio in Virgil's Mantua:

> The best days are the first
> To flee, sang the lovely
> Musician born in this town
> So like my own.
> I let the bee go
> Among the gasworks at the edge of Mantua.

Of course Jim's Italy is not merely the peninsula but also the literary tradition I mentioned earlier: There is the Italy of Catullus, Virgil, Ovid; and there is the Italy of frosty Protestants looking for sun, northerners who come south and like the bee almost die in the ecstasy of southern flesh. The Germans made their sensuous pilgrimage, notably Jim's beloved Goethe with his *Italian Journey,* and there were the great poets of our language: Keats, Shelley, Landor, Browning, Ezra Pound; American novelists discovered an Italy also: Henry James, Edith Wharton, and even William Dean Howells—the *other* literary figure born in Martins Ferry, Ohio.

In haste to arrive at Italy, I have bypassed some miseries. In 1963, the year he published *The Branch Will Not Break,* James Wright was fired by the University of Minnesota. Among the professors voting to deny him tenure was his friend the poet Allen Tate, which was hurtful. Jim missed classes because he got drunk; Jim got into barroom fistfights and spent time in the drunktank. It should be noted that Professor Berryman of the University of Minnesota, not renowned for sobriety, taught not in the Department of English but in the Department of Humanities.

Jim taught two years at Macalester College in St. Paul, then won a Guggenheim. In 1966, he took a good job at Hunter College in New York where he remained until his death. Soon after he moved to New York he met Edith Ann Runk—Annie—and they were married in the Riverside church in April of 1967. Although one cannot say that they lived happily ever after—Jim returned to the hospital with breakdowns—his fortunes in large part reversed themselves. Annie was tender, affectionate, and supportive of his poetry. Jim's work gained recognition, which can be tracked through prizes: In 1971 Brandeis gave him its prize in poetry; that year his *Collected Poems* appeared, for which he received the Pulitzer Prize; then the Academy of American Poets awarded him its generous fellowship. Increasingly, he and Annie spent summers in Italy or France; sometimes Jim took a term away from teaching and they would travel among hotels in Europe—quietly, soberly, enjoying pleasures of laziness, love, and work.

The year before he died was a good one, maybe more crowded with writing than any other time in his life. January through September, 1979, Jim and Annie traveled in Europe; he rose at four to work on his new poems. He wrote letters frequently, full of plans and vigor. Then, there was a sore throat.

Diagnosis was difficult. It was late in the autumn back in New York before his cancer was discovered, a little rough spot behind his tongue. At first it seemed curable: Oncology would shrink the tumor by x-ray and surgery would cut it out; Jim was worried that the operation would curtail his speaking of poems. But the tumor would not shrink and there was no operation. Annie wrote old friends who alerted each other by telephone. Jim's last outing was an appearance at President Carter's poetry party at the White House in January of 1980. Then he entered Mount Sinai. Annie arranged visits from old friends of his generation. Galway Kinnell was teaching in Hawaii then, but found a reading in New York that allowed him to visit. Also came Philip Levine, Mark Strand, Robert Bly, Louis Simpson . . . Because Jim looked bad—teeth out, hair patchy, thin—and because he was an old-fashioned male, he could not bear his women friends to see him. Jane Cooper and Jean Valentine prevailed, but only for a moment.

When I visited him the first time, on Saturday the first of March, it was NCAA basketball tournament time. I had seen a healthy Jim a year before, and we had talked excitedly about the confrontation of Michigan State and Indiana State, Magic Johnson and Larry Bird. Jim and I had always talked sports. Thus I arrived at Mount Sinai—to see my wretched racked friend—booming out noise about an approaching basketball tournament with a heartiness that tried to disguise fear and sorrow. Jim was polite but he was not in the mood to talk about sports. I quieted down; the subjects we spoke of were poetry, friendship, and mortality.

It was a room for four—noisy, shabby, and dirty. Behind him on the wall were tacked dozens of photographs, mostly of his friends' children. Jim couldn't talk—the tracheotomy—but he scrawled questions and answers on a yellow pad. The terrible thing was his coughing, as his throat tried to expel the machinery of its breathing-hole: Foam erupted, tinged with pink. Annie asked him if I could look at his new poems; he was still tinkering. So I first read *This Journey* as I sat beside Jim's bed in Mount Sinai, scarcely able to distinguish one word from another; I let my eyes scan across lines, down pages, and I murmured, "Wonderful, Jim, wonderful."

Three and a half weeks later Annie called me, the afternoon of March 25, to say that Jim had died that morning. The funeral at the Riverside church—in the Little Chapel where they had been married—was crowded with poets lamenting. The friends from California and Hawaii, who had visited Jim alive, did not fly in again for the memorial service, but Robert Bly was there, Louis Simpson, Gibbons Ruark, David Ignatow, Jane Cooper, Mark Strand, Tom Lux, C. K. Williams, Jean Valentine, John Haines, T. Weiss, Harvey Shapiro . . . The organ played "Shall We Gather at the River" but we did not sing it. The eulogy did not avoid the harshness of Jim's life.

As it happened, I had seen him one more time, only three days before he died, three weeks after my first visit. He had been moved to a hospice in the Bronx called Calvary. It was a relief to see him there after the squalor of Mount Sinai. His single room was quiet, clean, tidy. As I walked in the corridors while nurses attended to Jim, I saw a skeletal young girl with no hair, the skin tight on her skull; I saw a young man with a leg amputated, bandages over arms and head—yet tenderness and reverence were palpable in Calvary's air. In the corridor a young black woman sang softly to herself and with her arms clasped together danced a few steps. Jim's nurses and helpers touched him and called him pet names.

Annie was there with her niece Karen East; Jim was fond of Karen. I stayed for a couple of hours, mostly without speaking. At one point Jim started to write me a note, and paused after the third word. On his yellow scratch pad I watched him write, "Don, I'm dying"—and then, after a tiny pause, as short as a line-break—"to eat ice-cream from a tray." Jim stared continually at Annie as if he memorized her to take her with him. Once he stared fiercely at her back while she looked out the window at wet snow falling late in March in the dingy Bronx. He signaled to me that he wanted Annie. I relayed the message and she stood above him while he gazed and his jaw shifted from side to side. He held her hands, then took them to his lips and kissed them.

When Annie left the room briefly he was agitated. Although he was virtually speechless, he rasped one sentence: "Don, this is it." I nodded. When Annie returned he took up the manuscript of *This Journey,* which he had asked Annie to photocopy for mailing to several friends, who would work with her to make the final book. Because I was there, he could hand it to me, and he improvised a small ritual. He wrote on the manila envelope, among other words, "I can do no more." Ceremonially he asked Annie and Karen to sign as witnesses. He added the date and handed his last poems over.

William Carlos Williams
and the Visual

When I began reading poetry, early in the 1940s, William Car-
los Williams was old news. At a bookstore, I picked up a battered
copy of *New Directions 1937:* with Henry Miller, John Wheel-
wright, Gertrude Stein, E. E. Cummings, William Saroyan,
Richard Eberhart, Delmore Schwartz, Kenneth Rexroth—and
WCW's "Paterson: Episode 17," the marvelous "beautiful thing"
poem. But by the end of the decade I was studying at college
under new critics, reading Blackmur and Empson, enthusiastic
over *explication de text.* We practiced on the well-surveyed coun-
tries of John Donne and T. S. Eliot; we talked Eliot all day and
wrote Eliot all night. Whitman was off-bounds, impossible, an
embarrassment, the crazy cousin at the dinner party.

But what did we do with William Carlos Williams?

When I say "we," of course, I exclude Robert Creeley,
Charles Olson, Cid Corman, Louis Zukofsky, and others who
knew what to do with him—who attended not only to his
poems but to his theory. "We" is the rest, who swam with the
new-critical tide and found it exhilarating. Like Thomas Hardy,
WCW wrote poems in which it was difficult for us to find an
intellectual complexity for explication. We knew poems about a
red wheelbarrow, the road to the contagious hospital, and yachts
from anthologies like Untermeyer's and Williams's. A teacher
loaned me a copy of *The Wedge.* I bought *The Pink Church.* I
liked him; everybody claimed to like him—but I don't think we
read him very well.

It was the convention then to praise Williams for his *eye.* Out
of recollections of Imagism, or what Imagism might have been,

From *Poetry and Ambition: Essays 1982–88* (Ann Arbor: The University of
Michigan Press, 1988).

we praised him and pigeonholed him. We condescended to him as we admired him—and we ignored his inventions. Book One of *Paterson* made some of us take notice: Later books of *Paterson* rewarded attention less. When he wrote the late, triadic poems, many readers responded with more enthusiasm. It is still the late poetry by which he is best known, and not by the characteristic early work. For me, his early work remains the most shocking and the most useful.

NANTUCKET

Flowers through the window
lavender and yellow

changed by white curtains—
Smell of cleanliness—

Sunshine of late afternoon—
On the glass tray

a glass pitcher, the tumbler
turned down, by which

a key is lying—And the
immaculate white bed

"Nantucket" is typical of the early work—short, stark, clear, relentless, ecstatic, pure in its speech and delicate in its sound.

Put "Nantucket" up against "A Valediction: Forbidding Mourning" or "Ode to a Nightingale" or "Dover Beach." Or put it against "The Love Song of J. Alfred Prufrock," for that matter, with its honeyed Tennysonian conclusion; put it against "Sunday Morning," which is equally Tennysonian. If we measure a centipede against a Japanese beetle, both are tolerably understood as insects. But how are "Nantucket" and "Epithalamion" both *poems?* Older poems assemble lines and images into an order of thinking, appropriately complex, pendulum-arcs along the path of ambivalence. But "Nantucket" does not perform on this path. If you come to it out of literary history (as opposed to reading with the naked eye, which is always in short supply) it looks like something you might call Imagism, and you start talking about *eye.*

In reality, "Nantucket" has little to do with the movement which T. E. Hulme and F. S. Flint cooked up in London before the Great War; nor does it resemble H. D.'s early lyrics, nor Pound's from the time of *Des Imagistes*. In early WCW, maybe because of his rejection of his English father, his emphasis falls not on visual description but on the gestures of American speech, on the poem's visual shape which enforces rhythm, and on something which we might call a painterly stasis.

"Nantucket" has eye enough. But the visual adjectives are general: "yellow," "white," "white" again; also the nouns: "curtains," "sunshine," "tumbler," "a key." WCW does not write about an oblong-ended, brass, Yale key; the curtains are white but they are neither lace nor linen nor printed nor wrinkled nor ironed. When he writes of "yellow // changed by," the past participle is indirectly visual; the word asks recollection to color the curtain, and the reader to alter the tints of flowers as white curtains alter them. He does the same, in another area of sense, with "Smell of cleanliness," giving us no sense-image or metaphor, speaking in general or abstract language. WCW is master of abstract language. Again, "no ideas but in things" has no things in it, only ideas.

It is by his absences that we know a poet. WCW's absence of striking particularities, and of unusual word-combinations and metaphors, makes a gesture of simplicity and naturalness in diction. This is the shock of WCW. He writes with nouns and adjectives, no verbs except "is lying" and the past participles of "changed" and "turned." Not much action here: The vision is breathless with nouns. Egalitarian diction—no word better than its neighbor!—sets up "immaculate" to crash like a thunderball. Of course this violates egalitarianism. Why use egalitarianism unless you violate it?

Although a tradition of English and American poets—like Crabbe, Wordsworth, and Frost—used the demotic, WCW in the 1920s and 1930s was the most shocking. And he used it in connection with his other absence—of ideas. Now idealessness is not unprecedented, but critics write about ideas rather than about poems, which leaves idealess poems off the agenda. Of course ideas are perfectly fine objects to stuff into the container of the poem: One may also add old shoes, emotions, industrial waste. Poems contain everything like (in the words of the poet) the stomach of the shark. Mother Goose is a wonderful poet not notable for ideas. The critical neglect of Thomas Hardy's great poems derives from the difficulty teachers find in discussing poems that lack difficulty. Even Keats, in "To Autumn," writes a poem almost immaculate of idea. Of course Keats's ode is not without suggestions of value; it makes statement by shape—a quality we find in music, in Greek vases, in architectural design, in painting and sculpture, and for that matter in poems of intellectual content.

What a lovely small poem "Nantucket" is. One must qualify with a word like "small" and one must be sure that the qualification is not condescension. Or let me condescend to "Nantucket" only by acknowledging that it is not so ambitious as "Out of the Cradle Endlessly Rocking" nor *Paterson Book One*. We may love Robert Herrick without calling "Upon Julia's Clothes" as great a poem as "The Garden." And in poems like "Nantucket," "Upon Julia's Clothes," and "Baa, Baa, Black sheep" we begin to isolate poetry; it is more difficult to isolate the *poetry* of "Church Monuments" because ideas and theology distract us.

WCW makes me think of Herrick in other ways. Both give us models of joyous world-love. In "Nantucket" and in many other poems, WCW enacts a joy—unpretentious, accomplished in action not in reflection—like Herrick's double pleasure in Julia's motions and in the language by which he embodies her motions. Now WCW takes delight in his words also; no one is so scrupulous in movement of line-break and rhyme: "Yell*ow*" picks up "wind*ow*" and harks back to "fl*ow*ers"; consonants from "curtains" return in "cleanliness"; the bang-bang percussive "glass tray" is followed with "glass pitch-," "turned down," and "white bed." In "Nantucket" *ear* does ten times what *eye* does. If we try a portion in paragraph form—saying it aloud as if we were reading from the newspaper—we have: "On the glass tray a glass pitcher, the tumbler turned down, by which a key is lying. . . ." *Nothing*. The line on the page does the thing, providing we hear it according to its visual shape, the lines controlling rhythm. In the next to last line, he places a neat pause between "the" and the thunderball "immaculate"—then swiftly bang-bangs his coda: "white bed." Sound is scored by WCW's re-invention of the page.

The re-invention of the page. In *this* sense—a visual method for capturing speech—maybe WCW's eye was as important as we said, forty years ago. Let me try setting Whitman's tiny, imagistic "A Farm Picture" (see page 2) into lines that imitate WCW's spacing. (My version is arbitrary; other breaks might do just as well or better.) I omit capitals, re-spell "thru," omit two copulas, and come up with:

> thru the ample
> open door of
>
> the peaceful country
> barn, a sunlit
>
> pasture field
> with cattle and
>
> horses feeding,
> haze, vista, and the
>
> far horizon
> fading away

If it does not seem to resemble WCW, I mistake my point—which is double: First, the absences of Whitman's poem anticipate WCW (so does its emphatic stasis, which I will mention in a moment); second, the characteristic visual arrangement of WCW's early work—with its many pauses—provides a considerable part of the stylistic signature. Of course this Whitman poem, mistreated, lacks WCW's characteristic intimacies of sound, especially his frequent rhyming.

We need say one more thing about "Nantucket." Like many poems by WCW, it takes pleasure in stasis. Meister Eckhart among other mystics tells us what the soul longs for: repose. It is worth noticing the relationship to still-life, and recollecting WCW's closeness to his painter-friends. It is also worth remarking that for many poets painting is the second art. The perspective of painting-values, as it were mis-applied to the time-art of poetry, suggests or necessitates a useful conflict, as words-in-motion command stillness.

"Nantucket" provides repose. I compared "Nantucket" to "To Autumn" for its absence of ideas; WCW's poem also resembles Keats's in the value it suggests for the experience it embodies. This WCW poem does not begin by saying "so much depends / upon" but such insistence is implicit: An intense, even ecstatic value is placed upon the act of total attention, stasis becomes ecstasis, and soul flies out of body in astonished, acute notation of experience.

Pythagoras, Form, and Free Verse

"Pythagoras planned it," wrote Yeats. As an old man Yeats praised sensuous arithmetic and the aesthetic mathematics of form. "One asks for mournful melodies; / Accomplished fingers begin to play." "Mournful melodies" appeals to the story's shape in tragic art, which is also its content. But never overlook the accomplishment of fingers: Art is ratio of the vibrating string. "Measurement began our might: / Forms a stark Egyptian thought, / Forms that gentler Phidias wrought." Pythagoras was conduit, learning his arithmetic from Egyptians and handing it on to the Celts (we hear) by way of the Druids. The sculptor Phidias made "The Statues" where "His numbers though they moved or seemed to move / In marble or in bronze, lacked character"; yet this "plummet-measured face," this "intellect . . . calculation, number, measurement," these erotic "Calculations that look but casual flesh" by their form "put down / All Asiatic vague immensities. . . ."

The philosopher's mathematical aesthetics called beauty "the union of disparate or contrary elements." Harmony is a system of relations, form or ratio, and contrasts with matter: Beauty is attunement not explanation.

Eight years ago, on a panel at a poetry do, I heard a poet tell the audience that we were undergoing a revival of form in poetry. For evidence, we were told that sestinas were coming back— and *not only sestinas but villanelles!* The prophecy was correct, and in all the little magazines, villanelles and sestinas abound: each one worse than the next. Mostly, they are terrible because they are totally without form.

From *Poetry and Ambition: Essays 1982–88* (Ann Arbor: The University of Michigan Press, 1988).

The poem of our moment lacks form. Lack of sound-form speaks loudest among formal lacks, but sound is not the only way to click the box's lid: There is also visual form, syntactic repetition or resolution, metaphoric coherence, diction departing and returning to a norm—all devices capable of ratio or Pythagorean form. The poem of our moment is inchoate, its only form the narrative structure of the anecdote, less intricate or resolute than a joke.

Remember a notion of Pound's. When Amygism took over Imagism (brought it back to Brookline; fired quality-control and maintenance; hired a good ad agency) Pound declared that form had for the moment abandoned free verse. He spoke of Cézanne returning to cylinders and cubes when Impressionism got out of hand. Pound's recipe was Theophile Gautier or the Bay State Hymnbook; Eliot agreed: Mauberley and Sweeney four-squared themselves out of this reaction.

One reaction to the formlessness of our moment is the Bay State Hymnbook. Many folks are trying to write iambic pentameter: Most cannot scan. For fifty years, the people who live in poetry's neighborhood have been largely unable to scan. Influential poetry textbooks confused meter and rhythm; this confusion reflected losses in the English line and caused further loss. Correct meter is a trick easily learned, like riding a bicycle, but although its meter be perfectly performed, a poem may remain formally slack. Correct meter, alone, does not make form; it makes at least a grid. It *allows* form, but so does free verse or the prose paragraph. In the eighteenth century a man named Samuel Glover wrote an enormous poem call *Leonidas*—I forget how many thousand couplets—which was perfectly decasyllabic and perfectly without inversion: every even-syllable louder than every odd-syllable. *Leonidas* remained a formless poem.

In another way, it is formless to write a hundred-line poem of which seventy-four lines scan as iambic pentameter, fifteen have four feet, and eleven have six feet. This metrical chaos is no worse to read than *Leonidas*—but it is a new formlessness, a development of the last fifty or sixty years, the contribution of the neo-formlessalists. Chaucer, Shakespeare, Milton, Dryden, Wordsworth, Keats, Tennyson, Frost—and Samuel Glover—shared notions of what made a pentameter: Their lines added up to five.

Meter is not formally interesting in itself but only when a master or mistress performs it—and of course we must say the same of free verse. A distinction between free verse and metrical verse may be descriptive, but it does not denote degrees of formality. In this district, the only distinction worth making is between form and formlessness, ratio and chaos.

It may be useful to refer to a division of modern painting and sculpture into constructivism and expressionism. Constructivism concentrates on resolutions, shapes, grid-making, order, and assemblage: It is geometrical and archaic, Pythagorean and alchemical, secret with its golden section: Malevich, Suprematism, Mondrian, de Stijl . . . On the other hand there are the Blue Riders and the Spanish crazy men, with surrealism as a department of expressionism. Like all useful divisions, this one will break down, especially among the best artists (Heraclitus leads us rather than Pythagoras), when we encounter the draftsmanship of surrealism—de Chirico, Magritte—and the strong expression bugling out of something like Mondrian's *Broadway Boogie Woogie*. The great Samuel Beckett is a Pythagorean rationalist: Note his schemes of pebble-shifting and the arithmetic of the absurd in Krapp's tapes. But Beckett is not without expression.

Still, this distinction provides a way of looking.

Recent American poetry has been constructivist in two opposite ways. There was the metrical reaction enduring from Ransom, Tate, and Crane through Richard Wilbur and early Lowell. On the other hand, there was and is the constructivism of the advance guard—in visual poems, in sound-poems, in language poems. Grid upon grid. When a generative idea is aleatory, we should note that ideas of the aleatory at least emphasize *construction*.

Which doesn't mean, of course, that we *get* construction. But the avant-garde is at least far more aware of poetic form than the poets of our moment.

The poem of our moment demonstrates, even by its looks on the page, that nobody gives a damn about the shape of it. Lines get shorter down the page, lines get longer down the page. Only the ultra-conservatives with their stanzas, and the avant-garde with their linguistic ratios, seem to care about visual shape.

We still encounter among some Americans, of less than acute intelligence, the notion that it is politically reactionary to write in meter. Tony Harrison knows that one way to attack sonnet-culture is by means of the sonnet. It is simple-minded to think that you attack old things only by making the new.

If you can hear meter, it is pleasant to observe the Pythagorean grid of ratio in John Milton as his meter remains constant and his rhythm varies from pole to pole: Five lines apart we read "Rocks, caves, lakes, fens, bogs, dens, and shades of death," and "Abom'nable, inutt'rable, and worse." Eight loudish noises in one line, three loudish noises in the other (merely to *begin* noting rhythmic differences)—and the two lines are metrically identical regular iambic pentameter. Ratio like beauty is always *multum in parvo,* the combination or conflation or even identity of the disparate or even the opposite, in sound as in metaphor.

We find the same ratio when the verse is free—if William Carlos Williams or Ezra Pound does it, or Robert Creeley. No one among living Americans is more attentive to form, or more skillful with sound, than Robert Creeley. Here is one of his brief "Versions (*after Hardy*)":

> The weather's still grey
> and the clouds gather
> where they once walked
> out together,
>
> greeted the world with
> a faint happiness
> watched it die
> in the same place.

Creeley of course is a master of free verse, and surely most readers will find these lines both free and formal. Like many masters of free verse, like William Carlos Williams, Creeley writes many poems that scan as foot-verse—though they don't look as if they do. (The wittiest meter—as in Milton and Frost—looks as if it couldn't scan and does: unity and diversity.) As it happens, this poem—with inversions, extra syllables, and much manipulation of relative stress—is a dimeter: *c/cc/* | *cc//c* | *c/c/* || /cc/c | *c//cc* |

/c/ | /cc/. This meter is fairly wild, certainly witty, even extravagant . . . but it scans. People who believe in spondees, which are the Easter Bunnies of traditional prosody, will scan the last line: cc//.

But the metrical identity of this poem is only a portion of its form.

If you don't hear the meter, you should still hear the box lid clicking shut. Other arithmetic: Each stanza deploys fourteen words; in syllable count the eight lines are 5, 5, 4, 4 || 5, 5, 3, 4; in word count: 4, 4, 4, 2 || 4, 3, 3, 4. Listening to these eight lines, we can discover two loud noises in each line, and therefore call the line accentual . . . but, as always in accentual verse, there are questionable decisions: It is easy to say the first line with three accents, or the third line with one, or two, or three. Nonetheless, the approximation of a two-stress line contributes to the rhythmical and formal identity of this poem: like the meter, like the approximations of other arithmetic, word-count and syllable-count. These approximations of exactness are the tease available to improvisation.

Rhyme is obvious with *gather/-gether* and *-ness/place*. It is obvious enough to make us attentive, and our aroused mouths digest internal rhymes and repetition; we hear rhyme's assonance in *grey/they* (where spelling flashes a signal); we pick up the short *is* of the second stanza, and rise to the diphthongs of *die* and *same/place*—the strong coda of Creeley's assonance, which of course takes much of its power from three earlier instances: *grey, they, faint.*

There are also consonants—Creeley is a master of consonance: *weather, where, walked, world, with, watched:* Of twenty-eight words, six begin with *w.* With almost twenty percent of his words beginning with one letter; with almost the same number including one diphthong (and no words combining consonant and diphthong)—more than a third of Creeley's words contain one or the other of his interwoven mouthy obsessions.

Whether we call this free verse, or a loose dimeter, we must conclude: *It is formal.* It is made by a poet with a tongue in his mouth who knows or feels the values of sameness against the improvisations of variety—a poet in love with the ratios of Pythagoras.

⚘

Notes on the Image

body and soul

1. As W. J. T. Mitchell puts it, "To speak of 'imagery' . . . in temporal arts like . . . literature . . . is to commit a breach in decorum, or, to put it more positively, to make a metaphor." The poem's only genuine image is the squiggles of ink on paper which make letters and punctuation marks.

2. Here is a definition from a popular textbook: "Images are groups of words that give an impression to the senses. Most images are visual, but we can also make images of taste, touch, hearing, and smell. . . ." A sensible definition, no doubt—but it has little do to with what we mean when we use the word "image" in connection with a poem. When we speak of images in poetry, we speak of four or five different things, some of which have nothing to do with making "an impression to the senses."

3. Literary terms, by appointment in Samarra, eventually contain not only what they started with but the opposite of what they started with. "Spirit and image" meant "soul and body." But "image" has come also to mean precisely not-body, not-X, because the image is an imitation or a copy of X. From a copy or representation of a thing, the word can then move to mean the essence of a thing; therefore "image" comes to mean "spirit," which began by being its opposite.

As with literary terms so with literary movements. The manifestoes of the Imagist movement praised the particular over the abstract, the local over the infinite; and we were enjoined not to speak of "dim lands of peace." When Pound reported in a

From *The Weather for Poetry: Essays, Reviews, and Notes on Poetry, 1977–81* (Ann Arbor: The University of Michigan Press, 1982).

metaphor taken from electricity that the image is language "charged with meaning," we no longer heard about description and detail; we heard about quality and value, about intensity and intelligence. Here was Imagism's appointment in Samarra: The movement which started as an assault on the symbol ended by requiring that symbolism house itself in the particular without an explanatory genitival conjunction linking it to an abstraction.

Two lines of Pound's are sometimes cited as the image's apogee: "The apparition of these faces in the crowd; / Petals on a wet, black bough." Like most of us, I enjoy this morsel; but it is not only "an impression to the senses." The word "apparition" introduces magic—how infinite, how crepuscular, how fin-de-siècle—which by its connotation governs what follows. Pound the magician poet, as gifted as Ovid's deities, metamorphoses faces into petals; because the word "apparition" is poetic, the word "petals" takes on the association of beautiful flowers; and the word "bough" completes a natural scene. Thus the faces are by association pretty as they stand out against the dull crowd: bright petals torn by storm, blown by wind, stuck by rain to dark limbs. It is all accomplished by assertion.

4. We make poetry of our conflicts, our warring opposites, although we do not always pretend to; and we may not even know we do. When William Carlos Williams writes "no ideas but in things," his statement disexemplifies itself. It is an idea made of no things at all. And his famous image poem depends upon something besides an image; "so much depends / upon," claims WCW, with an imageless urgency.

5. Or take Ted Hughes, from a poem in *Moortown:* "The wind is oceanic in the elms. . . ." Is this an image? The wind which is invisible to the eyes becomes tangible and visible with the cooperation of the elms; the elms by responding make the wind visible—more, they make it audible: This image of course is a metaphor (airy wind compared to watery ocean) and the comparison takes place to the senses not visually but audibly. For the image to raise itself to sense-perception, the metaphor had to operate first.

"The wind is oceanic in the elms. . . ." Beyond the audible comparison there is comparison of size. The wind is as vast as the ocean, which is not a piece of sense data but an idea, a conceptual metaphor. But if it is imaginable we imagine it in terms of extent; I believe that "extent" is an abstraction of a visual experience.

6. "[D]im lands of peace" *does* seem like rotten language; we prefer this syntactical arrangement when it attaches particulars: "the camera of my eye," which is not visual or sensuous but conceptual, for an eye regarded as a camera looks no different from an eye regarded as an eye. The metaphor suggests not a datum of sense but an idea of function or utility . . .

But if we despise "lands of peace," do we also despise "sea of trouble"? The man suggested that the might "take arms against a sea," which is surely an image, fantastic as Cuchulain—which becomes less image and more metaphor when we add the genitive.

7. Lautréamont's is probably the most famous surreal image: the chance encounter on a dissecting table of a sewing machine and an umbrella. Of course one can see it if one tries, but it is not especially interesting to try. When we see, we don't imagine, we illustrate.

Surrealism is typically visual, perhaps excessively visual. If its pictures are literary, its narratives are pictorial. Many surrealist poems could be descriptions of paintings. And the name of each of them is The Strange Encounter. It is always the umbrella and the sewing machine, even when the umbrella wears shark's teeth and the sewing machine has goat's ankles.

8. There is also the metaphor that is perfunctory as metaphor, and vivid as image: "That time of year thou mayst in me behold. . . ." Obvious not because of overuse but because of natural symbolism, night as death and autumn as age . . . but: "When yellow leaves or none or few do hang" becomes more interesting not because of the image of turned foliage but because of the rhythm of its syntax, hurtling and hesitant by turns. Then: "Bare ruin'd choirs, where late the sweet birds sang. . . ." The audacity is imagistic and metaphoric together; a comparison compared over again, a likeness distanced by further likeness.

9. There are comparisons without images—"as futile as an old regret"—and of course there are images without metaphors: cold hands, sour cabbage, huge spider . . .

On occasion we may use image as an honorific gesture like "nice," from which we would wish to withhold the cold shower of definition. Is it possible that when we enhance "image"—calling it charged, calling it deep; when we refuse to call it "an image" unless it is unreal—that we are saying something like "I only respect an image when it becomes a symbol"?

Anyone who considers the ambiguity of "image" a modern degeneration should consult the OED. If I suggested using "image" to mean a sense datum, often but not always part of metaphor or component of symbol, I would accomplish nothing, because metaphor and symbol, words which we use as if they describe things that happen in language, are as imperfectly defined as image is.

Theory × Theory

In a day of literary theory, I want to take note of a characteristic relationship between theory and practice. Of course most literary theory, most of the time, is a bore—but so is most poetry. Surely we must acknowledge that good poets have often, even *usually,* entertained literary theory: They have talked about what they were doing; they have proclaimed why they do what they do; they have complained about what others do: manifestos, denunciations. Keeping to the English language, we can think of Jonson, Dryden, Wordsworth, Coleridge, Keats, Poe, Hopkins, Yeats, Pound, Eliot, Stevens, Frost . . . Some have argued only in letters, some in a few influential essays, some with a great body of critical work: all poets, all theorists.

But I am not sure that they have really "proclaimed why they do what they do," although they may have thought that they did. Maybe it is more accurate to consider that they made up theories in order to allow themselves to do what they had to do. Often, their stated theory has contradicted their poetic practice.

None of these poet-critics professes the theory-of-no-theory, which is the most rigid and confining of theories, as well as the most prevalent. In every generation the theory-of-no-theory shouts loudest in the third-rate—for whom, always, "the way to make poems is known."

Sometimes a good artist makes anti-theory noises. Barnett Newman said that aesthetics is to artists what ornithology is to birds. I suspect that these are the accents of an intellectual who needed to stop thinking in order to paint pictures. The sentiment condescends to the artist, brainless as a sparrow (with typical contradiction, it can also boast: instinctive and natural as a

From *Poetry and Ambition: Essays 1982–88* (Ann Arbor: The University of Michigan Press, 1988).

sparrow) and reminds us of a history of condescensions, like Plato's condescension to Ion.

When you admire something, you feel inferior to what you admire, thus envious or jealous; thence arises the need to assert counter-superiority; therefore condescension intimates inferiority. I assert: *All* assertions typically promote (a) themselves and (b) their opposites. The more vigorous (a), the more vigorous (b). So Barnett Newman recommended that artists speculate about aesthetics, as well he might.

I speak of "opposites." Paul de Man was more scrupulous. Reading some modern critics whom he admired, he noticed that after they made categorical assertions they always added "more tentative utterances that seem to come close, at times, to being contradictory to these assertions. . . ." But "a fundamental difference in the level of explicitness" prevents assertion and qualification "from meeting on a common level of discourse." Contradiction, yes; opposite, no. Rather, it is "as if the very possibility of assertion had been put into question."

And let discussion cease? It would seem so, on the principle that one should remain silent rather than to speak of what one does not know. On the other hand, we might note that the critic who questions "the very possibility of assertion" was known to be assertive. May one arrive at a true destination by means of a false journey? I suspect that in theory destinations are imaginary and in practice journeys are essential.

Also, I suspect that the doctrine of opposites, despite the scrupulosity of de Man's denial, has some utility: The stronger the taboo the stronger the desire. (Incest and cannibalism must be paradisal.) Heraclitus, who said that "up and down are the same," gives me my text: "Of the opposites, that which tends to birth or creation is called war and strife, and that which tends to destruction by fire is called concord and peace."

Literary theory is useful to the practitioner insofar as it contradicts what the practitioner does.

With Edgar Allan Poe the confrontation is classic. After "The Raven" achieved its notoriety, he wrote an essay to tell us how he composed it. "The Philosophy of Composition" is a theory of poetry and a fantasy of control: "[N]o one point in its composition is referable either to accident or intuition. . . . [T]he work proceeded step by step, to its completion, with the precision and rigid consequence of a mathematical problem." Telling us that he has decided to construct a poem, he must define "a poem": It shall not be long; it shall be composed of stanzas, with a rhyme scheme and metrics of considerable intricacy; it shall contain pleasing sounds or phonemic sequences. Last comes the annoying question of subject matter. The most interesting subjects, as apparently everyone knows, are death and young women. Ah!—it comes to Poe in a flash, Archimedes in the bathtub, *Eureka!*—"the death, then, of a beautiful woman is, unquestionably, the most poetical topic in the world. . . ."

Now it is moderately clear that Poe needed to write about dead women. Far from being the last item that enters the composition of Poe's poems, it is the first. Is the man a liar? Like most liars, most of the time, Poe tells the simple truth: He lies not to deceive others but to accommodate (and forgive) himself. "The Philosophy of Composition" is a lie that is accurate in its description of his method, for Poe could only dote on dead brides if he convinced himself that it was the last thing that came to mind. His formalism makes a model of constructivism in verse: intricate repeated stanzas of triple-footed meters and internal and feminine rhyme with the rhyme-sounds ingeniously elaborated by an obsession of tricks, a formal maze, a mathematical or Pythagorean resolved complexity of poetic devices. (Nothing in this sentence claims that the poem is any good.) His formalism serves a purpose not formal at all: the expression of necrophiliac passion antithetic to the moral manners of his society.

Of course it serves not one purpose only. If his formalism deflects his own attention from the theme, it also deflects the attention of his audience. For writer read reader, for reader read writer throughout. The reader whose dark attentions gather the forbidden *frisson* of this perversion is distracted by the formal elaborations of the poem and like Poe can claim to himself that, after all, subject matter is mere convenience.

As a rule of thumb: When a writer is most formal, manner of construction at the forefront of attention, then the writer uses form to evade confrontation of content. In such a confrontation, content triumphs all the more for its disguise. The luckiest writer uses evasive formality, unconsciously of course, with total lack of success: *The writer of genius is the writer who fails the most at what he or she tries hardest to accomplish.* Trekking through Arctic wastes north toward the pole, starving half to death in the endeavor, the fruit of the poet's passion is to arrive at Antarctica.

Thus: Fear of madness dominates the neoclassic poet. Yvor Winters wrote "In Defense of Reason" because his reason required defending. Thus: Imagism praised visual description in disgust over the infinitudes of symbolism, in order to revive a dead tradition and write symbolist poems. Thus: William Carlos Williams, defending plain talk and the American idiom, wrote verses dense with assonance like the Keats he grew up on. Thus: Jackson Mac Low pursues aleatory methods of construction, affirms a Buddhist disavowal of individuality, makes poems out of random computer-generated word-lists, and writes poem after poem which sound like no one in the world but Jackson Mac Low. Yvor Winters also professed the impersonal voice, and a Winters poem shows its markings at twenty miles. Eliot was another who famously spoke of impersonality—in order to allow a strong personality to speak the confessional *Waste Land* out of nervous breakdown.

For the most part I suppose that these motions of the mind's contradictions *must* be unconscious. But, really . . . it is difficult enough to understand one's own motives and intentions without speculating about somebody else's. Finally it is frivolous to worry about consciousness. As everyone knows, it is progressive California which gives the United States its most reactionary presidents. As everyone knows, it takes Richard Nixon to open American relations with the People's Republic of China.

The great middle or muddle of American poetry proclaims the theory-of-no-theory. The middle-muddle always does: The dominant mode of any moment lacks theory because "the way to make poetry is known; who needs to talk about it?" At the moment the McPoem validates itself on voice and on emotion. These are the poets whom John Hollander calls "journalists of compassion." At their common worst, they are specialists in slack free verse, writing poems that are autobiographical, narcissistic, brief, short-lined and end-stopped, with no attention to sound or syntax, with all attention to image, detail, and SELF. This poetry is above all personal; this poetry is self-made and in love with its maker.

And this poetry of individual voice performs the opposite of what it fondly claims: It suffers from impersonality and interchangeableness: Workshop Poem, McPoem, Clone-Poem, or Standard American Poem, a.k.a. SAP. The SAP settles (James Merrill's words) for "the holy poverty of some second-hand diction, pure dull 'message.' . . . " I have heard a McPoet, responding to someone's praise of poetic *art*—vowels or shapely stanzas—pour contempt on "poesy" with a sneer that bragged of his hatred for art, as if art prevented idea and feeling. I want to counter-assert: *No ideas without art. No art without ideas.*

And when I do, most avant-gardists (post-surreal) must object to the last clause. In the last century we heard that all art aspired to the condition of music, painting from a tradition as referential as poetry's. In the last fifty years the advance guard has aspired to the condition of analytic cubism (and Mondrian, and Malevich). Only two conditions are general enough to mention: We shall emphasize construction; we shall remain nonreferential.

Emphasis on construction, it must be noted, sometimes attends to the actual *structure* of the work, but more often to the *method of construction,* or, as often in conceptual art, its formula or description for reduplication. The reaction against content or exposition—clear in much abstraction, clear also in elements of Dada—in conceptual art and in much of the literary advance guard rejects especially the subjective and the emotional. One hears scorn for a "solemn feeling-tone and quasi-religious belief-system" (to quote Thomas McEvilley praising conceptual art) and praise for conceptual art's "expressive stance more like that of science and technology."

Now this "expressive stance" pays homage to the dominant culture, as the arts have typically done: the feudal system, the Catholic religion, the imperial state. For the last hundred and fifty years, much art has referred to science and technology in pursuit of an "expressive stance." When Eliot spoke of tradition by inviting us to recollect what happened when "finely filiated platinum is introduced into a chamber containing oxygen and sulphur dioxide," he employed the expressive stance (did he know what he was talking about?) of science and technology. Earlier, he had used medical technology for the same stance with "etherized." When Ezra Pound used the metaphor of language charged with meaning, his metaphor was electric. Earlier there was Walt Whitman and the locomotive, Henry Adams and the dynamo. For that matter, there was Edgar Poe who claimed "the precision and rigid consequence of a mathematical problem."

McEvilley continues: "The presentation of raw or unordered materials is not, as Kosloff has argued, a meaningless activity; it is the useful promulgation of a view of meaning as imposed arbitrarily on materials from without, for reasons not inherent in the materials themselves but in our plans and ambitions for them." But this is to praise a plan by which our expressive stance denigrates plans. Like all theory it contradicts itself. When critics defend meaninglessness by reference to notions of the marketability of reference, they find political meaning in the gesture of meaninglessness—and the Phoenix of meaning rises from the ashes of burnt meaning. It seems (by a series of quick reversals) that the Marxism of contemporary literary and artistic theory is meaning derived from meaninglessness for formal reasons by formal necessity. Such is *The Meaninglessness of Meaninglessness.*

When words cast doubt on words, doubt-casting is the meaning of the words. Skepticism about its own medium of language has been a project of much poetry forever: "We're ill by these *Grammarians* us'd; / We are abus'd by *Words,* grossly abus'd." Without such salt, the meat will spoil. But is there meat under this salt? I think so: although it is annoying that words carry a baggage of meaning with them—and nonsense is an arrangement of sense; although discourse or argument may be impossible; although mimesis is clearly illogical or implausible . . . Is Dante a Catholic? Does the brown bear sleep in the woods?

Perhaps on the other hand we should agree with the implications of Robert Graves's examiners at Oxford: "Mr. Graves, you appear to think that one poem is better than another."

Although most poets need theory to write out of, or more properly against, some folks will always use theory as a cover for writing badly. The worst writers thrive on movements because they get to join a club, which is both a security blanket and a way to gather attention. Dick Higgins says that if Edison had considered himself a member of the Electric Lightbulb Movement, he would never have invented the phonograph. I think of the scene in Europe late in the 1930s when constructivism and surrealism fought it out in the street—formalism against expressionism as usual. There were two competing shows in London, the same year, and only one artist showed in both exhibitions. This was Henry Moore (denigrated just now for something like a "solemn feeling-tone and quasi-religious belief-system") whose stringed figures, developed out of geometrical models at the Science Museum, were as constructivist as Gabo or Pevsner.

Of poets in my generation, only Robert Creeley could show in both shows.

Poetry and Ambition

1. I see no reason to spend your life writing poems unless your goal is to write great poems.

An ambitious project—but sensible, I think. And it seems to me that contemporary American poetry is afflicted by modesty of ambition—modesty, alas, well earned—if sometimes accompanied by vast pretense. Of course the great majority of contemporary poems, in any era, will always be bad or mediocre. (Our time may well be characterized by more mediocrity and less badness.) But if failure is constant the types of failure vary, and the qualities and habits of our society specify the manners and the methods of our failure. I think that we fail in part because we lack ambition.

2. If I recommend ambition, I do not mean to suggest that it is easy or pleasurable. "I would sooner fail," said Keats at twenty-two, "than not be among the greatest." When he died three years later he believed in his despair that he had done nothing, the poet of "The Eve of St. Agnes" convinced that his name was "writ in water." But he was mistaken, he was mistaken . . . If I praise the ambition that drove Keats, I do not mean to suggest that anyone's supreme ambition will be satisfied in this life. We never know the value of our own work, and everything reasonable leads us to doubt it: For we can be certain that few contemporaries will be read in a hundred years. To desire to write poems that endure—we undertake such a goal knowing two things: that in all likelihood we will fail, and that if we succeed we will never know it.

Every now and then I meet someone certain of personal greatness. I want to pat this person on the shoulder and mutter

From *Poetry and Ambition: Essays 1982–88* (Ann Arbor: The University of Michigan Press, 1988).

comforting words:"Things will get better!You won't always feel so depressed! Cheer up!"

But I just called high ambition sensible. If our goal in life is to remain content, *no* great ambition is sensible . . . If our goal is to write poetry, the only way we are likely to be *any* good is to try to be as great as the best.

3. For some people it seems ambitious merely to set up as a poet, merely to write and to publish. Publication stands in for achievement—universities and grant-givers take publication as achievement—but to accept such a substitution is modest indeed, for publication is cheap and easy. In this country we publish more poems (in books and magazines) and more poets read more poems aloud at more poetry readings than ever before; the increase in thirty years has been a hundredfold. So what? Many published poems are *readable,* charming, funny, touching, sometimes intelligent. But they are usually brief, they resemble each other, they are anecdotal, they do not extend themselves, they make no great claims, they connect small things to small things. Ambitious poems usually require a certain length for magnitude; one need not mention monuments like *The Canterbury Tales, The Faerie Queene, Paradise Lost,* or *The Prelude.* "Epithalamion," "Lycidas," and "Ode: Intimations of Immortality" are sufficiently extended, not to mention "The Garden" or "Out of the Cradle." Not to mention the poet like Yeats whose briefer works make great connections.

I do not complain that we find ourselves incapable of such achievement; I complain that we seem not even to entertain the desire.

4. Where Shakespeare used "ambitious" of Macbeth we would say "over-ambitious"; Milton used "ambition" for the unscrupulous overreaching of Satan. The word describes a deadly sin like pride. If I now call Milton "ambitious" I use the modern word, mellowed and washed of its darkness. This amelioration reflects capitalism's investment in social mobility. In more hierarchal times pursuit of honor might require revolutionary social change, or murder; but Protestantism and capitalism celebrate the desire to rise in the opinions of peers.

Milton and Shakespeare, like Homer, acknowledge the desire to make words that live forever: ambitious enough, and fit to the

OED's first definition of "ambition" as "eager desire of honor"—
which will do for poets and warriors, courtiers and architects,
diplomats, senators, and kings. Desire need not imply drudgery.
Hard work enters the definition at least with Milton, who is
ready "To scorn delights, and live laborious days," to discover
fame, "the spur, that last infirmity of noble minds." We note the
infirmity who note that fame results only from laborious days'
attendance upon a task of some magnitude. When Milton in-
voked the Heavenly Muse's "aid to my adventurous song," he
wanted merely to "justify the ways of God to men."

If the word "ambitious" has mellowed, "fame" has deterio-
rated enough to require a moment's thought. Fame tends now
to mean David Letterman and *People* magazine. For Keats as for
Milton, for Hector as for Gilgamesh, it meant something like
universal and enduring love for the deed done or the song
sung. The idea is more classic than Christian, and the poet not
only seeks it but confers it. Who knows Achilles' valor but for
Homer's tongue? But in our culture—after centuries of cheap
printing, after the spread of mere literacy and the decline of
qualified literacy, after the loss of history and the historical
sense, after television has become mother of us all—we have
watched the degradation of fame until we use it now as Andy
Warhol used it, as the mere quantitative distribution of images.
We have a culture crowded with people who are famous for
being famous.

5. True ambition in a poet seeks fame in the old sense, to
make words that live forever. If even to entertain such ambition
reveals monstrous egotism, let me argue that the common alter-
native is petty egotism that spends itself in small competitive-
ness, that measures its success by quantity of publication, by
blurbs on jackets, by small achievement: to be the best poet in
the workshop, to be published by Knopf, to win the Pulitzer or
the Nobel . . . The grander goal is to be as good as Dante.

Let me hypothesize the developmental stages of the poet:

At twelve, say, the American poet-to-be is afflicted with gen-
eralized ambition. (Oliver Wendell Holmes said that *nothing* was
so commonplace as the desire to appear remarkable; the desire
may be common but it is at least essential.) Robert Frost wanted
to be a baseball pitcher and a United States senator. At sixteen

the poet reads Whitman and Homer and wants to be immortal. At twenty-four the same poet wants to be in the *New Yorker.*

There is a stage at which the poem becomes more important than the poet. One can see it as a transition from the lesser egotism to the greater. At the state of lesser egotism, the poet keeps a bad line or an inferior word or image because *that's the way it was: that's what really happened.* The frail ego of the author takes precedence over art. The poet must develop, past this silliness, to the stage where the poem is altered to make it better art, not for the sake of its maker's feelings but because decent art is the goal. Then the poem lives at some distance from its creator's little daily emotions; it can take on its own character in the mysterious place of satisfying shapes and shapely utterance. The poem freed from its precarious utility as ego's appendage may possibly fly into the sky and become a star permanent in the night air.

Yet, alas, when the poet tastes a little fame, a little praise . . . Sometimes the poet who has passed this developmental stage will forget duty to the art of poetry and again serve the petty egotism of the self. Nothing is learned once that does not need learning again. The poet whose ambition is unlimited at sixteen and petty at twenty-four may turn unlimited at thirty-five and regress at fifty. But if everyone suffers from interest, everyone may pursue disinterest.

Then there is a possible further stage: When the poet becomes an instrument or agency of art, the poem freed from the poet's ego may entertain the possibility of grandeur. And this grandeur, by a familiar paradox, may turn itself an apparent one hundred and eighty degrees to tell the truth. Only when the poem turns wholly away from the petty ego, only when its internal structure fully serves art's delicious purposes, may it serve to reveal and envision. "Man can *embody* truth"—said Yeats; I add italics—"he cannot *know* it." Embodiment is art and artfulness.

When Yeats was just south of fifty he wrote that he "sought an image not a book." Many aging poets leave the book behind to search for the diagram, and write no more poetry than Michael Robartes who drew geometrical shapes in the sand. The turn toward a prophet's wisdom—toward gathering the whole world into a book—often leaves poetry behind as a frivolity. And though these prophets may delight in abstract revelation, we cannot follow them into knowing, who followed their earlier embodiments. Yeats's soul knew an appetite for invisibility—the temptation of many—but the man remained composite, and although he sought and found a vision he continued to write a book.

6. We find our models of ambition mostly from reading.

We develop the notion of art from our reading. When we call the poem more important than ourselves, it is not that we have confidence in *our* ability to write it; we believe in *poetry*. We look daily at the great monuments of old accomplishment and we desire to add to their number, to make poems in homage to poetry. Old poems that we continue to read and love become the standard we try to live up to. These poems, internalized, criticize our own work. These old poems become our Muse, our encouragement to song and our discouragement of comparison.

Therefore it is essential for poets, all the time, to read and reread the great ones. Some lucky poets make their living by publicly reacquainting themselves in the classroom with the great poems of the language. Alas, many poets now teach nothing but creative writing, and read nothing but the words of children. I will return to this subject.

It is also true that many would-be poets lack respect for learning. How strange that the old ones read books . . . Keats stopped school when he was fifteen or so; but he translated the *Aeneid* in order to study it and worked over Dante in Italian and daily sat at the feet of Spenser, Shakespeare, and Milton. ("Keats studied the old poets every day / Instead of picking up his M.F.A.") Ben Jonson was learned and in his cups looked down at Shakespeare's relative ignorance of ancient languages—but Shakespeare learned more language and literature at his Stratford grammar school—or by himself—than we acquire in twenty years of schooling. Whitman read and educated himself with vigor; Eliot and Pound continued their studies, or really started learning, after stints of graduate school.

On the other hand, we play CDs all night and write unambitious poems. Even sophisticated young poets—haunted by Hikmet, suffused in Sufi—know nothing of Bishop King's "Exequy." The syntax and sounds of one's own tongue, and that tongue's four-hundred-year-old ancestors, give us more than all the classics of all the world in translation.

But to struggle to read the great poems of another language—*in* the language—that is another thing. We are the first generations of poets not to study Latin; not to read Dante in Italian. Thus the puniness of our unambitious syntax and limited vocabulary.

When we have read the great poems we can study as well the lives of the poets. It is useful, in the pursuit of models, to read the lives and letters of the poets whose work we love. Keats. Yeats.

7. In all societies there is a template to which its institutions conform, whether or not the institutions promote products or activities that suit such a pattern. In the Middle Ages the Church provided the model, and guilds and secret societies erected their colleges of cardinals. Today the American corporation provides the template, and the university models itself on General Motors. Corporations exist to create or discover consumers' desires and fulfill them with something that satisfies briefly and needs frequent repetition. CBS provides television as Bic supplies disposable razors. The universities turn out degree-holders equally disposable; and the major publishers of New York City (most of them less profitable annexes of conglomerates peddling soap and paper towels) provide disposable masterpieces.

The United States invented mass quick-consumption and we are very good at it. We are not famous for making Ferraris and Rolls Royces; we are famous for the Model T, the Model A— "transportation," as we call it: the particular abstracted into the utilitarian generality—and two in every garage. Quality is all very well but it is *not* democratic; if we insist on producing only a hand-built Rolls Royce, most of us will walk to work. Democracy demands the interchangeable part and the worker on the production line; Thomas Jefferson may have had other notions but de Tocqueville was our prophet. Or take American cuisine: it has never added a sauce to the world's palate, but our fast-food industry overruns the planet.

Thus: Our poems, in their charming and interchangeable

quantity, do not presume to the status of Ben Jonson's "To Heaven"—for that would be elitist and un-American. We write and publish the McPoem—*a billion billion served*—which becomes our contribution to the history of literature as the Model T is our contribution to a history which runs from bare feet past elephant and rickshaw to the vehicles of space. Pull in any time day or night, park by the busload, and the McPoem waits on the steam shelf for us, wrapped and protected, indistinguishable, undistinguished, and reliable—the good old McPoem identical from coast to coast and in all the little towns between, subject to the quality-control of the least common denominator.

And every year, Ronald McDonald takes the Pulitzer.

To produce the McPoem, institutions must enforce patterns, institutions within institutions, all subject to the same glorious dominance of unconscious economic determinism, template and formula of consumerism. The McPoem is the product of the workshops of Hamburger University.

8. But before we look into the workshop, with its training program for junior poets, let us take a look at models provided by poetic heroes of the American present. The university does not invent the stereotypes; it provides technology for mass reproduction of a model created elsewhere.

Question: If in 1980 you manufacture Pac-Man, or a car called Mustang, and everyone suddenly wants to buy what you make, how do you respond? Answer: You add shifts, pay overtime, and expand the plant in order to saturate the market with your product. You make your product as quickly as you can manufacture it; notions of quality do not disturb your dreams.

When Robert Lowell was young he wrote slowly and painfully and very well. On a wonderful Library of Congress recording, before he recites his early "Falling Asleep over the Aeneid," he tells how the poem began when he tried translating Virgil but produced only eighty lines in six months. He found his struggle disheartening. Five years elapsed between his Pulitzer book *Lord Weary's Castle,* which was the announcement of his genius, and its underrated successor *The Mills of the Kavanaughs.* Then there were eight more years before the abrupt innovation of *Life Studies. For the Union Dead* was spotty, *Near the Ocean* spottier, and then the rot set in. No man should be hanged for losing his gift, most especially a man who suffered as Lowell did. But one can, I think, feel annoyed when quality plunges as quantity multiplies: Lowell published five bad books of poems in the disastrous last eight years of his life.

(I say "bad books" and would go to the stake over the judgment, but let me hasten to acknowledge that each of these dreadful collections—dead metaphor, flat rhythm, narcissistic self-exploitation—was celebrated by leading critics on the front page of the *Times* and the *New York Review of Books* as the greatest yet of uniformly great emanations of great poetical greatness, greatly achieved . . . But one wastes one's time in indignation. Taste is always a fool.)

John Berryman wrote with difficult concentration his difficult, concentrated *Homage to Mistress Bradstreet;* then he eked out *77 Dream Songs.* Alas, after the success of this product he mass-produced *His Toy, His Dream, His Rest,* three hundred and eight further dream songs—mostly the quick improvisations of self-imitation, which is the true identity of the famous "voice" accorded late Berryman-Lowell. Robert Penn Warren, late in his life a grand old man, accumulated another long book of poems every year or so, repeating himself instead of revising the same poems until they were right—hurry, hurry, hurry—and the publishing tribe celebrated these sentimental, crude, trite products of our industrial culture.

Not all poets overproduce in a response to eminence: Elizabeth Bishop never went on overtime; T. S. Eliot wrote bad plays at the end of his life, but never watered the soup of his poems; nor did Williams nor Stevens nor Pound. Everyone writes some inferior work—but these poets did not gush out bad poems late in their lives when they were famous and the market required more products for buying and selling.

Mind you, the workshops of Hamburger University turned out cheap, ersatz Bishop, Eliot, Williams, Stevens, and Pound. All you want . . .

9. Horace, when he wrote the *Ars Poetica,* recommended that poets keep their poems home for ten years. Don't let them go, don't publish them until you have kept them around for ten years: By that time, they ought to stop moving on you; by that time, you ought to have them right. Sensible advice, I think—but

difficult to follow. When Pope wrote *An Essay on Criticism* seventeen hundred years after Horace, he cut the waiting time in half, suggesting that poets keep their poems for five years before publication.

Henry Adams said something about acceleration, mounting his complaint in 1912; some would say that acceleration has accelerated in the years since. By this time, I would be grateful—and published poetry would be better—if people kept their poems home for eighteen months. Poems have become as instant as coffee or onion soup mix. One of our eminent critics compared Lowell's last book to the work of Horace, although some of its poems were dated the year of publication. Anyone editing a magazine receives poems dated the day of the postmark. When a poet types and submits a poem just composed (or even shows it to spouse or friend) the poet cuts off from the poem the possibility of growth and change; I suspect that the poet *wishes* to forestall the possibilities of growth and change, of course without acknowledging the wish.

If Robert Lowell, John Berryman, and Robert Penn Warren publish without allowing for sufficient revision or self-criticism, how can we expect a twenty-four-year-old in Manhattan to wait five years—or eighteen months? With these famous men as models, should we blame the young poet who boasts in a brochure of over four hundred poems published? Or the workshop teacher who meets a colleague on the crosswalk and buffs the backs of his fingernails against his tweed as he proclaims that, over the last two years, he has averaged "placing" two poems a week?

10. Abolish the M.F.A.! What a ringing slogan for a new Cato: *Iowa delenda est!*

The workshop schools us to produce the McPoem, which is "a mold in plaster, / Made with no loss of time," with no waste of effort, with no strenuous questioning as to merit. If we attend a workshop we must bring something to class or we do not contribute. What kind of workshop could Horace have contributed to, if he kept his poems to himself so long? No, we will not admit Horace and Pope to our workshops, for they will just sit there, holding back their own work, claiming it is not ready, acting superior, *elitists* . . .

When we use a metaphor, it is useful to make inquiries of it. I have already compared the workshop to a fast-food franchise, to a Ford assembly line . . . Or does "workshop" compare Creative Writing 401 to a sweatshop where women sew shirts at an illegally low wage? Probably the metaphor refers to none of the above, because the workshop is rarely a place for starting and finishing poems; it is a place for repairing them. The poetry workshop resembles a garage to which we bring incomplete or malfunctioning homemade machines for diagnosis and repair. Here is the homemade airplane for which the crazed inventor forgot to provide wings; here is the internal combustion engine all finished except that it lacks a carburetor; here is the rowboat without oarlocks, the ladder without rungs, the motorcycle without wheels. We advance our nonfunctional machine into a circle of other apprentice inventors and one or two senior Edisons. "Very good," they say; "it *almost* flies . . . How about, uh . . . how about *wings?*" Or, "Let me just show you how to fix a carburetor . . ."

Whatever we bring to this place, we bring it too soon. The weekly meetings of the workshop serve the haste of our culture. When we bring a new poem to the workshop, anxious for praise, others' voices enter the poem's metabolism before it is mature, distorting its possible growth and change. "It's only when you get far enough away from your work to begin to be critical of it yourself"—Robert Frost said—"that anyone else's criticism can be tolerable. . . ." Bring to class only, he said, "old and cold things." Nothing is old and cold until it has gone through months of drafts. Therefore workshopping is intrinsically impossible.

It is from workshops that American poets learn to enjoy the embarrassment of publication—too soon, too soon—because *making public* is a condition of workshopping. This publication exposes oneself to one's fellow-poets only—a condition of which poets are perpetually accused and frequently guilty. We learn to write poems that will please not the Muse but our contemporaries, thus poems that resemble our contemporaries' poems—thus the recipe for the McPoem. If we learn nothing else, we learn to publish promiscuously; these premature ejaculations count on number and frequency to counterbalance ineptitude.

Poets who stay outside the circle of peers—like Whitman, who did not go to Harvard; like Dickinson, for whom there was no tradition; like Robert Frost, who dropped out of two colleges to make his own way—these poets take Homer for their peer. To quote Frost again: "The thing is to write better and better poems. Setting our heart when we're too young on getting our poems appreciated lands us in the politics of poetry which is death." Agreeing with these words from Frost's dour middle-age, we need to add: And "setting our heart" when we are old "on getting our poems appreciated" lands us in the same place.

11. At the same time, it is a big country . . .

Most poets need the company of other poets. They do not need mentors; they need friends, critics, people to argue with. It is no accident that Wordsworth, Coleridge, and Southey were friends when they were young; if Pound, H. D., and William Carlos Williams had not known each other when young, would they have become William Carlos Williams, H. D., and Pound? There have been some lone wolves but not many. The history of poetry is a history of friendships and rivalries, not only with the dead great ones but with the living young. My four years at Harvard overlapped with the undergraduates Frank O'Hara, Adrienne Rich, John Ashbery, Robert Bly, Peter Davison, L. E. Sissman, and Kenneth Koch. I do not assert that we resembled a sewing circle, that we often helped each other overtly, or even that we *liked* each other. I do assert that we were lucky to have each other around for purposes of conversation, argument, and competition.

We were not in workshops; we were merely attending college. Where else in this country would we have met each other? In France there is an answer to this question and it is Paris. Europe goes in for capital cities. Although England is less centralized than France or Romania, London is more capital than New York, San Francisco, or Washington. While the French poet can discover the intellectual life of his times at a café, the American requires a degree program. The workshop is the institutionalized café.

The American problem of geographical isolation is real. Any remote place may be the site of poetry—imagined, remembered, or lived in—but for almost every poet it is necessary to live in exile before returning home—an exile rich in conflict and confirmation. Central New Hampshire or the Olympic Peninsula or Cincinnati or the soybean plains of western Minnesota or the lower East Side may shine at the center of our work and our lives; but if we never leave these places we are not likely to grow up enough to do the work. There is a terrible poignancy in the talented artist who fears to leave home— defined as a place *first* to leave and *then* to return to.

So the workshop answers the need for a café. But I called it the *institutionalized* café, and it differs from the Parisian version by instituting requirements and by hiring and paying mentors. Workshop mentors even make assignments: "Write a persona poem in the voice of a dead ancestor." "Make a poem containing these ten words in this order with as many other words as you wish." "Write a poem without adjectives, or without prepositions, or without content." These formulas, everyone says, are a whole lot of fun. They also reduce poetry to a parlor game; they trivialize and make safe-seeming the real terrors of real art. This reduction-by-formula is not accidental. We play these games *in order* to reduce poetry to a parlor game. Games serve to democratize, to soften, and to standardize; they are repellent. Although in theory workshops serve a useful purpose in gathering young artists together, workshop practices enforce the McPoem.

This is your contrary assignment: Be as good a poet as Sir Philip Sidney. Take as long as you wish.

12. I mentioned earlier the disastrous separation, in many universities, of creative writing and literature. There are people writing poetry—teaching poetry, studying poetry—who find reading *academic*. Such a sentence sounds like a satiric invention; it is objective reporting.

Our culture rewards specialization. It is absurd that we erect a barrier between one who reads and one who writes, but it is an absurdity with a history. It is absurd because in our writing our standards derive from what we have read, and its history reaches back to the ancient war between the poets and the philosophers, exemplified in Plato's *Ion* when the philosopher condescends to the rhapsode. In the 1930s poets like Ransom, Tate, and Winters entered the academy under sufferance, condescended to. Tate and Winters especially made themselves academically rigorous. They secured the beachheads; the army of their grandchildren occupies the country—sometimes grandsons and -daughters who write books but do not read them.

The separation of the literature department from the writing department is a disaster; for poet, for scholar, and for student. The poet may prolong adolescence into retirement by dealing only with the products of infant brains. (If the poet, as in some schools, teaches literature, but only to writing students, the effect is better but not all better. The temptation exists then to teach literature as craft or trade; Americans don't need anyone teaching them trade.) The scholars of the department, institutionally separated from the contemporary, are encouraged to ignore it. In the ideal relationship, writers play gadfly to scholars, and scholars help writers connect to the body of past literature. Students lose the writer's special contribution to the study of literature. Everybody loses.*

13. It is commonplace that, in the English and American tradition, critic and poet are the same person—from Campion to Pound, from Sidney to Eliot. This tradition started with controversies between poets over the propriety of rhyme and English meter, and with poets' defense of poetry against Puritan attack. It flourished, serving many purposes, through Dryden, Johnson, Coleridge, Wordsworth, Keats in his letters, Shelley, Arnold . . . There are *no* first-rate critics in the English tradition who are not also poets—except for Hazlitt. The poet and the critic have been almost continuous, as if writing poetry and thinking about it were not discrete activities.

When Roman Jakobson—great linguist, Harvard professor—was approached some years ago with the suggestion that Vladimir Nabokov might be appointed professor of Slavic, Jakobson was skeptical; he had nothing against elephants, he said, but he would not appoint one professor of zoology.

The analogy compares the elegant and stylish Nabokov—novelist in various languages, lepidopterist, lecturer, and critic—

---

* I am given to understand that at many institutions now Departments of English omit literature for theory. As a result, poems and fiction receive attention only from teachers of creative writing. Praise them. But I have not heard that student writers study work earlier than the twentieth century.

to the great, gray, hulking pachyderm, intellectually noted *only* for memory. By jokes and analogies we reveal ourselves. Jakobson condescends to Nabokov—just as Plato patted little Ion on his head; just as Sartre, who demanded that writers be *engaged* (in *What is Literature?*), makes charitable exception for poets; just as men have traditionally condescended to women and imperialists to natives. The points are clear: (1) "Artists are closer to nature than thinkers; they are more instinctive, more emotional; they are childlike." (2) "Artists like bright colors; artists have a natural sense of rhythm; artists screw all the time." (3) "Don't misunderstand. We *like* artists, in their place, which is in the zoo, or at any rate outside the Republic, or at any rate outside tenured ranks."

(One must admit, I suppose, that these days poets often find themselves in tenured ranks. But increasingly they enter by the zoo entrance, which in Hamburger University is the department of creative writing.)

Formalism, with its dream of finite measurement, is a beautiful arrogance, a fantasy of materialism. When we find what's to measure and measure it, we should understand style-as-fingerprint, maybe quantifying characteristic phonemic sequences. But it seems likely that we will continue to intuit qualities, like degrees of intensity, for which objective measure is impossible. Then hard-noses will claim that only the measurable exists— which is why hard-nose usually means soft-head.

Once I audited a course of Jakobson's, for which I am grateful; the old formalist discoursed on comparative prosody, witty and energetic and learned, giving verbatim examples from Urdu and fifty other languages, exemplifying the multiplicity of countable noises. The journey was marvelous, the marvel diminished only a little by its terminus. The last lecture, pointed to for some weeks, turned out to be a demonstration, from an objective and untraditional approach, of how to scan (and the scansion was fine, and it was the way one scanned the poem when one was sixteen) Edgar Poe's "The Raven."

14. If it seems hopeless, one has only to look up in perfect silence at the stars . . . and it *does* help to remember that poems are the stars, not poets. Of most help is to remember that it is possible for people to take hold of themselves and become better by

thinking. It is also necessary to *continue* to take hold of ourselves—if we are to pursue the true ambition of poetry. Our disinterest must discover that last week's nobility was really covert rottenness, et cetera. One is never free and clear; one must work continually to sustain, to recover . . .

When Keats in his letters praised disinterestedness—his favorite moral idea, destroyed when it is misused as a synonym for lethargy (on the same day I found it misused in the *New York Times, Inside Sports,* and the *American Poetry Review)*—he lectured himself because he feared that he would lose it. Lectures loud with moral advice are always self-addressed. No one is guiltless of temptation, but it is possible to resist temptation. When Keats worried over his reputation, over insults from Haydon or the *Quarterly,* or Shelley's condescension or Wordsworth's neglect, he reminded himself to cultivate disinterest; to avoid distraction and to keep his eye on the true goal, which was to become one of the English Poets.

Yeats is responsible for a number of the stars in the sky, and when we read his letters we find that the young man was an extraordinary trimmer—soliciting reviews from Oscar Wilde and flattering Katherine Tynan, older and more established on the Celtic turf. One of the OED's definitions of ambition, after "eager desire of honor," is "personal solicitation of honor." When he wrote, "I seek an image not a book," he acknowledged that as a young man he had sought a book indeed. None of us, beseeching Doubleday or Pittsburgh, has ever sought with greater fervor.

And Whitman reviewed himself, and Roethke campaigned for praise like a legislator at the state fair, and Frost buttered Untermeyer on both sides . . . Therefore let us abjure the old saw that self-promotion and empire-building mean bad poetry. Most entrepreneurs are bad poets—but then, so are most poets. Self-promotion remains a side issue of poetry and ambition. It *can* reflect a greed or covetousness which displaces the grand ambition—the kind of covetousness which looks on the life lived only as a source of poems; "I got a poem out of it"—or it can show only the trivial side of someone who, on other occasions, makes great art. At any rate, we should spend our time worrying not about other people's bad characters, but our own.

Finally, of course, I speak of nothing except the modest topic: How shall we lead our lives? I think of a man I admire as much as anyone, the English sculptor Henry Moore, eighty when I spoke with him last. "Now that you are eighty," I asked him, "would you tell me the secret of life?" Being a confident and eloquent Yorkshireman, Moore would not deny my request. He told me:

"The greatest good luck in life, for *anybody,* is to have something that means *everything* to you ... to do what you want to do, and to find that people will pay you for doing it ... *if* it's unattainable. It's no good having an objective that's attainable! That's the big thing: you have an ideal, an objective, and that objective must be unreachable. ..."

15. There is no audit we can perform on ourselves, to assure that we work with proper ambition. Obviously it helps to be careful; to revise, to take time, to put the poem away; to pursue distance in the hope of objective measure. We know that the poem, to satisfy ambition's goals, must not exist to express mere personal feeling or opinion—as the moment's McPoem does. It must by its language make art's new object. We must try to hold ourselves to the mark; we must not write to publish or to prevail. Repeated scrutiny is the only method general enough for recommending ...

And of course repeated scrutiny is not foolproof; and we will fool ourselves. Nor can the hours we work provide an index of ambition or seriousness. Although Henry Moore laughed at artists who worked only an hour or two a day, he acknowledged that sculptors can carve sixteen hours at a stretch for years on end—tap-tap-tap on stone—and remain lazy. We can revise our poems five hundred times; we can lock poems in their rooms for ten years—and remain modest in our endeavor. On the other hand, anyone casting a glance over biography or literary history must acknowledge: Some great poems have come without noticeable labor.

But as I speak I confuse realms. Ambition is not a quality of the poem but of the poet. Failure and achievement belong to the poet, and if our goal remains unattainable, then failure must be standard. To pursue the unattainable for decade after decade, like Henry Moore, may imply a certain temperament. If there is no method of work that we can rely on, maybe at least we can encourage in ourselves a temperament that is not easily satisfied. Some time when we are discouraged with our own work, we may notice that even the great poems, the sources and the standards, seem inadequate: "Ode to a Nightingale" feels too limited in scope, "Out of the Cradle" too sloppy, "To His Coy Mistress" too neat, and "Among School Children" padded . . .

Maybe ambition is appropriately unattainable when we acknowledge: *No poem is so great as we demand that poetry be.*

Polonius's Advice to Young Poets

When Polonius reached fifty, he looked at the poetry about him and he saw that it was not good. He saw more poets than ever before, more magazines, more books, more poetry readings, more audiences, and more dreck. Taking upon himself the burden of world-correction, he composed a series of rules, to which he attached parenthetic exclamations, explanations, anecdotes, and insults.

1. Do not live your life as if it were a fishing expedition, and poems were the fish.

(Some poets' greed is as boundless as Alexander's. "My sister's funeral was a drag," says one of them; "but I got a poem out of it.")

2. Read good poems at least two hours every day. Three-quarters of the poets read should be born before 1907 and outside Chile.

(Too many American poets read no poetry except contemporary work or work in translation. The latter leads to wonderful images about "jaws of the melon seed" and "bamboo under the mountain-color mountain," but does little for one's ear, one's syntax, or one's shapeliness. Henry King, William Cowper, Christina Rossetti, and Alfred, Lord Tennyson may help.

(Many American poets never read poetry at all, because books are expensive and you always need a new CD; books are old-fashioned; the Internet's *it;* if you read other poets it might spoil your original style because you would be influenced by them.

(Poets who read no poetry tend to exhaust their resources rather early.)

From *The Weather for Poetry: Essays, Reviews, and Notes on Poetry, 1977–81* (Ann Arbor: The University of Michigan Press, 1982).

3. Revise everything you write over and over again.

(Although your first draft may be inspired, and you may not know what you are doing, before you publish the damned thing see that you know what you have done. In retrospect, intend every word and every piece of grammar.)

4. Do not show anyone the draft of a new poem until you have read it over, all by yourself, every day for six months.

(Do not show it to your husband, to your wife, to your roommate, to your student, to your teacher, to your friend's spouse, to your spouse's friend, to Alice Quinn or Joseph Parisi, to your Workshop Director, or to me.)

5. Do not publish a poem in a magazine until three years after you have first shown it to someone. Keep looking at it, and change it whenever you find something to change. If you get tired of it you can always throw it away.

(Some old poets said ten years; some said five. But the world has accelerated, as everyone knows.)

6. Try to remember that quantity is not quality.

(Every American knows that if the automobile industry sells x-million cars it is a wonderful year, and this wonderful year has "a ripple effect" throughout the economy. A million fewer sales and we're sunk. Generally, farmers are happy to get more bushels of wheat from an acre this year than they did last year. Therefore our universities think that they have become better because they have become larger, and a Department of English which graduates twenty-seven Ph.D.s who cannot find jobs feels superior to a Department of English which graduates twenty-one Ph.D.s who cannot find jobs.

(Thus Polonius remembers sitting in John Berryman's living room to hear the poet, sober and drinking coffee by the gallon, announce that he had just completed a collection of more than three hundred new poems, and Polonius's prophetic stomach sank . . . And Robert Lowell, in mad Berryman-envy, rushed into mass-production of appalling unrhymed sonnets—and five books in eight years. And Polonius remembers the biographical note: "Ms. W—— published nine collections of poetry last year. . . ." And Polonius remembers the young poet who sent out a flier, advertising his availability for readings, that bragged of four hundred and twenty-six poems published by magazines in a period of three years.)

7. Do not commit dead metaphors, clichés, or thievery from other poets; be as hard on yourself as you possibly can.

(Most good poets cannot do it all alone. Most of us can fool ourselves even when we try hard not to. Create for yourself a jury of tough readers, to go over your poems during the years between starting and finishing. Someone who hates everything you write is useless to you; so is someone who loves everything you write. Find people who agree with your ambitions but who notice discrepancies between ambition and achievement. If anyone starts praising more than half of your lines, let that member of the jury be dismissed and another substituted.

(If you live in Maine near the Canadian border, or on a Kansas farm, you may find it difficult to construct a jury from your immediate neighbors. You must do it by mail. Write fan letters to poets and critics you admire, and some will write you back. [Beware of allowing letters to pen-pals substitute for energy given to poems.] The best way to get good, harsh, useful criticism is to dish it out. To sharpen your ability to criticize other poets increase your observation of Rule Two.

(If you are of a certain age, you may find it difficult to retain the jury you have constructed. Old friends die, stay drunk, go crazy, become famous or obscure, wear out. You must continually reinvent the jury, but it is difficult to find good readers among the young, if you are old and semi-famous. They are too impressed, and they praise bad work just because you wrote it. [As with most things in the world, there is a common converse—the young poet who wishes to convince himself of his incorruptibility, and therefore denounces every utterance that emerges from your pen or your mouth. Maim him.] You must search among old acquaintance, ex-jurors who have recovered their lost judgment, the rare young, the formerly young turned forty and no longer deferring to anybody.

(But as people have noticed in other connections, one of the consequences of aging is narrowed acquaintance. And who is blind Homer's peer? Blind Homer, if he continues to take pleasure in composing verses, presumably learns to take the absent friends inside. The internal critic, harsh but fair, is known as the Muse.)

8. Be open to change, to other poetries, to poets you have disliked in the past.

(If you hate Shelley or Jarrell, be sure to reread them now and again, trying to see what others see. If you are Objective, read Fantastic. If you are Fantastic, read *Sulfur*. Once again: no growth without contradiction!)

9. Do not date your poems. Do not submit multiply. Do not send the same poem twice to the same editor.

(It makes Polonius nervous to read a date on a poem—especially if it be a single day. He dreads the moment when he will read a poem dated "January 12, 2003, 8:02–8:04 P.M."

(It may come as a surprise, unless you have edited, that most editors *bother* over what they accept and reject. It annoys these editors when they discover that they have bothered to no avail. Therefore it is necessary to keep good records of where you have sent your poems. However, if you discover that you are devoting one-third of your time to postal flowcharts, revise your life. Marry the mailperson if you must, but remember what matters.)

10. Remember what matters.

(Remember that you love *poems,* those old stars burning in the sky forever: "To Earthward," "The Garden of Love," "Ode on a Grecian Urn," "The Return," "During Wind and Rain" . . . [here let the reader supply a list]. Remember that you work not for publication, not for NEA grants, not for listing in *Poets and Writers,* not for praise, not for notoriety, not for money, not for Guggenheims, not for Pulitzers, not for Greek Islands, not for *APR,* not for Yaddo, not for tenure. Remember that you work to make a star that will burn—outside you and even for a while after you—high in the sky.

(Remember that love is serious, and death is serious, friendship, justice, and aging are serious; remember that universities and magazines are not serious. Possibly you are serious, insofar as your poems are serious. Remember Keats and forget bibliographies.)

Starting and Keeping On

A few years ago I went to Nebraska for the National Book Foundation. Mostly, I visited Indian reservations, but one day I went to a high school in a tiny town and spoke to students. A nervous teacher suggested that I tell them how I began to write poetry. I told them the stories I've told so many times: At twelve I loved horror movies, and a neighbor boy suggested that I read Edgar Allan Poe, who led me to Keats and Shelley; I loved them all, and wrote revolting nineteenth-century poems until I was fourteen. Then a sophisticated sixteen-year-old introduced me to T. S. Eliot, Ezra Pound, Marianne Moore, William Carlos Williams, and I wrote revolting twentieth-century poems.

In the front row at the high school, a tall blonde boy raised his hand. "Didn't you do it to pick up chicks?"

"Of course!" I told him. "I was forgetting that part!" Surely one of the reasons I began to write poetry was to cut a romantic figure, to fascinate the cheerleaders, whom I couldn't interest by my athletic prowess. I wanted to be the solitary phantom walking the streets of the city at night, a black cape flowing behind me, eyes burning like coals. Pasternak said that the pose comes before the poem. The pose didn't work with the cheerleaders, but perhaps with girls who wanted to be actresses. Surely the girls wanted to be actresses in order to pick up guys.

There are silly reasons behind the major motions of our lives. (Of course all ambitious human endeavor serves seduction.) There are motives that endure, and that lead to endurance. Poets have usually started writing from love of poetry, poetry of the English past. They wanted to make objects like the objects that astonished them. Milton and Shakespeare and Keats looked to immortality, a notion which comes to seem naïve. (Rilke spoke

From the *Michigan Quarterly Review,* Fall 2000.

of the death of the sun.) Literature is a zero-sum game: To survive we must replace another poet, and if we replace somebody, we will be replaced ourselves. Needless to say, most poets never place at all—including many Poet Laureates, including many winners of many prizes.

Today, I find that most beginning poets look no further ahead than their own lifetimes, which is doubtless sensible. And maybe the motives, for starting to write, have become more reactive. We look to inwardness and the sensuous imagination in order to blank out the language and speed of commerce, cell phones on sidewalks, and to cast off the burden of information. Poems are not information, and information is the enemy of art. Under the assault of busy fact, poetry may become more a refuge than a strenuous art. And now, if poets take up their art from love of poetry, the art they love is contemporary or translated. It seldom includes the great sixteenth and seventeenth centuries of English poetry. We need also to know the old poetry of our language. Poetry makes poetry. We need old poets not for image-making so much as for sound, for structures not commonly used, for variety in syntax, for resolutions shaped by the nature of our language.

A poet's literary sources are more useful the more distant they are, the less like us: thus translations, thus the seventeenth century with its engines of irony and paradox. We use the foreignness of another age, embodied in an antecedent English. When we learn only from the poetry of our own age, we fall into the habits of the age.

When Eliot wrote about free verse, he said that no verse is free for a man who knows his job, and that traditional English meter lurks behind the arras—which is no longer true. Free verse lurks behind free verse, and therefore our poetry comes out of Whitman and the twentieth century. To absorb the older poets, we need one piece of equipment most of us lack. We cannot read the poets of the past if we don't hear their meter, and we won't learn to hear meter by reading contemporary verse. Nor can we learn by reading a book about prosody, any more than we learn to ride a bicycle by reading a manual. We learn the English metrical line by immersing ourselves in it and by experimenting with writing it ourselves. We learn the language by living in the country, not because we *should* write in meter, but in order to learn from our ancestors.

The life lived is the first source of poems, and we cannot live our lives in order to write out of them. We cannot control many other sources, but there are things that we can do, to help ourselves keep on. We need on purpose to plunder the store of the world. Our reading of literature must be interested or larcenous. Look at the origins and sources of Eliot's poetry. He read a book he found in the Harvard Union library, Arthur Symons on the symbolist poets. Discovering Laforgue's irony, Eliot arrived at his youthful tone. By the time he wrote *The Waste Land* he had studied the Jacobean playwrights and pillaged the sixteenth and seventeenth centuries. Still, the greatest influence on *The Waste Land*—besides Eliot's nervous breakdown—came from prose. Its major strategies derive from Joyce's *Ulysses*. Later even Walt Whitman, seemingly the far side of Eliot's moon, became a resource for *Four Quartets*.

When we read with an eye for what we can use, we take pleasure and then exploit our pleasure. We read with curiosity and greed. Think of Ezra Pound's acquisitiveness. Like Picasso, Pound hurtled from mode to mode. Pound's reading was *extensive*. He was a curious man, as Eliot was. Other poets have concentrated on a few antecedents, and learned them intimately. I grew up fickle, loving and learning from one poet after another, jumping from bed to bed. My late wife Jane Kenyon, who had read widely in English poetry, derived most of her craft from the *intensive* study of a few poets. I remember her studying Keats— reading all the poetry, reading all the letters, reading biographies and critics, reading all the poems again, reading all the letters again. She learned sound, especially the deliciousness of vowels; she learned density—as in Keats's injunction to Shelley: "Load every rift with ore." She used to repeat, "The hare limped trembling through the frozen grass," as if she were chanting a mantra. Later she read Elizabeth Bishop with a studious larceny. Just before she took sick, Jane began to study Emily Dickinson, and wrote Alice Mattison that she was beginning to discover some remarkable things about Dickinson's structures. We'll never know what.

There are resources even in literary criticism. We should read the poet-critics, like the table talk of Ben Jonson, when in his cups he talked with Drummond of Hawthornden. At one point Jonson said that John Donne warranted hanging for want of keeping the accent, at another that Donne was the best poet in the world, in some things. It's poet-talk, the original *Paris Review* interview. Read Coleridge, Wordsworth's "Preface," Keats in his letters, Pound, Eliot.

On the other hand there is disinterested reading, unpredictable gifts awarded to curiosity—reading without larcenous intention, sometimes resulting in accidental larceny. In middle-age I found Gibbon's *Decline and Fall,* and his prose entered my verse, especially in a long poem called *The One Day.* I was overwhelmed by the beauty and utility of Gibbon's syntax, by the way he imparted ambivalent judgment in the construction of his sentences, irony by grammar and word-order. He will tell us that the emperor coerced or perhaps persuaded; the emperor persuaded or rather coerced. At first we want to say, "Make up your mind, Mr. Gibbon," but then we realize that we are instructed to take the two verbs, qualified by "rather" or "perhaps," and gather a range of possible judgments. Gibbon's prose displays disparate feelings and ideas, apparently contradictory, and combines them into the single body of a sentence. Embodiment of oxymoron is poetry's task. In poetry as in human life, north is south and south is north. Bloom is Odysseus, Odysseus is Bloom.

Some poets read the philosophers, but reason tends to deny that north can be south, and I take part in the old war between the philosophers and the poets. Still, in my disinterested reading I have been able to steal from philosophers who make startling apothegms—like Neitzsche, like Meister Eckhart, like Heraclitus: "God is day and night, winter and summer, war and peace, satiety and hunger; but he changes like olive oil which, when it is mixed with perfumes, gets its name from the scent of each." The identity of opposites in Heraclitus resembles Freud's thinking, and resembles the dynamic paradoxes that drive poetry. Emerson the maker of sentences invented the notion that God is dead by saying that God was not dead. Addressing the students at Harvard, he made a string of negative assertions, including "God is not dead." To suggest that God is not dead is to suggest that God might be dead. Every denial suggests affirmation, every affirmation denial.

Poets find resources in the other arts by making analogies to poetry. More poets seem to take inspiration from painting and sculpture than do from music. Maybe the time-art of poetry makes use of analogy to a space-art. (There are musical exceptions: For Whitman, Italian opera was a major resource; American jazz has left its mark, not only on Americans.) Painting and painters have been resources for many poets. I feel closer to sculpture, to weight and touch over illusion. Da Vinci exalted painting over sculpture because it carried its own light; I like the real heft and thinginess of sculpture. For a few years I spent time with Henry Moore, and learned useful attitudes toward art and work. He was determined to compete, not with his contemporaries, not with Epstein or Hepworth or Archipenko, but with Michelangelo and Donatello. From listening to Moore on sculpture, I learned more about writing poetry than I did from talking with older poets. Frequently he quoted notions from Rodin: Rodin said that an old craftsman told him, when they worked in a stonemason's establishment, to carve those roses as if they were pushing right up at you. *Never think of a surface except as the extension of a volume.* In poetry, the energy of its import—what William Stafford called its underneath language—pushes upward against the surface of its statement.

And Moore said, quoting Rodin again: If you are a young sculptor making a maquette and it's not going right, don't keep on jabbing at it with your tools; drop it on the floor and see what it looks like then. Comical as it is, this advice can help a poet. When the poem won't come together, change its form. Turn long-lined end-stopped free verse into short-lined enjambed free verse, or into syllabics, or into a sonnet sequence.

Hall's Index

A young poet friend calls my letters the Dead Metaphor Bulletin. It is *possible* that I am a crank about dead metaphors. Another friend sent me a completed manuscript, which I read with pleasure, and when I wrote him I congratulated him on writing a long book with only four dead metaphors in it. They were the usual things, often nouns used as verbs, often monosyllabic or disyllabic, often taking their origins from archaic sources—words like "shield," "cradle," "plough," and "dart." In minor pique, he answered me alluding to "Hall's Index."

The phrase "dead metaphor" is a dead metaphor, henceforth known as *DM*. The phrase implies that the metaphor was once a living organism, like a human being, but died and became a corpse. When we use such words in our poems, we populate *DM* our poems with zombies.

A defense of poetry argues that the art fulfills a social function by using fresh *DM* language, keeping the language new or lively *DM*. "Fresh" compares language to bread or lettuce. (When you call air "fresh," you compare it, say, to strawberries; when you call it "crisp" you compare it to potato chips.) When we hear that the city is blanketed with snow, we should understand that the city is covered with snow as a blanket covers a bed and its occupants. But reading "blanketed," in reality we respond only to a portion of the word—the portion abstracted into the notion of covering. We don't feel the irony in the metaphor— blankets warm us—because our mind cancels the literalness of the word and takes in only the word's abstracted sense. Its physicality is lost. If we use "blanket" to mean "cover" in a poem, lacking the image of woolen fabric and the feel of warmth, we write poems using language that is shallow *DM* or stale *DM*.

From *The Writers' Chronicle,* 1997.

When we speak, when we write letters or newspaper head-
lines, we use dead metaphors and we understand each other. The
dead metaphor is not a criminal activity—but it is an activity at
odds with poetry. If a poem is to alter us, or to please us extrava-
gantly, it requires close attention from both poet and reader. Close
attention to language is the contract *DM* that writer and reader
sign. The terms of the contract require that each word be fully
used—so that its signification, implication, association, and import
may impinge upon us, move us, and reward intelligent attention.

One dead metaphor will not sink *DM* a poem. Theodore
Roethke's "The Meadow Mouse" is a small powerful lyric, orig-
inal in language: "My thumb of a child"; "The paralytic stunned
in the tub, and the water rising—". But the poet went careless
for one word when he wrote that he brought the mouse inside
"Cradled in my hand." Cradles are no longer commonplace ob-
jects but everyone knows what a cradle is; we can all visualize a
cradle. Used as a verb, the particularity of "cradle" has deterio-
rated, diminished, and abstracted into "hold in a protective man-
ner." In news magazines, people cradle Uzis—and the writer
does not intend to compare automatic weapons to infants. The
abstracted verb has no wooden sides nor rockers; it comforts no
babies. Although "The Meadow Mouse" survives *DM* one egre-
gious dead metaphor, the word is a blemish *DM* on the poem.
When a poem strings *DM* such words together, a necklace of
putrescence, the poem stinks *DM*.

A poem is no better than its skin. A poem requires a skeleton,
and doubtless a soul or at least a brain, but without skin this body
cannot stand or walk, dance or sing. Translations are scams be-
cause skin seldom translates. (We learn from leading translators
that Goethe and Pushkin made poems out of dead metaphors; I
don't believe it.) Translation is a useful scam, so that languageless
readers may gather notions of what Cavafy or Tu Fu are up to,
but Frost's "poetry is what gets lost in translation" is a definition
of poetry. Poetry lies in the minute shades *DM* that distinguish
among words commonly known as synonyms. Poetry happens in
the differences between the words listed together in Roget:
"chaste, virtuous; pure, purehearted, pure in heart; clean, cleanly;
immaculate, spotless, blotless, stainless, taintless, white, snowy;
unsoiled, unsullied, undefiled, untarnished, unstained . . ."

The poem's skin is its words, and words are phonemic se-
quences, combined by the poet for beauty of sound, which are
also bundles *DM* of history and circumstance, so that a "dart"
is not only d-a-r-t but a feathered projectile hurled by English-
men in pubs, or poisoned and ejected from blowguns, or
Cupid's arrows—and abstractly a verb for quick movement,
useless in a poem. In late Robert Lowell we found "minnows
darted"—and early Robert Lowell must have whirled in early
Robert Lowell's grave. Minnows have darted in *several* poets'
poems. When a poet uses "dart" for "the act of sudden acceler-
ation or movement," and compares this motion to a small fish's,
the poet violates the contract with the reader. For one thing,
minnows move quickly but not in the manner of darts. Min-
nows speed for a few inches, stop abruptly, and squirt off again
at an angle, often a right angle. The dart has not been invented
that pauses and alters direction. When Shakespeare had lovers
dart glances at each other, iconography supported his verb:
There is a quiver on Cupid's back.

Intelligent people have devoted much thought to the nature
of metaphor and other figures of speech. I do not disparage this
thinking, but in this practical guide *DM* to incompetent lan-
guage, I am unwilling to explore *DM* distinctions among meta-
phor, metonymy, synecdoche, and algorithms. I speak merely of
inadequate diction, physical words used in a sense abstracted
from particularity, of which the particularity is universally avail-
able or even unavoidable. I speak of poets using false color *DM,*
words that would be as bright as Matisse if familiarity had not
turned them gray and tan. Headline writers find delight in dead
metaphor. I believe that PTA TAKES AIM AT VIOLENCE is deliberate
wit, the dead metaphor as pun. But I doubt it was conscious salad
DM to write TOMATO SALES MUSHROOM IN CONNECTICUT. Re-
cently an obituary in the *New York Times* spoke of a mountain
climber who PAVED THE WAY ON MT. EVEREST. The same paper told
us later that REBELS IN PERU LEAVE DOOR AJAR ON ASYLUM.

Commonly, when I accuse my friends of dead metaphor, they
rightly point out that all language is ultimately metaphoric, and
they entertain me with derivations: "Cliché" is a French print-
ers' word meaning stencil or plate, a pre-assembled block. Yes.
And mostly a word's metaphoric origin is buried *DM* in ety-

mology or antiquarianism. When Richard Wilbur, in "Lamarck Elaborated," writes of "the tactless finger-bone" and how nature "inspired the nose," he speaks to that portion of his audience (I suppose considerable) who will understand that to inspire is to breathe in, and that something is tactless when it lacks touch.

It's not only a matter of Latin. Once in a poem I wanted to speak of the shape hay makes on the ground after a mowing machine has cut it. I used the noun "wake," and the context excluded Finnegan's sort. My noun was visually appropriate but deplorable in its inefficiency—because the reader would not *see* the dead-metaphorical wake of a boat, which has been abstracted into "anything that follows." The wetness of "wake" is suppressed (or comically present) in the spread hay drying under the sun. A magazine sent me a proof of my poem containing "wake" just as I returned from a gathering where I had denounced dead metaphor with special attention, as it happened, to "wake." I telephoned the editor, frantic with a revision and apologizing for my gaffe. He accepted my change and told me that he had no idea what I was talking about. For a substitute, I turned not to a new metaphor (I found none handy) but to a word that would carry the sense without intruding the false color of a dead metaphor. I used "aftermath." When I looked the word up in the OED I was amused: "Aftermath" originally meant the second mowing of a field, "aftermowth."

It doesn't now. Few readers will know the derivation, so that common sense will allow the word in its abstracted sense of "something that follows." George Orwell made a distinction between moribund metaphors and dead ones. "Aftermath" would be dead because readers do not recognize its physical origin; "wake" would be moribund. (Although I recognize Orwell's distinction, I choose not to follow his classification here; it is convenient to use "dead metaphor" to signify the sort of thing that most of us mean by "dead metaphor.") Another example like "wake" and "aftermath": Once I denounced "dart" to a friend and asserted that I would prefer a boring substitute to the dead metaphor; I said I would rather write "move quickly" than "dart." As my friend pointed out, to move quickly is to move in the manner of a live person rather than in the manner of a dead person. Since this use of "quick" survives only in "the quick and the dead," I permit myself "quickly" without considering it a dead metaphor.

Maybe I am inconsistent or arbitrary. If I read the word "churn," I think butter, yet poets I respect use the word for any agitated motion. (When Pound wrote "So-shu churned in the sea," in the second Canto, he alluded to Ovid's metamorphosis in which a ship turns into rock.) Yet I use the word "flail," as in "flail about," although I know what a flail looks like. Maybe I deceive myself that the particularity of "flail" has nearly evaporated *DM*. I deplore "shoulder"—as in "take on a burden" (PRESIDENT SHOULDERS BLAME FOR . . .)—but I am seldom disturbed by "hand" as in "proffer" (PRESIDENT HANDS OVER DECISION . . .). I used "handy," above, without calling it a dead metaphor. If Hall in his language violates Hall's Index, praise the Index and blame Hall.

Along with "dart," another favorite dead metaphor, among contemporary poets, is "cup." In poems (and in prose and in all discourse) we are always cupping things, and often our actions bear no resemblance to the shape of a cup. I remember a poet cupping a dead rabbit. Another frequent dead metaphor is "echo," used for any loud noise, without the possibility of a literal echo. Poets use "echo" also to indicate any repetition. It has become a poetical word, like "pattern," that prettifies and remains vague. "Mirror" is just as common—used as a verb meaning "to copy or reproduce"—as "echo" is. If we pause in revision between "echo" and "mirror," as verbs of duplication, we cannot be searching for the right word. Other common dead metaphors: "erase," "dwarf," "tool," "flower," "veil," "fog," "fade," "haunt," "haunted."

Illness provides ten thousand wounds *DM* to the language, which Hall's Index would nurse *DM* back to health *DM*. The dead metaphor is a cancer *DM* in the poem's language which only revisionary scrutiny can cut out *DM*. We are crippled *DM* when we use "crippled" except in its literal sense. What's more we are sick *DM*. Maybe the dumbest dead metaphor is "blind." We should never use the word except to indicate sightlessness. Writing poems, we must save "cup" for a thing that you drink coffee from. A "harbor" must be a refuge for ships not for poets. A "mirror" is something that hangs on a wall. It's only in revision that we uproot *DM* the dead metaphors that inspiration provides—or we may need the help of friends. Jane Kenyon read my drafts first, and triumph would rise in her voice when she told me, "Perkins, here's a dead metaphor!" The brain notoriously overlooks its own errors while it discerns the errors of others.

Earlier I mentioned that the sources of many dead metaphors are archaic: "king," "reign," "scepter." Not long ago most of our ancestors farmed, and the vocabulary of agriculture supplies many dead metaphors. The fullback plows *DM* through the line. If the defensive line finds this assault harrowing *DM*, how many sports writers have observed a harrow breaking soil? In our poems we sow *DM*, we plant *DM*, we reap *DM*, and we enjoy harvest *DM*. Because our language and literature derive from an island nation, our dead metaphors navigate *DM* the seven seas. Endlessly we drift *DM*. Clouds drift, our minds drift, practically everything drifts. To express the contrary fixity, we anchor *DM* ourselves. (An anchor is apparently synonymous with a chemical binding solution, since we might as well be glued *DM* to a chair as be anchored to it. Another kind of fixity is more drastic: We are paralyzed *DM*.) Needless to say, we harbor *DM* to protect; that is, we harbor as we cradle—and a harbor resembles a cradle as much as an echo resembles a mirror. Other nautical relics: "rudder," "flotsam and jetsam," "keel." Architecture supplies another set: "architecture" itself, "tower," "arch," "vault," "buttress," "foundation."

The word "forge" is used by people who never saw one. Joyce has the young Stephen Dedalus vow "to forge in the smithy of my soul the uncreated conscience of my race." Granted that the mature author used rhetorical inflation to satirize his younger self, Joyce and his readers could not forbid themselves from seeing the image of an actual forge, because they lived in an age of the blacksmith. Also, Joyce made his metaphor more concrete by extending "forge" into "smithy." Sometimes we may resuscitate the dead by extending and developing the metaphor, therefore enforcing the physical. "Forge" departs from the abstract "create" when the physical "smithy" brings the blacksmith alive. Can one make a dead metaphor walk? Possibly by speaking of zombies. But it is chancy; we are more likely to link *DM* dead metaphors together.

What about "spur"? When Milton wrote that "fame" was "the spur," the poet was the horse and his avid pursuit for honor dug sharp points into his own ribs. The element of pain—giving and getting—could not be overlooked. When Yeats was an old man he wrote "The Spur": "You think it horrible that lust and rage / Should dance attention upon my old age; / They were not such a plague when I was young; / What else have I to spur me into song?" Yeats's "plague" is a dead metaphor—but "spur"? Yeats wrote late in the 1930s when people rode horseback more rarely than they did in Milton's England. But Yeats was born in 1865, and celebrated hard-riding country gentlemen. I think that pain remained inside "spur," and the poet was the horse with his own "lust and rage," and dug painfully into his own side. Today, when the headline tells us that CHRISTMAS SALES SPUR ECONOMY, no horse gallops across newsprint.

Medieval or ancient warfare decimates *DM* language, urged on by phalanxes *DM* of cliché. Armor *DM* yourselves against this onslaught *DM*. Avoid: "shield," "siege," "sword," "invade" and "invasion," "army," "weapon." Another class of dead metaphors slips from the military to the sadistic: "kill," "torture," "whip," "scar." Another dead metaphor is offensive: "He slaves over his geraniums."

Is the dead metaphor a contemporary epidemic *DM* or flood *DM?* The dead metaphor has always been with us, as a glance at old magazines will confirm. Nor is it confined to one form or division of poetry. Two of our Language Poets use more dead metaphors than the rest together; neo-formalists score high on the Dead Metaphor Meter. Certain poets who specialize in the ironies of received language—John Ashbery, heaven knows—use dead metaphors to desired or purposeful effect. Once when Ashbery heard a poet claim that poetry cleansed *DM* the language, he murmured that his own work "gave it a blue rinse." Sometimes a poet uses a dead metaphor as part of an idiom, where an alternative would be paraphrastic. What can you do except "cap" *DM* a nuclear pile? The practice I deplore is the unwitting use of dead metaphors in the pursuit of poetic effect: the unrealized comparison as false color.

Of course, the ways of failure are infinite. A poem without a single dead metaphor will most likely be wretched anyway.

Size and Scale

Henry Moore talked about the difference between size and scale in sculpture. The *size* of a piece is its measure in inches or meters. Its *scale* is its monumentality—impact, power, import. There are sculptures in hotel lobbies that loom huge—enormous in an atrium, twenty-five feet tall—but remain minuscule in scale and therefore disgusting. On the other hand, if the size of a piece is small but its scale is large, this disparity strengthens the object. There's an often-photographed carving by Moore from the 1930s, referred to as his "Chacmool" because of its archaic Mexican source. It looks huge pictured in catalogues but it is only thirty-seven inches long. A photograph of a 1976 two-part reclining figure, an alternate to his twenty-seven-foot Lincoln Center piece, occupies a full page in a Tate catalogue, looking enormous *and* monumental. In fact, the photograph renders a maquette, and the real bronze is eight-and-a-quarter inches long. There are wit, conflict, and energy in this opposition of size and scale. Sculptural equality of large size and scale happens often in a public place, like the Lincoln Center pool, where the sculpture's size and scale compete with the buildings around it. Other outdoor sculpture must compare itself to trees and hills.

Whenever Moore talked about sculpture I tried finding analogy to poetry. Sometimes I draft poems in which size is only *a little* too big for scale. I have had the thought: "Cut twenty percent, one line out of five. It doesn't much matter which lines I cut." On the other hand, there are poems in which size overwhelms scale, bluster or rhetoric or inflation disguising small import. Examples? Old examples of size exceeding scale disappear into the scholar's study. One needn't go back so far as *Leonidas.* William Morris's interminable poems, and many of Conrad Aiken's, embody huge size and small scale. In modern work as in ancient, failed long poems are forgotten: Stephen

Vincent Benét, Jeremy Ingalls. Inappropriate grandiosity disfigures some contemporary work, even in short or middle-length poems. Robert Penn Warren's size frequently exceeds scale. The progress and regress of James Dickey's poems provide examples: In an early poem like "The Heaven of Animals" we find a taut direct correlation between size and scale. By the time of "Falling" and "May Day Sermon," rhetoric and drive expand beyond the poem's potential, and it becomes the globe in the Marriott lobby. When some poets age into celebrity, and find more time for writing, they inflate like the walrus in Macy's parade. Or maybe mania takes over. Compare the average density of Berryman's *77 Dream Songs* with the average density of *His Toy, His Dream, His Rest*. Compare the energy and power of *Lord Weary's Castle* and *Life Studies* with the slackness of late Lowell.

Notions of "average density," not to mention scale or monumentality in poetry, demand elaboration or at least speculation. Let me begin definition by way of number. Scale is determined by the number of units, successfully resolved, relative to the size of the whole, and relative to their disparity. Mere numerosity does not provide variety enough: Scale derives also from the difference or opposition of the units. Probably dissimilarity contributes more to scale than number does—the diversity of the units (mostly emotional, but also physical and intellectual), their distance from each other or their apparent opposition. Ten million items similar in nature make an easy wholeness but remain boring; when disparate things—hate and love and dark and light and melanoma and astronauts and dogturds and daisies and fleas and vaginal orgasms and daylilies—come together to make a whole, we have a complex single object in which scale may equal or exceed size. Sometimes I think that poetry exists primarily to embody elements that appear impossible to combine or reconcile: opposing notions occupying the same point in the human psyche at the same time; or opposites simultaneously true, as in Heraclitus; or as in Catullus: "Odi et amo." Such combinations occupy our inward places.

Many small poems in English and American literature show monumentality, and their brevity lends to their power. In English, for a short poem huge in scale, think of Thomas Wyatt's

"They Flee From Me." It is multiple and it is brief. There are monumental sonnets by Shakespeare, Milton, Keats, Hopkins, and Hill. Think of Hardy; always think of Hardy. Emily Dickinson is brief and monumental. *The Waste Land,* medium length, is a triumph of scale over size. Some tiny poems by Robert Creeley and William Carlos Williams loom larger than other poets' book-length assemblages.

Of course Wordsworth's first *Prelude,* not to mention Milton's epic, embody size and scale together. So does "Song of Myself" but not "Evangeline." In far fewer lines, but not so brief as a sonnet, Marvell's "Horatian Ode" is huge in scale, immeasurably greater than its size. The same is true for Marvell's few best lyrics—while his lengthy unread satires lack scale; they were intended for their political moment, shallow or crude in their contrasts and contradictions. When their moment vanished so did they.

⮥

Naming the Skin

The form of a poem is the flesh of its art, and all good poems are formal. ("No *vers* is *libre*. . . .") As I argued in "Pythagoras, Form, and Free Verse," the best Creeley is as tightly formal as the best Wilbur. I'll say it again: Clonky and approximate terms like *sonnet,* and *iambic tetrameter,* even if they name attributes of the poem, may apply with accuracy to poems which are formally disgusting. Meter is real enough, but it has value only when it contributes to the intricate, intimate sound-form of the whole. Sound-form is a thousand small disparities and resemblances, essential to poems whether they are metrical or free of meter.

Conflict makes energy. There is no beauty and no form without conflict and its resolution. Form in a poem uses all the qualities of language in its accomplishment of tension and release. Sound-form uses pitch, duration, volume, the sequence of all these qualities and resemblances, or contrasts among them. It centers itself in two different areas of the body: in the limbs or muscles that respond to sequences of rhythm; and in the mouth that chews and sucks, especially on the resemblances among phonemes.

Infants identify objects by taking them into their mouths. Just so, we do not read a poem unless we chew and suck on it for a while. Most critics have been inhibited, in early life, by prohibitions against thumb-sucking; many poets appear embarrassed about their mouths. I used to accuse a poet-friend, who never wanted to listen to words like *assonance,* of being the victim of MOUTH-GUILT.

Form is not only sound-form, but it is always tension and release. For instance, a poem's diction may approach decorum, vi-

---

From *Poetry and Ambition: Essays 1982–88* (Ann Arbor: The University of Michigan Press, 1988).

olate it, and then resolve itself. Wordsworth, Whitman, and Williams use common speech in conflict with Latinate abstractions. Form is also syntax, from the periodic sentence, which provides its own tension and resolution, to combinations like the sequence of simple clauses extended by prepositional phrases in many of James Wright's poems, where a syntactical plainness contrasts with startling leaps of image. Form is the conflict and resolution that exists within the single metaphor; and form is also (as so often in Shakespeare) whole communities of metaphor, subsumed together, joining the apparently unjoinable. Form is also the development, conflict, and resolution of action or thought.

Narrative form by definition requires conflict and resolution, from the smallest anecdote to *Madame Bovary* or *The Tempest*. The model is genital: A progress of conflicts builds tension and culminates in release. This observation needs repeating as we approach an erotic poetic—but by itself it lacks critical utility: for the same stick-figure terms describe the structures of kitsch. An episode of *Seinfeld*, an installment of *Batman*, a Stephen King novel, and a thirty-second TV commercial may mimic the same erotic structures.

When we look into the erotics of sound-form, we discover that it is pre-genital, as I suggest in "Goatfoot, Milktongue, Twinbird." To summarize: Freud suggested that literary form resembled foreplesure, which is a reminiscence of the generalized sexuality of the infant. Sound-form derives from the whole eros of the body, starting from the infant's bodily pleasures. When we read with body as well as mind, our skin becomes alert to muscular rhythm, limbs writhing, motion of the baby's limbs that becomes adult spasms in intercourse; even more profoundly, sound-form uses the mouth's pleasure in lipping and tonguing the phonemes of milk and honey. Poetry derives its origins from the baby's gurgling and cooing in the utterance called autistic. If I am right about the etiology of sound-form, we reconstitute the origins of poetry only when we read with our bodies as well as our minds. Then poetry's wholeness reaches at the same time the conscious intellect, the dreamy associations of memory, and the sensory organs of the body—skin, mouth, and limbs.

This should not need saying but experience suggests that it does: If poetry's lineage derives power from the crib it does not remain there. If George Herbert and Emily Dickinson connect back to this cooing and gurgling, they put the crib to adult uses. Sometimes when people praise the sound of verse, they are dismissed as anti-intellectual. This objection depends upon the idea that intellect may be contained by abstraction and by reasonable discourse. But the whole human intellect thinks with its brains and with its marrow-bone. Insofar as intellect is translatable into abstraction, insofar as it can be paraphrased in synonyms, the language of intellect is inadequate to represent or embody human experience.

Our claim for poetry is not that it belongs to the body, but that it integrates body and mind, reason and unreason, that its fineness of articulation depends not only upon the generalizing intellect—which it usually includes—but upon tongue and skin as well. Sound-form is minute and pleasurable, but it is also expressive. We think not only by detached heads speaking general nouns, but by joyous mouth, by tapping foot, by swooping hand. Of all the arts, poetry embodies best the whole of human experience—because it combines in the same material of syllables abstract thought, historical allusion, dream, recollection, thigh, and mouth.

You would never know it, to read most of our critics and book reviewers. You would never know it, to sit in most classrooms. For all the manifestos of our critical leaders, be they new-critical, Marxist, Freudian, or deconstructionist, the troops in the trenches (reviewing, teaching) decade after decade provide paraphrases, summaries of content, and implications of intent. Poetry turns into white sugar on top of ideas and anecdotes. In classrooms the troops paraphrase poems and teach their students to do the same in papers and on final exams. Textbooks used in poetry courses reinforce the knowledge that everyone shares: A poem is something with an Answer which might as well be printed in the Back of the Book. The Answer is a prose equivalent to the poem, viewed as the idea the poet started with, before the poet charmingly decorated it with poetry. Book reviewers continually tell us what a poet's poems are *about*. The famous critics of our moment, as well as the classroom teachers, almost uniformly ignore the sound a poem makes. And so do most poets.

Talk is the enemy of poetry.

The counter-truth is the saw which affirms poetry's derivation from common speech, announced by Dante when he preferred Italian to Latin for the *Divine Comedy,* developed by Wordsworth, Whitman, Frost, and Williams. When a truth becomes a saw, when everybody knows it, that truth becomes a lie. If we suspect that admirers of Charles Bukowski and Anthony Hecht agree that "poetry derives from common speech," we had better start looking for what is wrong with the suggestion.

In America now, dogmas of the idiom promote not freedom of expression but narrowness of possibility. Naturalness of language becomes a limitation. To break a line anywhere except at the end of a clause—to use enjambment for emphasis and for the pleasure of sound-form—is derided as unnatural; only boring rhythms are tolerable. The name of William Carlos Williams is linked to the natural, to words of one syllable, or to the lowest common denominator. But read the poems: Like Robert Creeley, Williams is a master of the strange, stuttering line-break, and the line-break often serves to draw attention to his loud, sensuous assonance. (See pages 132–37.)

The tyranny of talk makes for a poetry, unlike the poems of Williams or Creeley, which is flat, plain, and unorganized—without rhythmic tension or conflict, and without the erotic mouth-pleasure of repeated diphthongs. It makes for the quickly readable, disposable poetry of notation, diary-entries slowed down by line-breaks according to the clauses of a simple syntax. If this poetry were distributed by Columbia Records, it would be called EASY READIN'.

In an issue of *Exquisite Corpse* (a poetry magazine with useful bad manners, usefully discontent with much of the usual scene; also with some bad ideas) a reviewer quotes Denise Levertov saying that contemporary poems are often "musically 'flat.'" The reviewer takes issue with Levertov, and quotes some lines by a contemporary, beginning:

> At the northern edge of this country
> where the rain halts only
> to be snow, the great glaciers wander
> the slow, indifferent centuries. . . .

The reviewer is disgusted by the musicality here, created by en-jambment, and asks: "Who actually talks like this today . . . ?" The reviewer invokes a shade: "Walt Whitman's diction . . . is far more contemporary and concise."

Now these lines are mildly decorative; the poet *uses* the line; is that his offense? Or is the word "halts" too fancy for our critic? Pity. Then the reviewer asks us to look at Whitman, who is ludicrously invoked as "contemporary and concise." Few read-ers seem to have noticed Whitman's conciseness, but what about his contemporaneousness? The great thing about Whitman is not his commonness, his limitation to the idiom of soldiers and horsecart-drivers: It is his openness to everything; he does not limit himself by poetic dogmas. Where another Victorian could not have uttered *privy,* he utters it happily; but he also *thee*'d and *thou*'d, used French and Spanish . . . EASY READIN' avoids complex syntax, foreign languages, historical or literary allusions, and big words, but Whitman feels free to use anything he damned well pleases. Look at the sentence which begins Whitman's "Out of the Cradle":

> Out of the cradle endlessly rocking,
> Out of the mocking-bird's throat, the musical shuttle,
> Out of the Ninth-month midnight,
> Over the sterile sands and the fields beyond, where the
>   child leaving his bed wander'd alone, bareheaded,
>   barefoot,
> Down from the shower'd halo,
> Up from the mystic play of shadows twining and
>   twisting as if they were alive,
> Out from the patches of briers and blackberries,
> From the memories of the bird that chanted to me,
> From your memories sad brother, from the fitful risings
>   and fallings I heard,

From under that yellow half-moon late-risen and swollen
    as if with tears,
From those beginning notes of yearning and love there
    in the mist,
From the thousand responses of my heart never to cease,
From the myriad thence-arous'd words,
From the word stronger and more delicious than any,
From such as now they start the scene revisiting,
As a flock, twittering, rising, or overhead passing,
Borne hither, ere all eludes me, hurriedly,
A man, yet by these tears a little boy again,
Throwing myself on the sand, confronting the waves,
I, chanter of pains and joys, uniter of here and hereafter,
Taking all hints to use them, but swiftly leaping beyond
    them,
A reminiscence sing.

This immense sentence is nobody's common speech, and it
never was: Twenty-two lines, varied in length, without meter
but with a strong falling rhythm, this sentence of two hundred
and eight words ends, by means of a grammatical inversion, with
its verb. It uses grammatical parallels: *Out, Out, Out, Over, Down,
Up, Out;* and then *From,* eight lines in a row. Slowly by repeti-
tion with variation it accumulates material; it sets a scene and
foreshadows the structure of the whole poem; then it departs
from its prepositional structure, its line-after-line of positioning
details, to approach its grammatical subject first in apposition—
"A man, yet by these tears a little boy again"—and after two
participial clauses names its subject: "I." Two more appositional
nouns, two more participles, and we arrive at object and verb:
"I . . . a reminiscence sing."

If Whitman had benefited from the advice of a workshop, he
would of course have avoided the embarrassing and pretentious
"sing," not to mention the unidiomatic (for his day as for ours)
grammatical inversion, not to mention the fancy Latinate ab-
straction of "reminiscence." Let us do him the favor of a rewrite
job:

> I remember once
> when I was a kid
> on Long Island
> in like September
> there was this bird . . .

(It's not only more idiomatic, it's more concise.) But we don't need to rewrite Whitman into the talk-poetry of our moment; thousands of people are doing it every day.

If there is print behind Whitman's sentence, it is the King James translation with its Hebrew prosody of parallel grammatical structures. If there is spoken language behind it, it is the powerful sentences, often periodic, of eighteenth- and nineteenth-century oratory—ten thousand Fourth of July orations denouncing the British Empire. The classic construction of the periodic sentence builds, graduates, gathers, accumulates and enlarges itself, becoming more tense and intense, until finally it achieves release or resolution, comes to rest or repose in the achievement of its verb. Tumescence, orgasm, and release.

Whitman's lines are voluptuous, and arouse the bodily reader's skin to an erotic receptivity which the rest of the poem magnificently fulfills. When he first published it, the first line was "Out of the rocked cradle. . . ." Revising, he picked up the falling rhythm of the second line and anticipated it in the first, beginning his sensuous music, which is more the pleasure of motion—rocking, from cradle through sexual intercourse—than the pleasure of the poem in the mouth.

But it is both, and it is both at once. Although some poets are leggy—moved by muscle and dance, by leg-and-limb sensuousness; Robert Frost's greatest pleasure in life, after Elinor and poetry, was walking fifteen miles a day—others like Dylan Thomas are mostly mouth. (A friend of mine, mixing admiration and distaste, described Dylan Thomas's style of reading aloud as "beating off his lips in public.") Shakespeare and Keats—both of whom could do more things at once than most poets in the language—reach simultaneously both mouth and leg.

Therefore it is useful, when we talk about sound-form, to insist that we talk about discernibly different qualities of sound. Even within mouth-sound, we are comparing phonemes in their pitch, their duration, their volume, and in motions that the tongue takes to make them. Mostly we delight in resemblances, as in assonance; but the mouth requires contrast as well, to set off resemblance, like a silver coin mounted on black velvet. In leg-sound, we surely take account of syntax; therefore we observe pitch in another sense—not the characteristic high and low of a vowel, but the lowering pitch of a phrase set off by commas or by parentheses, and the raised pitch of a question. In both leg-sound and mouth-sound we are affected by the length of time it takes to move from one word to another, so that duration is common to both; syntax and punctuation, as in the comma or its gestural necessity, also affect the time we take moving along.

A line I have recited ten thousand times ends Thomas Hardy's "During Wind and Rain." The poem as a whole is written in a simple diction with familiar details and descriptions, only three metaphors in its twenty-eight lines; no similes at all. Plain language sets itself against a firm and artful stanza, and sound seldom calls attention to itself—until this last line. Then, in a poem spoken during wind and rain, lamenting the inevitable ends of things, centering on families that work and play together only to grow old and die, Hardy writes: "Down their carved names the rain-drop ploughs."

This line is a banquet to the mouth, as erotic as it is calorific, a total *pleasure*—except that of course it speaks out of mourning, depression, and loneliness: Conflict makes energy. The mouth's banquet begins with the stately slow pound of the beating foot. All syllables except *the* are loudish, even *their;* most are long as well. The first and last syllables repeat the same extended diphthong, great for chewing on; the last syllable elongates itself further by adding the *z*-consonant. Framed inside this frame is another pair of diphthongs, an *abba* arrangement, with *names* and *rain.* Slowness and length are accomplished not only by long double-vowels; there is also the consonant-string, so that we have to pick our way over the boulders of four consonants—*r, v, d, n*—to make the journey from *carved* to *names;* then there is the great enforced hiatus between the two *p*'s of *drop* and *ploughs;* we cannot say "droploughs." In an earlier version of the poem Hardy wrote "drops plough," where the one word slides easily into the other, and the line ends without the prolonging *z*. We may be grateful for revision.

If we cannot hear the difference between *drop ploughs* and *drops plough,* we need to learn to read poetry all over again. And if we can read the first sentence of "Out of the Cradle" without a happy exhaustion that resembles sexual arousal and its fulfillment; if we can read Keats's "To Autumn" in silence without tiring our throats and without feeling excitement in our skin; if we can read Robert Frost for one hour without the leg-weariness that should follow a long walk—well, either we are in very good shape or we need to send our bodies back to first grade.

Let Hardy's line stand as example of thinking by muscle and tongue. If we read it with our bodies as well as our heads, its pounding slowness and its held diphthongs and its roughening consonants deepen and elongate the sense. Its last syllable extends itself by the repeated diphthong, by the long consonant, *and* by a metaphor that requires decades of water to cut into stone. If we read it only to paraphrase, we might as well be reading it translated into German, translated back into English as "Across their etched inscriptions the drop of rain cuts," or "The drop of rain digs into their incised surnames."

These paraphrases resemble not only translation; they resemble the footnotes, interpreting metaphor, that Norton uses in its anthologies.

Maybe this needs saying also: It is *boring* to read people talking about sound, to read print that tells us "four consonants—*r, v, d, n*"—and I am sorry to be boring. When we read poems silently, we do not respond to poems by making sentences in our heads about the *abba* arrangement of diphthongs. Instead, we take pleasure, and the pleasure we take is surely erotic, and we need not worry about where it's coming from. But when we understand that other readers do not receive the same signals—when we realize that most teachers merely paraphrase everything—and that the EASY READIN' folks deny sensuousness—we may look back at the poem to try to name what excites us.

Naming the skin is boring—it is easier when one can read aloud—but the skin is not boring.

Another note: I suppose that I am trying to look into the erotic nature of the "musicality" of verse—but let us avoid the musical metaphor, which introduces at least two confusions and does more harm than good. In the first place, this metaphor compares things that are too close to each other and not close enough; it is like describing a hen by comparing her to an eagle. Music and poetry both make noises, as hens and eagles both have wings, but music exists largely independent of idea, and the noises of poetry function in conjunction with sense. Music makes allusion by onomatopoeia, like "piping of plenty," but it is never so referential as "carved names." Even when words make nonsense, their disconnection from sense is a statement: "I am deliberate nonsense"; "I am a series of prepositions which cannot be understood as meaningful." When Chomsky tried to make up a perfectly meaningless sentence, "The stone is dreaming of Vienna," he sounded like a weekend surrealist.

Then there is another problem: Often music and poetry are compared in a way that has nothing to do with noise but with a distaste for subject-matter, with symbolist vagueness, with a fraying and blurring of denotation in the service of suggestiveness. Thus a poem may be called "musical" although it pays no attention to sound.

Let us ban the metaphor that ascribes musicality to poetry. Poetry makes pleasing and useful noises. Or it does not.

There is a different analogy, comparing poetry to another art, which I find more useful. Music and poetry are time-arts, and one thing follows another. Poetry's form, however—especially sound-form—creates an illusion of stillness, like the repose after orgasm, or like the stasis which Stephen Dedalus defines for Cranly in *Portrait of the Artist as a Young Man*. I like the analogy which compares poetry to sculpture, the work of art achieving a marble or a bronze repose. Carved into the shape of flesh, readable only with the flesh's help, poetry reaches the voluptuous solidity of stone.

One more comparison: Some poems are like rivers, some like mountains. I prefer the mountain-poem, because poetry already flows as a river does; when a river tries to become a mountain, the conflict is energetic. But maybe the river and the mountain are simply two kinds of poem. In which case, it is best that

mountain incorporate river, or river mountain: motion and sta-
sis together.

When I talk about sound-form—as I tend to do—I concen-
trate on mouth-sound (my heart is in my mouth) but leg-
sound is just as pleasurable and possibly more expressive. Leg-
sound works by syntax and uses pitch. It exists in good prose,
in masters as different as Hemingway ("In the fall the war was
always there but we did not go to it any more"), Gibbon, and
James. In poetry we control the sentence not only by syntax but
by line-breaks. Frost is the master of "sentence-sounds," as he
calls them, and it was his pleasure to break the sentence across
the line:

> I'm going out to fetch the little calf
> That's standing by the mother. It's so young,
> It totters when she licks it with her tongue.
> I shan't be gone long.—You come too.

So natural, and yet so tightly made. Meter and line enforce par-
ticular stresses—"I *shan't* be *gone* long"—and we don't feel
forced. So often in Frost the sentence in its connections mimics
the mind's motion, and does it with the foreplay-teasing of delay
before fulfillment, a thinking-with-legs which defies translation
or paraphrase. Or look at Robert Creeley's "The Hill":

> It is sometime since I have been
> to what it was had once turned me backwards,
> and made my head into
> a cruel instrument.
>
> It is simple
> to confess. Then done,
> to walk away, walk away,
> to come again.
>
> But that form, I must answer,
> is dead in me, completely,
> and I will not allow it
> to reappear—

Saith perversity, the wilful,
the magnanimous cruelty,
which is in me
like a hill.

Here is an agonized teasing, as the self-accusing voice stumbles
in awkwardness toward moral insight, achieved in Creeley's rare
simile at the end. Rhythm mimics or embodies the mind's mo-
tion. Creeley is master of syntax, of sentence-sounds, with
maybe the most original and compelling ear of any contempo-
rary poet. In his New England voice, relentless in self-examina-
tion, and in his delicate leg-motion control of sentence, syntax,
and pitch, this master of free verse is Frost's true heir. Look for
comparison at Frost's awkward mimetic syntax beginning "Di-
rective": "Back out of all this now too much for us."

Among my contemporaries, maybe the Black Mountain
poets make the best noises, the most various and adaptable and
ingenious combinations that achieve conflict and resolution.
Denise Levertov had an ear even sharper than her eye. Their
masters were masters: Of all modern poets, surely Pound is the
most sensuous; the skin of his poems, when he chooses, is per-
fectly sexual. Williams is almost as fleshy, wholly unpuritanical in
his erotic richness of sound. With Williams the lines and line-
breaks themselves are erotic. There is nothing sensuous in the
prose version of WCW's famous wheelbarrow: "So much de-
pends upon a red wheelbarrow glazed with rainwater beside the
white chickens." Or break the lines at the expected, obvious,
syntactical breaks, like most inept free verse; there is nothing
erotic about an EASY READIN' version either:

> so much depends upon
> a red wheelbarrow
> glazed with rainwater
> beside the white chickens

This arrangement of lines is obvious because the lines break
where the phrases pause. If you were saying the prose sentence
aloud, and had to pause three times because you were out of
breath, you would pause where these lines end. The arrangement

slows the sentence down, and maybe it causes us to pay more attention to the visual imagery—the wheelbarrow is redder, the rain wetter, and the chickens whiter—but it is rhythmically boring. The final version, with its etymological wit, with its unnatural line-breaks between parts of compounds, with its mouthy concentration on assonance, is a poem of intense sensuousness:

> so much depends
> upon
>
> a red wheel
> barrow
>
> glazed with rain
> water
>
> beside the white
> chickens

This arrangement releases the sound, and sound releases meaning or import. The poem becomes exact, fixed, and permanent—like a carving. The words are exactly the same as they were in the prose sentence above, or in the four-line version, but now have become a poem.

When you look at its shape, its visual shape alone announces that it is deliberate. Just to the quick glance, the visual arrangement says, "I am orderly. I am arranged on purpose. There is nothing sloppy or careless or inadvertent in me." But the sound is the big thing, not the look of it. The real poem has much pause, much silence—and it has pause in places where, if you were saying the sentence as prose, it would not pause at all: between "wheel" and "barrow," between "rain" and "water." These line-breaks give us two nouns for one, separating the original components of a compound word, giving us twice as much thinginess. (Even in the first line, the line-break splits a verb phrase into its parts, hanging a preposition from a verb that originally meant "hang from.") This visual arrangement, turned audible, releases the sound of the poem, giving a sound-pleasure like the eye-pleasure of the thinginess. By line-break and visual shape, the poet's language becomes sensuous. The two long *ay*'s of "glazed" and "rain-" come in one line, as later the two long *eye*s of "-side" and "white." Both "rain" and "white" come at the ends of lines, so that we hold onto these longish diphthongs. We taste the pleasure of repeated sound.

Williams is a bad example for those who preach simplicity. Look at Williams's "To Waken an Old Lady," with its mixtures of natural and unnatural. After the hurtling beginning,

> Old age is
> a flight of small
> cheeping birds

in which simple language conflicts with outrageous metaphor and with swift hesitations at unnatural line-breaks, Williams ends the poem with the birds momentarily resting,

> and the wind tempered
> by a shrill
> piping of plenty.

Abstraction ends it, directive of feeling, with an enjambment between adjective and noun which allows alliterative nouns to frame the last line, with onomatopoeia (*e*-sounds in the unstressed syllables repeat the cheeping), and doubtless with classical allusion, for "piping" recalls not only birdsong but the pipes of Pan whose music stills the wind.

Such are the resolutions—allusive, rhythmical, mouthy; erotic by analogy and by reference to forepleasure and infantile sexuality—that make the poem's art.

To concentrate on any one quality, of the many qualities essential to poetry, is to fail complete reading: to concentrate on image, on thought, on gross form like pentameter or villanelle, or on the erotics of sound-form. If conflict makes energy, wholeness or manyness of attention helps to make conflict, and in a poem every word must do everything at once. When poets concentrate on making Beautiful Sound—Swinburne and Poe—they often parody themselves; we find ourselves bored by a movement all in one direction, by the denial of manyness, ambivalence, and conflict. Rough needs smooth as smooth needs rough, naturalness needs unnaturalness, simple needs complex, and up requires down—for the wholeness of art. There can be no resolution if there is no disparity, for there is nothing to be resolved. Total concentration on sound-form—or on any single quality—makes a poem as isolated as masturbation.

Concentration on sound-form is scarcely a common problem among contemporary American poets; the common problem is the lack of any attention to sound or form.

The question is: If we lack it, where do we go to find it? Clearly much of the answer must lie within the poet, for the sources of the mouth-and-leg pleasures that make the poem's skin remain in our own dark places, possibly in places darker and deeper than the strata where we find metaphors. To reach these places in ourselves, we use our reading of poems by others. Contemporary masters of sound—back from Creeley and Levertov (Simpson, Wright, Kinnell) to Rexroth, Roethke, Williams, and Pound. But we can also learn these sensuous pleasures by reading language remote from our own, in which we are less subject to possible imitation: Keats and Shakespeare, Marvell, Jonson, and Wordsworth. When pronunciation differs because of world and time, it usually differs uniformly, so that altered phonemes remain identical.

We must read aloud; we must listen. We must roll vowels on our tongues, chew at consonants; we must keep the beat with arm and leg.

And we must read the original language instead of translation. Of course some translators make good noises but they do not make the noises of the original. We can translate gross form, using the same meter or rhyme scheme; we can translate the thrust of the original, the larger erotic structure; but we cannot translate the intimacies of sound-form: Almost always a translation omits the oldest and most primitive sources of eros in poetry, present in the original, which provide poetic art's connections back. If we concentrate on reading translations, we lose out on forepleasure.

Although our lack of sound-form may partly derive from attentions to translation, I think it mostly represents a residual puritanism, MOUTH-GUILT, from shame over infantile sexuality. Thumb-sucking. Many years ago the American psychoanalyst A. A. Brill characterized poets as people who like to chew and mouth beautiful words. I agree. If poetry only begins there, with sound-form, at least it *begins* there—with the sensuousness of words rolled on the tongue, bumping against the insides of the lips; with the cadence of thrashing limbs. For dogmatists of naturalness, a line like Keats's "Thou watchest the last oozings, hours by hours" is disgusting—because it is orally erotic. This disgust, if it be consistent, must also condemn Hardy, Pound, and Wilbur—and it should also condemn Williams, Levertov, and Creeley. Poems that lack sound-form may mimic the plot structure of excitement and orgasm, but their texture rejects mouth, skin, and muscles; it is sex without foreplay, roll over and fall asleep.

On Moving One's Lips,
While Reading

Miss Stephanie Ford stepped to the blackboard. My first-grade teacher was angular, elderly, and black-haired. The day before, Miss Ford had announced, "Tomorrow, we will begin to learn to read." The whole school year, we had prepared for this day. It was a moment, I told myself at the age of six, that I would remember forever. My house was a temple of reading. Every night after supper, when my parents finished the afternoon newspaper, and my father the work he brought home from the office, they concealed their faces behind books. For my mother it was often a mystery: Agatha Christie, Erle Stanley Gardner. My father read historical novels: Kenneth Roberts; *Anthony Adverse.* Reading was what grown-ups did; now I, eager to overcome the obstacle of infancy, would join the reading world.

Miss Ford drew a series of sharp lines, making large printed letters, which we had learned as the alphabet, stringing together T, H, A, and T—white on black. She stood back and raised her long wooden pointer. "That," she said in her stiff clear voice, "is 'that.'" If her enunciation was stilted, it was not cold, because she moved her lips in an exaggerated fashion—she opened her mouth wide; her tongue curled and snapped—so that we might understand or imitate the oral formation of sounds. This angular, elderly, black-haired person taught us to read by acts of mouth and body.

We had studied the alphabet for weeks by chanting it aloud in unison and copying it in pencil on large yellowish lined sheets of paper. All through grammar school, much of our learning was memorization and repetition by rote, "two plus two is

From *Principal Products of Portugal* (Boston: Beacon Press, 1995).

four," whatever the subject: state capitals, the presidents with their years of office. Eight years later, when we started Latin in high school, we singsonged conjugated Latin verbs for Mr. Brown who always wore brown. Meanwhile we repeated multiplication tables, the dates of battles, poems, the principal products of Portugal, and the Gettysburg Address.

We did not speak pieces competitively as our parents and grandparents had done; entertainment by movies and radio had replaced recitation of poems and oratory. A pity. Loss of recitation helped to detach words from the sounds they make, which is the castration of reading. This loss took the name of educational reform, which attacked not speaking pieces but memorization in general. Beginning in the late 1920s, spreading over years into the educational trenches, American educators crusaded against memorization. Doubtless the crusade was largely good. There are better ways to learn history, social studies, and geography. Reasoning by rule is more useful for mathematics than memorizing tables for consultation. (As for balancing a checkbook, our calculators will do that for us.) Learning French or Spanish by talking it, or reading real examples of its literature, will bring us inside the syntax of a culture better than the rote imprint of conjugations.

But when they discarded recitation of dates and declensions, educators threw out as well the practice of reciting and performing literary work, and with it the habit of understanding literature by hearing it, by absorbing the noises it makes. An older culture centered on the written word as performed aloud for edification and entertainment. Before the automobile took farmers to the movies, before the radio's chatter ended the millennia of our silences, our entertainment was local: piano solo, drama group, chorus, barbershop quartet—and recitation or performance of the written word.

When we looked at print a hundred years go, we imbibed it as *sound* (with or without committing it to memory) at school or church, in nursery or living room. People performed literary art, or popular entertainment, even while doing other tasks. Memorization let the woodworker recite "The Raven" or "The Heathen Chinee" while turning a lathe, and the mother chant "Baa, baa, black sheep" for her baby while her hands assembled a pie. On Sunday the preacher read from the book, prophet and gospel; on worknights after milking, an elocutionary cousin performed chapters from Scott and Dickens. At school we recited gems of political oratory and stanzas from the poets.

In a few blessed backwaters, school children still do prize speaking once a year. My town of Danbury, New Hampshire, is a surviving culture of the nineteenth century, like those Greek colonies in the Italian hills, founded four centuries before Christ, that still spoke Greek after the Second World War. Prize Speaking Night at Danbury School is a measure of what we were, a memory alive reconstituting the old world. I recommend it.

Technology exists to make memory unnecessary; we invented the alphabet so that we needed no longer memorize Homer. But the alphabet was a device for the preservation of noise not of information. For a long time the written poem was a mnemonic device, and the spoken poem was the poem itself. It was more than a thousand years before humans invented silent reading. Literature was something heard not seen. Almost until print took over, literary performance (and perception) was sound not sight, mouth and ear not eye and mind. When silent reading became common, roughly during the Renaissance, literature flourished—but: *This silent reading remained a noisy matter.*

Until recently, when we have read silently we have heard every word. Spending our childhoods listening to people read aloud or recite, ourselves reciting and performing in school and for the fun of it, we could not read in silence without inwardly hearing the sounds of the words. Even people too shy to read aloud heard print make noises in their heads.

Even now, if we read literature properly, we hear the words on the page—in our own minds. Hearing the words, we make constant unconscious decisions about tone, feeling, and import; we remain alert to the gestures of words. Hearing the words, we cannot skim; passivity is impossible. By imagining how the words would sound if spoken aloud, we understand their tone. If we see on the page the sentence "Mr. Rumble nodded his head," our inward voicing requires us to understand whether Mr. Rumble disapproved, or was outraged, or merely passed on information ("No, it's not raining").

If we do not hear the words inside our heads, we are reading passively. Speed reading is sloppy reading, an abomination, and turns the reader into a slack-jawed receiver of surfaces, of mere information. We hear about Mr. Rumble's head gesture but we pass over its implication. When we allow words to be abstracted to the page or screen, detached from the body and the sensations of the human, we abandon the site of feelings. Do Mr. Rumble's palms sweat? Does he feel the start of an erection? Does his toe hurt? Mr. Rumble looks bland and speaks without affect, like a voice generated by a computer. Who knows what Mr. Rumble is thinking?

Of course sometimes we need only information. By necessity all of us must learn a selective difference in modes of reading. We must read quickly in order to process newspapers, manuals of instruction, and business journals—or we would go crazy; it would take us a month to read the Sunday *Times,* hearing every word. We would lose our minds if we listened with an inner ear to the instructions that come with 1040A.

On the other hand, when we read for joy—for beauty, for intelligence, for understanding—we must hear the words in order to read well. If we move our lips when we read silently, fine; it will slow us down, and we will read better. Whether moving our lips or not, we must test literature's words in our mouths. When I read good poems, in perfect silence, after twenty minutes my throat muscles feel tired.

Most people have become passive readers, and passive reading is diminished literacy. Television takes most of the blame, but there were earlier reasons: The motor car invented shopping and the movie, for Americans who lived outside cities. There was also radio, wonderful radio: We stopped singing for each other and let Rudy Vallee take over. We listened no more to public recitations of "Little Orphan Annie" because radio soap operas were available every day. We didn't need "The Owl and the Pussycat" because we had Fibber McGee and Molly.

But . . . when the automobile replaces walking, we need to take up jogging. We can learn to read again, and maybe to move our lips, by becoming conscious of the sound of words. Taped books help. Commuting, we hear words acted, language made human by emphatic mouths, lips, and tongues. (It helps if the book is literature and entire.) Hearing books helps restore blood and flesh to language, bringing sound back to literary experience. But, listening to tapes, we are only receptors: Actors do the action; other voices, other minds make decisions of tone. Better is reading aloud ourselves, preferably as a regular part of the day, and such reading aloud is not only for parents entertaining children. My late wife and I read a hundred books aloud, thirty minutes a day of *Huckleberry Finn, Madame Bovary,* the *New Testament,* Fitzgerald's *Odyssey,* and enormous quantities of Henry James. It's a local perversity, perhaps, but James feels superb on the tongue. I've read every syllable of *The Ambassadors* aloud twice. I've read aloud *Portrait of a Lady,* wonderful late stories like "The Beast in the Jungle," *The Golden Bowl,* and *Wings of the Dove.* Maybe they read aloud so well because James dictated them.

The voice that reads late James aloud must not be monotone. To read parenthesis within parenthesis the reader must drop pitch and build it up again, and a sentence by Henry James becomes an exercise for voice-athletes to train by, pitch and pause in particular. Representing James by your mouth, lips, tongue, contracted throat, and vocal cords, you accomplish literary analysis by means of your vocal equipment. Your larynx could write a doctoral thesis on the Jamesian parenthesis.

⚛

The Way to Say *Pleasure*

1

Poetry and pleasure. I think of a radio talk-show host who oper-
ates out of New York. When I did a new book of poems a pub-
licist set me up to talk with him at noon live from a restaurant.
The man was brisk, shrewd, attractive, funny, and mindless. Once
he turned reflective. "I don't know, Don," he mused; "I didn't use
to care about poetry and that sort of thing. . . . Nothing but
the almighty dollar. . . . But last summer I bought a boat. . . . I
spent weekends just floating on the lake, doing nothing, and . . .
you know what I mean?"

Thus was the art of Dante and Homer—not to mention
Keats, "Casey at the Bat," and Marianne Moore—identified with
doing nothing. (I remember a functional definition delivered by
a professor of philosophy: "Your house burns down; they say: 'Be
philosophical. Don't think about it.'") Of course poets them-
selves praise lethargy. The author of "Sleep and Poetry," as well
as "Ode on Indolence," died at twenty-five: Still, Jack Stillinger's
newest edition of Keats's *Poems* runs to five hundred and thirty-
five large pages while the *Letters* come in two volumes. Walt
Whitman praised loafing; he also figured that *Leaves of Grass* was
twice as long as the New Testament. We all agree, working like
hell, that poetry reminds us of leisure which rhymes with pleas-
ure if that's the way you pronounce it. What else does it remind
us of?

(a) Making love (b) Eating (c) Thinking (d) Playing games (e)
September (f) Walking (g) Standing still (h) Listening to music (i)
Looking at pictures (j) Touching sculpture (k) Smelling garlic (l)

From *Poetry and Ambition: Essays 1982–88* (Ann Arbor: The University of
Michigan Press, 1988).

Goodness (m) Sin (n) Giving (o) Duplicate bridge (p) Receiving (q) Arguing (r) Dancing (s) Watching dancers (t) Watching athletes (u) Looking at flowers (v) Smelling flowers (w) Doing nothing (x) Osso bucco (y) Suffering (z) Death

2

"Poetry is the supreme result of the entire language," says Joseph Brodsky. Poetry is what language is for, what language exists to move toward. Language becomes poetry insofar as the poet employs the whole word: its vowels, consonants, characteristic pitches, volume, duration; its sequences as they connect with surrounding sequences, for prosody is always contextual; its history: etymological development back and forth across ideas often encompassing contradictions and swift alternations of feeling; each word's associations by sound and shape with other words of its own language and other languages, not to mention allusion potential and genuine; its syntactic moves within the sentence by which it walks, for syntax is sinew. And at some point or other the poet must attend to the word's contemporary lexical reference.

Say that a short poem includes a hundred words. Say that each word includes a hundred edges and dimensions: The tiny poem flashes a potential ten thousand facets the poet must be aware of, wary of; the reader intent on pleasure must take in the ten thousand things.

Ordinary prose uses ten facets a word. Poetry is the supreme result of the entire language. Except as poetry, language is poorly used—and for that matter most poetry is language poorly used. As I write these paragraphs, how much of *paragraph* do I use? Insofar as translation can substitute for the original, so much is language not used for its supreme result; insofar as *paragraph* equals *caput* equals *Absatz* equals *parrafo*, so far is the word as nourishing as sawdust. What do we say when we say *pain? Emotion? Imagination?* Saying these words to each other, we nod our heads as if we agreed. We conspire to understand each other. But poetry—the supreme result—embodies or enforces a fierce nominalism. What does *pleasure* mean?

And tear our Pleasures with rough strife,
Thorough the Iron gates of Life.

Marvell's wholeness takes part of itself from the violence of "tear" (referring not only to maidenhead or peritoneum but to engines of warfare) rubbing against the lexical softness of "pleasures" and altering it. Part derives from the *f*-sounds in "rough" and "strife," part from the volume that rises four equal steps in the last four syllables of the first line. Word multiplied by word cuts a thousand facets in one couplet.

Poetry is not only the supreme result, it is the only possible result of language taken to extremity. And it is so particular, so contextual, and so historical that it will not suffer paraphrase or translation.

3

"If it ain't a pleasure it ain't a poem," said William Carlos Williams in a reading at Harvard. Between poems he talked about the vernacular, about poetry's sounds, about the vividness of direct impressions of experience. All art gives pleasure, he said; his asides enacted examples of his own.

But people take pleasure in all sorts of things. The critic's pleasure as she writes about Keats is clear, an attractive enthusiasm, as she imposes implausible structures to make the Odes uniform. The Nietzscheans of deconstruction take pleasure in argument, in talking for victory. As for pleasures of sound, people find pleasure in Poe and Liberace; what do we accomplish by calling them wrong? More people take pleasure in the dramatic structure of a Miller Lite commercial, one Sunday afternoon, than enjoy Shakespeare and Chekhov in a decade. Art including poetry is pleasure if you are the sort of chap who likes that sort of thing.

Charles Baudelaire wrote the inscription carved on our boudoir-schoolroom: "Pleasure is a science, and the exercise of the five senses requires a special initiation, which is reached only through inclination and need."

The pleasure of sculpture happens first in hands that would touch: texture and shape; later in muscles that would lift: bulk, volume, heft. The eye seeing stone conducts to hand and muscle for response. Some sculpture uses shapes of lightness, flight, airiness (Calder, Ritchie) that require the imagination of weight in conflict with weightlessness.

We watch ballet with our legs.

For literature mouth is the receptor. Commonly we speak of ear but ear is less sensuous than mouth; say it lies halfway between the mouth which has no brains and the eye which is intellectual. For most critics, the reading eye drills straight back into the brain with no stop at the mouth or the muscles. For the whole-reader of literature, the eye is channel of entry, and the material that enters there is first tasted and chewed by the mouth, then distributed to muscles of the limbs. When we imbibe literature audibly, at a poetry reading, our ears funnel to our mouths. The thinking brain, an invaluable if late participant in the sequence, also attends life's feast; it sits below the salt.

Some mind-pleasures in poetry are literary, like allusion; others are psychological like catharsis; there is also the chess-playing pleasure of logic. All come long after we taste the work's verbal tangible (chewable) body. Many readers ignore (fear?) or remain senseless to primary body-pleasure. When critics write about poetry, usually they might describe work translated from another language. If the level addressed is translatable, what gets left out? The notion that there is a noumenal poem underneath the flesh of linguistic circumstance denies the skin of literature. Brodsky, who reads Auden magnificently, would have us translate Russian poets keeping their meters intact, but Tsvetayeva's trochee brought into English sails us to the shore of Gitchi Gumee—or "The Raven" with caesuras. The spirit that resides in prosody dies in translation. It is false to think that we can encode and translate an essence: Platonism is anti-poetic. Information gives pleasure but never so much as a headrub.

It is literature if, when you read it aloud, or hear it clearly when reading in silence, it gets better. Of course Shakespeare and Frost and Bishop and Dryden and Hardy and Dickinson and Whitman are best aloud. So is great prose like Henry James, Thoreau, Hume, and Gibbon. We must read literature with our bodies. A neurosis of the academy detaches head from body. Literature is unseparable. Literature is coherent. Literature is not talking heads. We must not read Henry James with our eyes. We may read him with our toes maybe or our hair follicles but never never never never with our eyes. He made his greatest work walking up and down saying it aloud. We should read him aloud whether or not we make a sound.

5

Reading is maybe three thousand years old. For the first half of its life no one read in silence; reading in silence did not become commonplace until after Gutenberg. Rich Romans paid slaves to read aloud while they dressed, bathed, and took walks—and even when they read in solitude they read aloud. When they heard a slave read they listened with their mouths. Even a century ago much of our culture connected the word with the mouth. Again, by 1930 this outloud culture was mostly dead and there's no point in whining about it. But in the 1930s American poets forgot how to scan; *Understanding Poetry* is a gravestone over the corpse of meter. Connections between print and mouth are largely canceled.

Bodiless intellects tell us there's no author, and quite likely no text: In the ancient war between the poets and the philosophers—theorists are philosophers; none reads a poem except Harold Bloom—the removal of the author from the text is the intellectual's final solution. Plato finally expels the poets by a nifty expedient: Looking them in the eye he declares that they don't exist. Remember Richard Wilbur's couplet:

> We milk the cow of the world, and as we do
> We whisper in her ear, "You are not true."

6

When we bring the body back to the book, the book exists for the mind to receive, to mull over, to react to, to learn from. We must not be aesthetic airheads praising style over substance as if we cheered Democrats over Republicans. *Let it all in:* But its wholeness enters only through the body's door. Doubtless the alphabet was a mistake, but I suppose that silent reading is worse. Nonetheless if we are aware of absences inherent in silent reading we can recover the sensuous loss. After practice in reading aloud, we can sense the physical words (in throat, mouth, and muscles) as we read in silence.

Thomas Henry Huxley once accused poets of "sensual caterwauling." I like that. Serious people deplore sensuous mouthy frivolities. I suppose that the most gorgeous lines in our language belong to John Keats in the Odes, and among the Odes "To Autumn" contains the most mouth juice. Everybody knows it, but let me chew on a couple of lines anyway:

> Then in a wailful choir the small gnats mourn
>> Among the river sallows, borne aloft
>>> Or sinking as the light wind lives or dies. . . .

Load every rift with béarnaise! Assonance is loud with "light" and "dies," subtle with the short *o*'s, and the liquid consonance thrills the tongue: "wailful," "choir," "mourn," "river," "sallows," "borne," "aloft" . . . Leg-pleasures of rhythm, separate from meter and aided by meter, follow close behind mouth-pleasures. Of course it is too obvious for mention, this sensuous caterwauling, this chewing and mouthing, except that . . . When Helen Vendler wrote three hundred pages on Keats's Odes, paraphrase- and source-hunting, she did not consider it worthy of remark that these poems occur in lines, in meter, in stanzas, with rhythm, assonance, and consonance—or that they make a noise when spoken aloud.

7

The body's reading opens up bodily pleasures which leave us vulnerable to pain. Sensitivity to pleasure does not enlarge without at the same time an enlargement of the sensitivity to pain. Now the bodily pleasure of poetry is itself unmixed; it is there or it is not there. Ugly language is not painful but disgusting or boring: The mouth does not hurt reading bad poetry; the leg muscles do not ache. The whole poem, past its sensuous mouth- and leg-connection, includes pain by reference not by form. Granted that there are some small poems, like Herrick on Julia's clothes, that carry no pain; the pleasures that they carry are nei- ther profound nor long-lasting. The pure song of their joy is brief, pleasing, and shallow: It is not Marvell's "Horatian Ode," nor "London," nor "Home Burial," nor "Burnt Norton," nor the five dozen best sonnets. Although the brief joy-song is fairly rare, it is what unreading people call *poetry*—childlike, happy, brainless, dear, impractical, and pure: sunbathing on a boat.

Great poems in paraphrase sound like the mutterings of a de- pressive poised on the bridge: One of the many troubles with paraphrase is that the body's pleasure (like Tsvetayeva's trochee) will not translate. When Shakespeare's sonnet speaks of his own dying while he gazes at his youthful love, his joyous vowels sing along with the intricate resolutions of his metaphors: The one set of words brings ecstasy and despair together at once. At once everything is whole and rent—and *everything is neither if every- thing is not both.*

As we walk with a set smile among children studying at school, our despairing thoughts sing forth in lines profound in pleasure. The king bows his head for the executioner's ax as on the silk sheets of a bed.

8

Literature is largely although not entirely the product of maniacs.

Any notion that connects genius with abnormal psychology is routinely dismissed with the epithet *romantic.* Conventional minds need to dismiss the notion of functional aberration. But discovery necessitates eccentricity because the center is already known. Of course it must be noted that neither mania nor any- thing else guarantees discovery.

The incidence of bi-polar mood disorder in artists, especially in writers, rises high in proportion to the rest of the population. Bi-polarity implies gross swings of mood, but not necessarily the madness of delusion or suicide. Some manic-depressives—including Robert Lowell and Theodore Roethke—enter institutions for thought-disorders not just mood-disorders. In any case, bi-polarity is painful and wasteful: Mania is self-deceptive and depression self-destructive. At extreme manic states one lacks judgment so thoroughly that one is unlikely to write well; in extreme depression one cannot lift a pencil. Recent pharmacological discovery allows many patients respite from these extremes.

But also: Manic inspiration can make great art. The confidence and energy of a limited manic state is the divine afflatus, the sense of possession or transport, inspiration, the vatic voice that speaks unbidden. Mania characterizes not only poets but saints, mystics, mathematicians, and inventors. The poet's inspiration is a heightened ability to perceive and embody previously unrecognized identities. It reaches past pleasure to joy. Pleasure is the body's and allows the poem its entry. Joy is the spirit's and responds to what mania provides: the insight that recognizes and establishes connections and resemblances. Metaphor is the spirit's rhetoric as mania is its chemistry; the psyche which we experience as immaterial works through material means.

Mania is essential to the survival of the species, and to the large machine of civilization; it enhances not the individual but the collective. Manic-depressives may kill themselves when they are down but when they are up they give birth. Creation needs destruction. By inventing epics and wheels when they are inspired, manics provide for the whole machine. When they are low they provide nothing—but they do not break the machine. (They break themselves and people around them.) When they write books they write out of their experience, much of which is hopeless. They report on loss and despair, which are endemic to all life, in the flesh and body of their art which is pleasure. This marriage of dark and light, this wedding of pain and pleasure, makes literature's bi-polar wholeness. Poetry weds the unweddable and embodies the conditions we live under: twigs of dread, nest of pleasure.

There are some pleasures without pain. These are closest to the surface of the skin. Take the word *pleasure* itself. The way to say *pleasure* is to take a long time in the saying: Drag it out, and while you say it, lick it all over like a nipple. Hit the *p* lightly, then glide over the slippery *l*, touching it lightly with the tip of the tongue; slide languorously over the diphthong, curl around it the way a cat curls on top of the VCR, let it roll and ride on the long journey from its *a* to its *e*; let it spend a week in the sun while it makes the journey. When the chant of this diphthong regretfully concludes itself, next reach to the alternate and contrasting pleasure of the *zh* consonant. Then, after a mini-vowel, there's the rolling conclusion of an *r*, *l*'s cousin making a fit coda. A coda is what you need by this time. *Pleasure* is a weekend of a word; you need a rest, after you learn the way to say *pleasure*. BREAKFAST SERVED ANY TIME ALL DAY.

Other pleasures without pain: keeping time with the foot, dancing while you sit in the chair. Otherwise, this pleasure is called rhythm, which includes expectation, disappointment, and fulfillment. We feel rhythm bodily in the shifting of weight (or the imagination of weight) and in the motion of muscles to shift it. The bang-bang-bang of "small gnats mourn" receives itself within ten syllables shaped swinging by pairs sorted out into relative volumes; the great lounging precise sentences of Henry James, or of Marianne Moore his disciple, swing the leg also—to a tune longer in the interval, that locates itself first in muscle then in mind.

Like narrative, rhythm sets up and disappoints-fulfills. Because disappointment is not supposed to be pleasurable, I suppose that we have reached past the borders of pleasure-without-pain into the country of pleasure-pain. Like narrative, like metaphor, like any resolution involving two (or more) disparates coming together, rhythm is sexual. The development of story, like the development of line, sentence, paragraph, essay, poem, or metaphor, advances and recedes, separates and concludes, arcs and subsides. Is love-making a pleasure?

But, as I have said before, structure alone is not enough—because the overall structure we ascribe to *Macbeth*, "To Autumn,"

The Death of Ivan Ilych, copulation, and *Walden* may with equal justice be ascribed to a well-made TV cop show.

Once we go past the nerves on the skin's surface, pleasure and pain come together. We find no "sunny pleasure dome" without "caves of ice." "All the instances of pleasure have a sting in the tail." "Pleasure is the first good," pain is the second. In "Alexander's Feast" Dryden sings: "Rich the treasure, Sweet the pleasure; / Sweet is pleasure after pain." Sweeter than it is before pain *or without it.* For all things are a flowing, sage Heraclitus says. Although we are bent on pleasure, we acknowledge that love has pitched his mansion in the place or even the palace of excrement; for nothing coheres that is not fragmented. When desire gets what it wants desire dies. Nothing proceeds except by the rhythm of opposites. We breathe out to breathe in to breathe out. No pleasure is profound that does not embrace pain: The progeny of this embrace is beauty.